DEADLINES ON THE FRONT LINE

Recent military history by Paul Moorcraft

African Nemesis: War and Revolution in Southern Africa; 1945–2010
Axis of Evil: The War on Terror (with Gwyn Winfield and John Chisholm)
Guns and Poses: Travels with an Occasional War Correspondent
Inside the Danger Zones: Travels to Arresting Places
The Rhodesian War: A Military History (with Peter McLaughlin)
Mugabe's War Machine
Shooting the Messenger: The Politics of War Reporting (with Philip M. Taylor)
Total Destruction of the Tamil Tigers: the Rare Victory in Sri Lanka's Long War
Omar al-Bashir and Africa's Longest War
The Jihadist Threat: The Re-conquest of the West?
Dying for the Truth: The Concise History of Frontline War Reporting
Superpowers, Rogue States and Terrorism: Countering the Security Threats to the West
Total Onslaught: War and Revolution in Southern Africa Since 1945

On mathematics

It just doesn't add up: Explaining Dyscalculia and Overcoming Number Problems for Children and Adults

Recent fiction

Anchoress of Shere
Regression

DEADLINES ON THE FRONT LINE

Travels with a Veteran War Correspondent

PAUL MOORCRAFT

Pen & Sword

MILITARY

AN IMPRINT OF PEN & SWORD BOOKS LTD.
YORKSHIRE – PHILADELPHIA

First published in Great Britain in 2018 by
PEN & SWORD MILITARY
an imprint of
Pen & Sword Books Ltd
Yorkshire – Philadelphia

ISBN 978 1 52673 9 490

Typeset in 10/12.5 & Times New Roman
by Aura Technology and Software Services, India

Printed and bound in England by TJ International Ltd, Padstow, Cornwall

Pen & Sword Books Limited incorporates the imprints of Atlas, Archaeology, Aviation, Discovery, Family History, Fiction, History, Maritime, Military, Military Classics, Politics, Select, Transport, True Crime, Air World, Frontline Publishing, Leo Cooper, Remember When, Seaforth Publishing, The Praetorian Press, Wharncliffe Local History, Wharncliffe Transport, Wharncliffe True Crime and White Owl.

For a complete list of Pen & Sword titles please contact

PEN & SWORD BOOKS LIMITED
47 Church Street, Barnsley, South Yorkshire, S70 2AS, England
E-mail: enquiries@pen-and-sword.co.uk
Website: www.pen-and-sword.co.uk

Or

PEN AND SWORD BOOKS
1950 Lawrence Rd, Havertown, PA 19083, USA
E-mail: Uspen-and-sword@casematepublishers.com
Website: www.penandswordbooks.com

Contents

What the Critics said about Paul Moorcraft's Previous Books on Travels in War Zones

What the hell am I doing here? (1995)

'Gripping tales from the life and wars of an irrepressible foreign correspondent.' James MacManus, *The Times*

'An erudite potpourri of good reporting, whimsical colour, historical perspective and wit. Moorcraft takes a jaundiced-eyed, literate and often sensitive frolic across the news fronts of two decades.' Allen Pizzey, CBS News Correspondent

'Paul's been around and doesn't it show.' John Humphrys, BBC

'I am amazed he's still alive.' Sir John Keegan, Defence Editor, *Daily Telegraph*

'One of our era's foremost scholars of international communications as well as one of our leading professional journalists. He is truly a scholar-journalist of which there are few .... A superb writer.' Loyal Gould, Emeritus Professor of Journalism, Baylor University, Texas

'... unlike many of the instant experts of journalism, he is also a scholar .... It rips along, making it difficult to put down ... solidly entertaining story in the style of the old-fashioned and probably politically incorrect Kiplingesque adventure story. As a good yarn, it is all the better and more convincingly detailed because it is founded on strong journalism.' Professor Damien Kingsbury, Journalism Department, Deakin University, Australia

'... an exceptional book, which is well worth buying due to its humour and the remarkable experiences of the author .... This professional journalist's brilliant account of his many adventures makes marvellous reading and is highly recommended.' Oliver Lindsay, *Guards* magazine

'Fascinating reading .... Passion, pace and wit here by the bucketful ... bracingly honest.' Colonel Michael Peters, *Despatches*

'He writes vividly, with pace and authority ... .' Alan Ward, Department of War Studies, Royal Military Academy, Sandhurst

'Thoroughly readable and, ironically, very enjoyable. Candid in his opinions of both sides in each war, the fascinating expeditions into war zones reveal the reality of rule by the gun and the value of cigarettes as a hard currency ... . Stimulating read ... part travel book, part history, part autobiography, Moorcraft talks sparingly of his personal life.' *Wanderlust* magazine

'Paul Moorcraft is an academic with a considerable reputation ... but the Cardiff-born teacher is also one of those journalists who cannot resist the call of trouble wherever it develops in the world.' Mario Basini, *Western Mail*

Guns and Poses: Travels with an occasional war correspondent (2001)
'Gripping collection of despatches from many of the most war-torn countries of recent times ... told with comically little machismo.' *Times Literary Supplement*

'Gripping tales from the life and wars of Paul Moorcraft, an irrepressible foreign correspondent.' *Legion* magazine

'... a footloose freelance with a consuming curiosity about human behaviour from the battlefield to the bar-room. He minces no words about the shambolic state of our poor old world.' *Good Book Guide*

'Paul Moorcraft has crammed more drama, intrigue, adventure and good old-fashioned hard-core journalism into his existence than most of us will manage in a lifetime .... *Guns and Poses* is absorbing as a historical read and as the memoirs of a man who lives life large.' Cara Bouwer, *Business Day*, Johannesburg

'… a type of professional detachment that rejected the temptation of advocacy journalism … thought provoking and readable.' Stephen Williams, *African Business*

'Bin Laden escaped Paul Moorcraft, but a hundred other fascinating people did not. This is recent history written with humour and sometimes pathos. The print is in black and white but the prose is in full colour.' Graham Bound, *Focus* magazine

Inside the Danger Zones: Travels to Arresting Places (2010)

'… unforgettable journey … insightful information … very entertaining.' The *Citizen,* Johannesburg

'Driven by a desire to test the limits of his own courage, he has spent more than three decades dodging bullets in the world's most dangerous regions.' *Western Mail*

'Full of verve … a compulsive book.' Professor Stephen Chan, The *Round Table*

'Easy-going style … tongue-in-cheek humour … a knowledgeable book.' *Defence Focus*

'An author with a history that reads like 007's back-story.' *Surrey Advertiser*

'Refreshingly self-effacing account … healthy sense of colour-blindness … few punches are pulled …. There is something of William Boot (the bumbling protagonist in Evelyn Waugh's masterful *Scoop*) in Moorcraft's account.' Adrian Johnson, *RUSI Journal*

'The author and the book defy all metrics … he is a national treasure. The book is really that good. An anthropological primer to the war zones of the world, their peoples and cultures.' Steve Johnson, *CBRNe World*

Shooting the Messenger: The Politics of War Reporting (2011)

'*Shooting the Messenger* should be high on the reading list of aspiring strategists.' David R. Mets, US Air Force Research Institute

'… a cracking history of war reporting and its political impact, unreservedly recommended reading for practitioners, scholars and journalists alike.' Kenneth Payne, *RUSI Journal*

'… well-written, well-researched, accessible study … highly recommended.' *Choice*, national US library journal

'… an invaluable title for any collection strong in either military history/military issues, or journalism studies.' *Midwest Book Review*

'I must admit I thought it was rather good, and enjoyed the read. Some welcome deadpan humour from time to time …. With input right up to the Libyan war, this book covers a lot of ground in an accessible way. Recommended as a reader for the more serious student of journalism, but also for those less serious but interested in their news all the same.' Guy Gabriel, Albany Associates

'Penetrating look at the complex issues surrounding war reporting.' Mark Kukis, Baghdad correspondent, *Time* Magazine

'… crisp, provocative history that dispels many of the myths about war reporting.' Philip Seib, author of *The Al Jazeera Effect*

'Essential read for anyone interested in what generals and politicians are doing to shape and restrict good war reporting … gives the big historical picture as well as the small anecdotal and entertaining details that make this book a great read.' Philip Smucker, author of *Al Qaeda's Great Escape*

The Jihadist Threat: Re-conquest of the West? (2015)
Shortlisted for the British Army Military Book of the Year, 2016

'Book of the Month …. A mine of valuable information, this compelling title has much to enthral even those who take even the slightest interest in home and international affairs …. The language and even his brand of humour make it very accessible.' *Soldier* magazine

'A great overview of the current Islamic threat.' Five stars. Army Rumour Service

Superpowers, Rogue States and Terrorism (2017)
'In these uncertain times Paul Moorcraft's latest book is first class, and well worth reading. Don't expect a dry-as-dust academic tome; Moorcraft manages to combine the relaxed communications skills of a well-travelled and experienced journalist with the deep knowledge of an expert in the field of strategic studies. He writes wittily and engagingly and with a geopolitical awareness that is almost tactile. His coverage of the forces at play in Middle East politics is compelling, as is his balanced and mature assessment of the "threat to the west"…Highly recommended.' Professor Paul Cornish, Australian National University

About the Author

Professor Paul Moorcraft is an internationally respected expert on crisis communications, especially relating to security issues. He completed his studies at six British, Middle Eastern and African universities, thereafter lecturing fulltime (consecutively) at ten universities in the UK, US, Africa, Australia and New Zealand in journalism, politics and international relations. He was most recently a visiting professor at Cardiff University's School of Journalism, Media and Cultural Studies. He worked fulltime for *Time* magazine in Africa, then for the BBC and most of the Western TV networks as a freelance producer/correspondent. He has worked in thirty war zones in Africa, the Middle East, Asia and the Balkans, often with irregular and, sometimes, jihadist, forces. Most recently he has been operating in Afghanistan, Iraq, Palestine/Israel, Nepal, Sudan, Zimbabwe, Syria, Turkey, Sri Lanka and, for a pleasant change, the Maldives.

Professor Moorcraft spent five years as a senior instructor at the Royal Military Academy, Sandhurst, and later the UK Joint Services Command and Staff College (JSCSC). He also worked in Corporate Communications in the Ministry of Defence in Whitehall; the MoD recalled him for service during the Iraq war in 2003. One of his main roles in Whitehall and as a member of the directing staff at JSCSC (later the UK Defence Academy) was advising on and teaching media operations (media ops). Professor Moorcraft also worked in media ops in Bosnia, Kosovo and Iraq.

Paul Moorcraft is a regular broadcaster (BBC TV and radio, as well as Sky, Sky-Arabic, Al Jazeera, etc.) and op-ed writer for international newspapers (including the *Guardian, New Statesman, Washington Times, Canberra Times, Business Day,* etc.). He is the author of a wide range of books on military history, politics, crime and mathematics. He co-authored *Axis of Evil: The War on Terror* (Pen and Sword, 2005). His *Shooting the Messenger: The Politics of War Reporting* (Potomac, Washington, 2008) was co-authored with Professor Philip M. Taylor. An updated version was released in 2011 (Biteback, London). The first of many editions of *The Rhodesian War: A Military History* (with Dr Peter McLaughlin) was published by Pen and Sword books in 2008. *Mugabe's War Machine* (Pen and

Sword) came out in 2011. *Total Destruction of the Tamil Tigers: A Rare Victory of Sri Lanka's Long War* was released by Pen and Sword in 2012. Three volumes of memoirs have been published; the most recent was *Inside the Danger Zones: Travels to Arresting Places* (Biteback, London, 2010). He is an award-winning novelist as well as the author of a publication related to his charity work (*It Just Doesn't Add Up: Explaining Dyscalculia and Overcoming Number Problems for Children and Adult*s (Tarquin, St Albans, 2015)). *Omar al-Bashir and Africa's Longest War* was released by Pen and Sword in June 2015. *The Jihadist Threat: The Re-conquest of the West?* (2015) was shortlisted (6 out of 2,000) for the British Army Military Book of the Year, 2016. *Dying for the Truth: The concise history of frontline war reporting* came out in 2016 (Pen and Sword). His most recent for Pen and Sword books are *Superpowers, Rogue States and Terrorism: Countering the Security Threats to the West (2017)* and *Total Onslaught: War and Revolution in Southern Africa (1945-2018)* (2018).

Paul Moorcraft is the director of the Centre for Foreign Policy Analysis, London, founded in 2004 and dedicated to conflict resolution. He was Head of Mission, for example, of fifty independent British observers at the Sudan election of 2010. He lives in a riverside cottage in the Surrey Hills, near Guildford.

Timeline

1948	Born in Cardiff, Wales
1967-1972	Educated at Swansea, Cardiff and Lancaster Universities
1973-75	Senior Lecturer at the Royal Military Academy, Sandhurst
Late 1975	Studied in Israel
1976	Lectured in politics, University of Rhodesia
1977	Lectured in politics, University of Natal
1978	Lectured at University of Cape Town
1979-1981	Editor in chief, College Press, Rhodesia; vice chairman of Press (Quill) Club; stringer for *Time* magazine
1981-82	Lectured in international relations at the University of the Witwatersrand, Johannesburg
1982-87	Wrote books and made films on South Africa
1984	First work in Afghanistan
1986	Films in Mozambique, Namibia and Angola
1987-1990	Based in Spain
1990-93	Based in Wales, taught at Cardiff University. Gulf War film. Second film with Renamo. Trips to Romania and Balkans. Film on forts in West Africa. Elected local local councillor. Visiting professor, Baylor University, Texas
1993-94	Based in Geelong, Australia. Election in South Africa. Travels in the Balkans
1995	Taught at Bournemouth University
1996	Moved to Shere. Made first film on Sudan. Recovered in Guildford hospital from cerebral and intestinal malaria
1997	Based in Hamilton, New Zealand. Trip to Cambodia/Vietnam
1997-2000	Rejoined MoD as Senior Lecturer, Joint Services Command and Staff College. Travels in Bosnia, southern Africa, Germany, Kosovo, Ukraine, Turkey and work in US
2000	Work in Defence Procurement, Abbey Wood, then Main Building, Whitehall. Trips to Gibraltar, Cyprus. Left MoD
2001	Edited *Defence Review* in London. Worked in Israel, Afghanistan, Iraq

2003	Returned to MoD. Worked in Iraq
2004	Set up Centre for Foreign Policy Analysis, a think tank dedicated to conflict resolution. Worked in Darfur
2005	Worked in Nepal
2006	Sudan, Turkey
2007	Started work in Maldives
2008	Syria, China
2009	Just survived brain tumour operation
2010	Sudan election
2011	South Sudan referendum
2012	Started working in Sri Lanka
2014	Visits to Sudan, Sri Lanka and India
2015	Worked in Sudan and Maldives
2016	Book on Jihadist threat shortlisted for British Army Military Book of the Year

Foreword

Hell, I'm getting on now, and I still don't know what I want to do when I grow up. I've spent the best part of the last forty years travelling and talking to really odd — often homicidal — people in unusual and dangerous places. Much of my reporting was done within the cosy intellectual parameters of the Cold War. Then, post 9/11, came the so-called clash of civilizations, and a series of travels in Islamic lands: returning to Afghanistan, despite vowing never to go back there, fresh locations in Iraq and Darfur, and indulging in the tragic *déjà vu* of conflicts in Israel/Palestine. I thought the world had been turned upside down by the assaults on the Twin Towers, but the economic crash of 2008/9 threatened to do to capitalism what years of communist intrigue had failed to do. Until about 2012 I thought that perhaps al-Qaeda had better hurry up, or the Western world would implode before bin Laden's disciples (or Brussels bureaucrats) could aspire to complete their mission. And then we should consider the march of Chinese power, Putin's revival of the Cold War and the menace of jihadism.

I covered many wars on most continents, yet I was always more interested in vivid characters rather than battles or bullets. Some dark times intruded, but mostly black humour was the best antidote to death and suffering. Besides, some of the stories in this book are about nice places. Irwin Armstrong, the cameraman who often accompanied me, used to complain in regions such as Darfur that we worked too often in difficult dry places where we couldn't get a beer occasionally. So I dragged him off to make some films in more bibulous zones such as the Maldives and Nepal.

I kept going too long and started to worry that I was not fit to lead younger journalists into war zones, let alone look after myself. Somehow, like a punch-drunk boxer, I was often persuaded to do 'one more trip'. I had suffered a number of wounds and tropical diseases, but in 2009 a brain tumour nearly finished me off. *Inter alia*, I lost nearly all my vision, so I decided I needed a niche market: to work as a blind observer in African elections. Hence various further adventures in Sudan, accompanied by probably more competent but certainly more visually able observers.

Originally this book was to be called *Hacks, Heroes and Harlots* before my rather prim publishers changed the title. 'Hacks' referred to journalists, not horse-rides, and 'harlots' is a reference to the famous quote that the media have power without responsibility, 'the prerogative of the harlot throughout the ages'. Being a rather primly brought-up fellow, I don't know much about real harlots, so don't expect a tour of exotic bordellos. We may come across a few real heroes, however.

The *introductory* chapter briefly sketches some of the adventures in my first three books of travels, so loyal readers may want to speed-read this section, though there are new insights (I hope) and fresh material.

The photographs are my own, except where indicated otherwise. I have few acknowledgements, mainly because most of the people I met in this line of work did everything they could to hinder, discourage, or, occasionally, shoot me. I would, however, like to thank Tony Denton for endless computer and design help. I applaud Irwin Armstrong's patience for entering into war zones with someone as clumsy as me. I salute Tim Lambon, formerly deputy foreign editor of Channel Four News, for covering, and kicking, my butt so often. And thanks to Jenny who gave me her arm, when I often needed to dispense with my white cane. Thanks, too, to Henry Wilson for commissioning yet another book for Pen and Sword. I hope readers will enjoy the adventures as well as the humour, especially as it's often at my own expense.

Surrey Hills
UK
April 2018

Chapter 1

The Story so Far

I can't really explain how I started on my long journey without maps. Despite my deep roots in Wales, perhaps I became addicted to exile, to always being a foreigner, a lone stranger in an unfamiliar setting. Maybe I found wandering more stimulating than belonging.

I began with all the keyboard courage of an academic. My degrees in politics and defence studies were of no practical use. True, I had been a senior civilian instructor teaching war studies at the Royal Military Academy, Sandhurst, where I played rugby, rode horses, and did some shooting, all equally badly. But I was the proverbial round peg in a square hole, almost convinced that I was the only sane man in a lunatic asylum. Looking back, Sandhurst appeared to be Hogwarts with lots of guns. One of the more polite names I was called in the officers' mess was 'rebel'. So moving back to Israel and then to a rebel colony, Rhodesia, seemed appropriate: I wanted to experience war, not talk about it.

I had first visited Israel in 1970 to indulge in an idealistic Kibbutz adventure. I returned to the country in 1975, funded by a scholarship to study the aftermath of the 1973 Yom Kippur war. I had some help from the Hebrew University, Jerusalem, and from General Arik Sharon, the then prime minister's security adviser. I also took a few months off while I was there to enjoy the best job I ever had: working as a life-guard at a swimming pool. I did little except admire the tough gun-toting Lolitas from the Israeli army as they changed personality and became minxy civilians in bikinis.

I became interested in the idea of comparative siege cultures to include Israel, Rhodesia and South Africa, which I planned to work up into a doctoral thesis. My next trip would be to southern Africa.

The lure of Africa – Rhodesia

'Rhodesia is a well-armed suburb masquerading as a country.' The first sentence I ever wrote about the place just about summarized my political views on the rebel colony. I was intellectually curious about the rebellion against the British Crown. How could the white Rhodesians, outnumbered by blacks 25 to one and ostracized by the world, hang on to power for so long? How could they argue with arithmetic? Rhodesia and more especially South Africa had almost ceased to be geographical

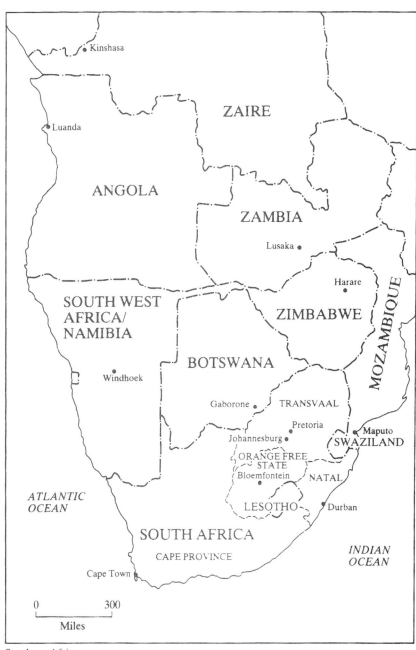

Southern Africa

entities. To the outside world they were more a *condition*, a disease. South Africa was no longer a country but a map of the mind, in which anyone could find his/her own place. What's more, as a boy I had been seduced by the African tales of writers like Henry Rider Haggard. As a student I had been touched by Africa's apparent mysticism. Armed with conventional wisdom, curiosity, and just a touch of romanticism, I set out for the continent in March 1976.

At Jan Smuts airport in Johannesburg I was met by Andy Gancewicz, a big, aggressive, kind-hearted Pole with whom I had worked briefly on the *Western Mail* in Cardiff. Andy thought I was demented when I said I was thinking about travelling to Rhodesia.

'There are lots of jobs here in Jo'burg. Why go to a place where the Afs are knocking the hell out of the whites? There's a war on.'

'That's precisely why I want to go. To find out why.'

A letter arrived from the University of Rhodesia offering me an interview for a temporary post teaching politics. They included a return airfare to the capital, Salisbury. For the previous two weeks the road linking Rhodesia with South Africa had been closed because of guerrilla attacks.

'You must be mad to teach politics in the middle of a civil war,' Andy said. 'I hear that the last five white politics lecturers were deported.'

'If they want a lunatic, I have the right qualifications.'

*****

Despite the war, Rhodesia was a very friendly place. In my five years of travelling throughout the country both blacks and whites were almost always courteous and easygoing, with little of the sullen black resentment and white aloofness I had encountered in South Africa. The historian Lord Blake put it well: 'Apartheid south of the Limpopo was a religion, north of it a dubious and impractical expedient.'

UDI — the Unilateral Declaration of Independence in 1965 — was both a bluff and a blunder. Except for a few hotheads, the Rhodesian armed forces would not have resisted a British military intervention. Rhodesia broke away from Britain to avoid black rule, but Prime Minister Ian Douglas Smith became totally dependent on a South African government that eventually became more determined than London to establish a moderate black leader in Salisbury. Faced with its own pressures in the 1970s, Pretoria sought to distance itself from Rhodesia's failing white government, but also wanted to show that sanctions didn't work and couldn't be seen publicly to ditch a white ally.

Until 1976 Rhodesia's diplomatic history was a long melodrama punctuated by angry encounters on ships and trains, foolish estimates, and silly superlatives. The country's fate would be decided largely on the battlefield. White Rhodesians were sucked into a war that by the late 1970s they were manifestly losing: if the 1979 Lancaster House talks in London had not intervened, military defeat was around the corner. I spent most of my five years there trying to understand why the whites couldn't see that they were bound to lose.

I stayed mainly in Salisbury, where roughly half the white population of around 240,000 lived. I did travel around the country on convoys, in helicopters, occasionally on horseback, and very occasionally on foot, but it was a difficult war to get to grips with. Even when I switched to fulltime writing, few journalists were allowed near the actual fighting. There were few 'battles' and most of these were in cross-border raids into Mozambique and Zambia. The war was mainly one of fleeting skirmishes and death from the air by way of 'Fireforce' helicopters. Short of actually enlisting or accepting conscription, few hacks (as journalists called themselves) witnessed any real action. So I hung around the press bar: falling off the high bar stools and risking the stale sandwiches were not entirely ignoble introductions to the Rhodesian art of war.

Salisbury, now renamed Harare, became my favourite city in Africa. Like many writers based there, I wrote books and articles full of righteous indignation about racial injustice; like them I lived well and enjoyed myself. Two friends who wrote for the most liberal British newspapers, the *Guardian* and the *Observer,* regularly

Salisbury, the capital of the rebel Rhodesian republic. Jameson Avenue in the 1970s. 'My favourite city in Africa'.

thundered on about opulent white lifestyles while themselves sitting comfortably surrounded by servants, a pool, and a tennis court.

You could live in Salisbury and see very little of the war. The city was mesmerized by the killing in the countryside and yet, paradoxically, seemed entirely untouched by it. Salisbury was simultaneously remote, charming, claustrophobic, and seductive.

The conversation was often about the 'situation' — the war — but the ambience was of the colonial heydays of the 1950s: squash at the club, bridge and tennis parties, cocktails at the Reps theatre bar, racing at Borrowdale, and endless dinner parties with servants to do the washing up. Rugby and cricket were important even though South Africa was the only opponent.

Yet the polite 'business as usual' was often a deliberate act of temporary oblivion, especially for the men. By the end of the war the military call-up extended to age 60. Some younger men spent 'six months in, six months out' of the army every year; some were on continuous call-ups. One-man businesses collapsed. Many urban wives concentrated on pottery and bridge, but the women on the farms lived with the everyday reality of mined roads, cattle-maiming, poisoned wells, attacks at night, the Agric-Alert security system warning of a guerrilla raid on the next-door farm, the crash of broken glass, the rattle of AKs, the rush of adrenalin and the dash for weapons besides the bed, shouting at the children to lie down in the corridor between the bedrooms, the smell of fear, cordite … and eventually the awful, sickly sweet, overpowering stench of death. It was on isolated farms, half-sleeping, listening, waiting for different sounds amidst the drumming of the cicadas, that I learned about bush war.

The TV and radio harped hypnotically on a few basic themes: the chaos in black states, disorders elsewhere in the world (especially in countries such as Britain that attracted southern African émigrés), and the monolithic communist threat. Smith claimed to have 'the happiest blacks in the world', bar a few troublemakers misled by professional Moscow-trained agitators. Few whites could put themselves in the shoes of blacks and realize that they would fight too if they were deprived of an effective vote, given inferior schooling, medical services, and land, and treated as second- or third-class citizens.

Although the whites did fight long and hard, and despite the ubiquitous weaponry and uniforms, Rhodesia was not a militaristic society. They much preferred beer and *braais* (barbecues) to military parades. Later, as black rule became imminent, the whites looked back with sorrow and resignation rather than anger; with a bruised pride in having survived so long against the odds. Few outsiders could doubt their courage, or their stupidity.

As I explored the inequality of life in Rhodesia, I began to understand the reasons for the war. From a liberal perspective in the UK, it was as though a giant local bowls club – Surrey with the lunatic fringe on top – was defying the

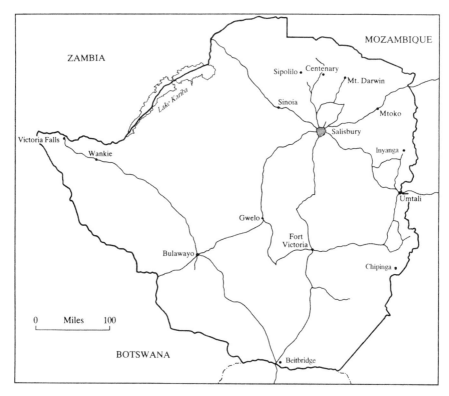

Rhodesia in the colonial period.

world. In many ways Rhodesia was unsophisticated and behind the times, a living museum. Rhodesians tended to look back to the days when Britain was Great; before socialism, as they saw it, gutted the bulldog spirit.

I started to understand the Rhodesians' love affair with the land — the rolling hills of Inyanga, the majestic wildlife, the mysterious balancing rocks, the crystal-clear, champagne quality of the air, the invigorating climate, the sense of space, the sensual perfume of jasmine in the suburban gardens, and the rugged wild aromas of the bush — but not with its native people. White Rhodesians paid more attention to their roses, their Currie Cup cricket, horses, dogs, and the level of algae in their pools than to the black people whose land they shared in unequal proportions. Rhodesia may have appeared boundless to the white man because his 5 per cent of the population owned 50 per cent of the agricultural land and all the political power. It could not last.

The whites tried to tame Africa in their own image. Wherever the British settled they planted trees and gardens, built churches with neat rows of pews, and ran lending libraries. In Rhodesia, throughout 1977 and early 1978, Ian Smith tried to design a very complicated and tidy constitutional settlement that would establish the kind of majority rule with which whites were prepared to live. In short, tame blacks.

A racial Armageddon looked possible, so in trooped the 'vultures' of the foreign press corps. The run up to the first multi-racial election in April 1979 brought a wave of hacks. The 'Gang of Four' — Smith and his 'moderate' black allies — wanted maximum publicity, so for once it was relatively easy to get press accreditation. It was a time of madness for Rhodesia: wild press parties were the order of the day. The hacks had lots of real money, US dollars and British pounds, and liked a good time. Most of the indigenous white males were 'out in the bush slotting gooks', so the press corps attracted hordes of bored local females, many of them tanned, blonde Amazons. This did nothing to improve relations between the soldiers and the press.

A Fire Force trooper, Mtoko, 1977. By Chris Dehon.

Then I received my call-up papers. Technically, male residents under 38 could be conscripted if they had lived for two years in the country; as I had become a resident only a few months before, I was not theoretically eligible for call-up. In one respect I was quite keen to see the war from the inside, but on the other hand I could not fight for a lost, and immoral, cause I didn't believe in. Besides, I had just started stringing for *Time* magazine and been elected vice-chairman of the Press Club. Many resident journalists did serve part-time in the police, but I told the call-up board I would leave the country.

They said they would imprison me.

'Try it,' I said. 'Great publicity just before your damn election.'

The next morning I received a letter which said a mistake had been made. I was given a year's deferment.

The war went on. I criss-crossed the country on behalf of *Time* with Peter Jordan, a daredevil photographer. Peter and I were in a vehicle that could ford rivers and travel cross-country: a hire car. We were stopped once by the 'terrs', but luckily and surprisingly our press passes – and a lot of cigarettes – persuaded them to let us go.

A 'turned-terrorist': an on-side auxiliary, 1979. By Allen Pizzey.

I also managed to survive an unpowered landing in an air force Alouette helicopter, a brilliant piece of flying that saved my life. I also came out of a crash landing in a Dakota which had lost some of its landing gear. I was beginning to earn my spurs as a war correspondent.

I was young, fit and busy and lots of pretty girls fluttered around. The wine was terrible – you could get bilharzia from it, it was said – but the beer was good. To echo William Wordsworth, not only was I alive, but I was young in that revolutionary frenzy. I mourned the deaths, not least of my friends, but I was entering that potentially fatal zone for a young correspondent: I started to believe that I was invincible, that only the people to my left or right would get 'their' bullet. The first and only white correspondent killed in Rhodesia was my occasional squash partner, Lord Richard Cecil. His forebear, Lord Salisbury, lent his name to the capital. Ironically, as a former Grenadier Guards officer, he was the most militarily competent correspondent. Richard's rifle was not able to fire when he was surprised by a single armed guerrilla who fired two shots at him from a range of a few feet. The hacks had nicknamed the handsome young adventurer 'Young Winston', not always endearingly, because he was criticized for breaking the rules of neutral journalism by bearing arms. It was a lesson I was to ponder in many later close encounters.

The Lancaster House conference in London in late 1979 saved the Rhodesians from themselves and perhaps me from myself. A new constitution and a ceasefire were agreed. In December 1979 Lord Soames took over as governor: the first time in the long imperial recessional that a white colonial official had replaced an African premier.

New elections were scheduled for February 1980 and over 350 foreign correspondents flocked into Salisbury. As the local Press Club representative I tried to make them welcome, using the opportunity to plug my recent book on Rhodesia. The 1,300 troops in the British-led Commonwealth monitoring force

Rhodesian propaganda posters.

faced a mountain of problems in maintaining the ceasefire. The well-fleshed British governor, Lord Soames, was sitting on a powder keg.

Exactly 2,702,275 men and women, under the watchful eyes of 570 British Bobbies standing by the polls, voted in the middle of the rainstorms of February 1980. Everyone waited for the results. Would it be peace, or coup and all-out war in southern Africa? A possible white-led military coup was just hours away before the military supremo, General Peter Walls, insisted that 'he would not copy the rest of Africa'. After all the killings, the old Sandhurst principles prevailed.

On 18 April 1980 Zimbabwe became independent. A right-wing British Conservative prime minister, Margaret Thatcher, had caused, by accident, the first electoral triumph of a Marxist in Africa.

Robert Mugabe had won. The history of the Rhodesian security forces was one of tactical and operational brilliance but strategic ineptitude. The initial aim of the war was to prevent the passing of power to any black government, no matter how moderate. An admission of racism, if only within the high command and Cabinet, might have produced a more coherent grand strategy. But no clear political programme — beyond a vague preservation of the *status quo* — was ever articulated.

As one senior Rhodesian officer admitted to me: 'We relied ninety per cent on force and ten per cent on psychology, and half of that went off half-cocked. The guerrillas relied ninety per cent on psychology and only ten per cent on force.'

The insurgents had a clear vision of their purpose: to break the back of white supremacy and establish a black majority government. This gave them remarkable stamina and their cause the strength to weather numerous political crises and almost consistent military defeat in the field. In the pattern of all colonial wars, the Rhodesian settlers simply gave too little, far too late.

I stayed in the new Zimbabwe for just over a year after the colonial war spluttered into a tribal conflict. Salisbury was renamed Harare and became more cosmopolitan. The TV was Africanized. Everyone was 'Comrade' this or that. New TV heroes appeared: Yasser Arafat, Gaddafi, and other great thinkers of the age. After an initial improvement with the end of sanctions, the shortages grew worse and more inconvenient. The disappearance of toilet rolls particularly irked my posterior. The harder the currency the softer the toilet paper, I was to learn on many future travels.

There were many initial improvements for the majority Shona people, especially the fat cats in the ruling party. Schools were re-opened, new clinics were built, and some underutilized white land was re-apportioned to the peasantry. The schools and clinics had been destroyed by the guerrillas and now white taxes were used to rebuild them, or so many disgruntled 'ex-Rhodies' argued. For most whites the lifestyle and servants remained, despite niggling shortages, high taxes, and the impossibly dull TV. Some of the new programmes were so bad that at times I longed for the boy-meets-tractor themes of Soviet drama.

A white architect put it this way: 'The whites are spiralling up on their social life but spiralling down on their business.' Comrade Mugabe's drive to a one-party

'Robert Mugabe:
I found him charming
and highly intelligent.'

Marxist state did little to encourage foreign investment. Nor did destabilization by the South Africans, who stirred up tribal dissidents and held up trade at border posts.

One white businesswoman was more fatalistic: 'We had paradise here; now we're becoming part of the normal world.'

I interviewed Robert Mugabe and found him charming and highly intelligent, the smartest politician – black or white – that I had encountered in Africa. I was surprised by his almost BBC received pronunciation and also by his mincing manner, such a contrast to the image of a revolutionary who had led a brutal insurgency.

I also spoke to the defeated white leader, Ian Smith, who seemed quite positive about his initial contacts with the austere Marxist prime minister. Later, Smith would return to his old mantra: the economy, education, law, and medical services would collapse under black rule, and the Ndebele and Shona tribes would

Bishop Abel Muzorewa and his wife, Maggie, the first day in the prime minister's residence. 'I found him charming and far less smart.'

fall on each other's throats without whites to stop them. Sadly, most of Smith's prophecies were self-fulfilling, partly because of white intransigence.

At least Smith had the courage of his convictions and stayed in Zimbabwe. I didn't. I was 'taking the gap', the local colloquialism for emigrating. I regarded many black and white Zimbabweans as my friends. I had admired the courage and decency of many white Rhodesians, but detested their unthinking arrogance towards their voteless compatriots. I had come to love the country but none of its rulers. I had enjoyed an exhilarating five years as a writer and I wanted to keep some good memories. The transition from white to black rule had been spellbinding, but I didn't want to see the country die.

I decided to take up an offer to teach politics at South Africa's most liberal and distinguished university: 'Wits' or, to be formal, the University of the Witwatersrand. Down South was where the action was. The transformation of Rhodesia to Zimbabwe meant the replacement of an efficient, racist, white élite with an inefficient, tribal, black élite. It was inevitable and, ideally, should have happened without bloodshed.

I handed in my police uniform; I had eventually served as a reservist in the dying days of the British South Africa Police, but only after Mugabe won and the police force fell apart. I also found another police uniform in my house as

I tidied up to leave. My female housemate admitted she had been in Special Branch. I hadn't known – which speaks volumes for my skills as an investigative journalist.

'I confide in you and you're a spook,' I said testily.

She was not a bit contrite: 'I helped to give you a clean bill of health. You've been such a nosy bastard for the last five years, and they were convinced that your books on the country were a cover, and your Sandhurst background, and your friendship with Ken Flower [the intelligence chief] and his daughters …. It was me who helped to get your clearance to go everywhere. They were thinking of deporting you.'

We had not been lovers, but I had loved her like the sister I never had. I should have been angry and hurt. I wasn't. Much later, she said she had been joking about my security clearances, but I still wonder.

In June 1981 I tenderly embraced my glamorous longterm companion. With the inevitable sad determination of a traveller, I said goodbye to her and the country I had loved, yet had to leave.

I did return for visits, even after Mugabe had banned me from the country in 1986. In 1987 I sneaked in and got married by accident on Lake Kariba's beautiful Spurwing Island. I woke up with a wife, and hangover, though it took a little while for both of us to realize the mistake. I continued to visit clandestinely, and even published a book in 2011 on Mugabe. Despite the self-destruction of the economy, the country had made me fall in love with her and the whole of Africa, despite the numerous wars I covered on the continent.

A rare photo of Ken Flower (left) visiting my flat in Salisbury for an election party.

I would dream of the long drives through Matabeleland, the granite castle *kopjes* set against the setting sun, the smooth trunks of the upside-down giant baobabs with their coppery sheen, the *mukwa* (bloodwood) trees with their round bristling pods hanging like medals, and colourfully dressed African women trudging along dusty tracks with massive bundles on their heads. They all convinced me that if I left Africa it would break my heart. Then I would read a newspaper and the idiocies of the politicians would almost convince me to bribe my way onto the first flight out. Africa is about strong passions of love and hate. Europe breeds indifference; everything about Africa evokes emotion — the vibrant colours, the rains on the dry earth, the storms, the spontaneity of its peoples … the sheer lack of conformity to nearly everything man-made.

Apartheid South Africa
I loved the country, but hated the government. The conflict in this strange, fascinating, achingly beautiful land was far more complex than the comfortable stereotypes imposed from thousands of miles away. I never saw it as a straightforward case of good versus evil. South Africa, unlike Rhodesia, was not a case of thwarted decolonization. The three million or so Afrikaners were a genuine white African tribe. They had nowhere else to go. Africa was home.

South Africa was unique (in sub-Saharan Africa) in having a large poor white population, and apartheid, initially, was the racism of poor whites. But the ruling National Party enshrined racism in its constitution when it won power in 1948. That was a bad PR move just three years after the fall of Hitler. The Afrikaners were honest or stupid enough not to disguise their degraded political philosophy. Like Ian Smith in 1965 — from Western European and American perspectives — the Afrikaners should have learned to lie like white men.

Much as I came to despise apartheid and its vicious implementation, I had few doubts about the genuine philosophical, even moral, impulse behind the Afrikaner desire for self-determination. The nineteenth-century history of southern Africa records the savage duplicity of British imperialism, especially during the Boer War. Welshman David Lloyd George had shown sympathy for the Boer struggle and so did I. The Welsh were like the Afrikaners — too near the English and too far from God. I did my best to learn Afrikaans, that feisty derivative of Dutch that was the official language alongside English. Though when I gave a carefully scripted speech in Afrikaans, I was told I sounded like 'Adolf Hitler reading a nursery rhyme in Dutch'. Unpopular though it may be now, when I started living in South Africa I was predisposed to understand the Afrikaner, not indulge in knee-jerk moralizing. I was wary of the African National Congress not because of their aims – which I supported except for their socialism – but their methods. Yet I knew the ANC would win in the end. I came to support sanctions and to accept, finally, the armed struggle, although not attacks on civilians. Revolution and war were inevitable as long as the whites, 13 per cent of the population, controlled 87 per cent of the land. If the government was serious about its homelands strategy then the only logical solution was a white homeland approximating to the size of the white population. The apartheid rulers, however, tried to hang on to the lot.

Many Afrikaners were utterly sincere in their belief that the Bible ordained the policy of separate but equal. I thought they were sincerely wrong in believing that God wanted them to keep blacks from the ballot box. Among the wealthy English-speaking liberal community, however, politics was more etiquette than conviction. In South Africa 'liberal' had a special meaning. The terms 'left' and 'right' bore little resemblance to northern European models. Most South African liberals, for example, opposed universal franchise.

There was no doubt about the volcanic impatience of the young blacks in Soweto. South African cities appeared more ripe for revolution than Russia in 1917. For a black radical I could see the attraction of the South African Communist Party. To him, apartheid was synonymous with capitalism. But in the countryside and homelands, where blacks had been shoehorned into gulags without fences, I found great passivity. In 1976 I didn't think that a successful revolution was imminent because of the sheer efficiency of the security forces. As in most authoritarian systems, the thing that worked best was the secret police.

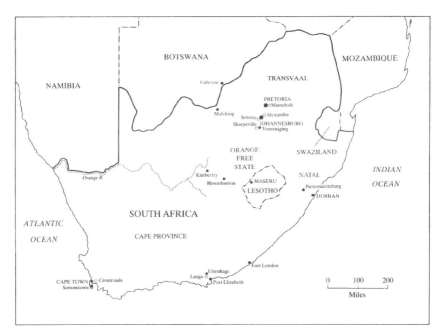

South Africa.

South Africa, unlike Russia in 1917, had not been defeated in war. It was a continental superpower, a military and economic giant while remaining a moral pygmy. In this sense apartheid worked. It had created a cargo cult on a vast scale for the whites in the 1960s and 1970s. And it had worked psychologically. As intended, it kept the races emotionally apart.

My introduction to Afrikanerdom was in the cradle of the culture, Cape Town. My stint at the University of Cape Town was enlivened by elegant vineyards and the finest Cape Dutch architecture. I also taught at the University of Natal, in Durban, and later at the University of the Witwatersrand in Johannesburg. At both Cape Town and Durban I was an academic locum during the sabbaticals of the respective professors of politics. It was a useful financial and intellectual background for my writing. I also taught occasionally at the most liberal Afrikaans-language university in the beautiful town of Stellenbosch. It was their Oxbridge.

I had a privileged perspective of apartheid in these universities. In Cape Town, I had a so-called 'Coloured' (mixed-race) girlfriend, whom I met at the university. We both loved eating out, dancing, and the cinema. And we enjoyed making love. The apartheid laws made it illegal for us to do any of these things together. I didn't intend indulging on my own, so we were forced to break the law. I had no problem in contravening this kind of legislation, but – even though Cape Town was more racially tolerant than other South African cities – I knew my friend felt understandably awkward in public places. Because she could almost 'pass for white' — to use the local parlance — there were rarely any rude comments. Only

The beautiful location of Cape Town University.

once were we asked to leave a restaurant. Of course, once was more than enough. We spent much of our time in my flat, where she felt more comfortable. Life in South Africa for 'non-whites' was not a street of joy.

My friend warned me that the security police, who were not above raiding the beds of mixed couples to examine the sheets, might try to plant drugs in the flat. Deporting a foreign journalist and university lecturer in politics on a drugs charge would be more expedient, she explained, than the bad publicity of arraigning me on offences against the Immorality Act. She also explained some of the more arcane mysteries of apartheid: the various grades of 'Coloured' — Cape Coloured, Malay, Griqua, Indian, Chinese, 'other Asiatic', and 'other Coloured'; how the Race Classification Board worked; the sixteen different grades of pigmentation based upon a person's public acceptance as being white, black, Malay, and so on; tests such as whether the hair was crinkly enough to hold a pencil, or the width of the nose …. Not only was apartheid doomed, it was damned.

When I argued with white reactionaries and white liberals about one person, one vote I would ask a simple question: why should Archbishop Desmond Tutu, a Nobel laureate, be denied the vote when an illiterate, unemployed Afrikaner railway worker was enfranchised?

I eventually settled in the artists' quarter of Johannesburg, in Melville, in June 1981. At first sight, and even after regular visits, Johannesburg was an ugly, scary city. It was the biggest conurbation south of Cairo, with six or seven million inhabitants then, and part of the Vaal triangle, which included Pretoria and interlocking industrial towns. Census figures were very rough guesses. Not much more than 100 years old, its existence had nothing to do with natural beauty, convenience, rivers, or trading routes. It was founded on top of a gold reef. Brash, fast, crime-ridden, well-armed, and architecturally a dump, Jo'burg had three redeeming features: wealth, energy, and an excellent climate. I started teaching international relations at the University of the Witwatersrand, the largest English-language college in South Africa, and arguably the most distinguished university in Africa.

Beyond occasional forays into the battles in the townships, I lived a comfortable suburban life, along with most of the rest of white South Africa. The 1976 Soweto insurrection had been forgotten. Until the townships erupted again in 1984, the white suburbs were immersed in what writer Nadine Gordimer called a 'dreadful calm'. Most whites regarded politics just as Californians thought about earthquakes; the black townships were out of sight and usually out of mind. The torture chambers of the police HQ at John Vorster Square were just around the corner from the Market Theatre, where white liberals could learn about black suffering from playwrights such as Athol Fugard.

Until the war lapped around their cities in the mid-1970s, Rhodesians didn't want to talk politics or war. In the early 1980s in affluent South Africa it was the same. Sport, the new pool or BMW, Waterford crystal, Gucci shoes, Dunhill belts, Georg Jensen silver, and Balenciaga dresses came before ritual jokes about President P.W. Botha. The war was 'out there', on the border with Angola, a thousand miles to the north. That suited the government, which hadn't even told its own citizens that its army had invaded Angola in 1975.

My talks with government ministers suggested that they too wallowed in wishful thinking. The Afrikaners were desperate to avoid foreign contamination — hence the absurd bans on films such as *Guess Who's Coming to Dinner?* and works by Daniel Defoe, William Faulkner, and even *A Book of Common Prayer*. I used to keep awake in the cinema by counting the cuts, after exchanging my brain for a packet of popcorn.

Pretoria said it was not only part of the West, but was in the vanguard of Western Christendom's battle with Moscow's evil empire. The Afrikaner government had a Ptolemaic view of the world: Pretoria, not Berlin, was the centrepiece of the Cold War. Pretoria therefore had to allow a free press, as integral to its defence of Western values, though it had to curb Moscow's total onslaught, aided wittingly or unwittingly by the local and foreign media. The government wanted to be treated as part of the West and explained that there were similar problems with terrorists elsewhere. 'Look at the IRA.' On the other hand, it said, treat us differently. There are special problems with democracy in Africa. 'Look what's happening north of us.'

South Africa was third and first world, Australia dumped on Nigeria. You could change worlds by travelling a mile or so from the rich white Johannesburg suburb of Sandton to the desperate poverty of the nearby black township of Alexandra. The third-world analogy permitted a soothing psychic balm. For the comfortable whites the problems were not happening in the next township, which they very rarely visited, or in the dustbowls of the black homelands hundreds of miles away; no, the starvation and turmoil were another *world* away. It was much easier to ease the conscience by discovering black Africa in the Market Theatre. It boasted a bar and even a multiracial restaurant.

The complacency was shattered when Alexandra went up in flames in the 'unrest' which began in 1984. Ex-Rhodesians in Johannesburg were once again planning to become *uhuru*-hoppers. Most of them could claim British citizenship, but Afrikaners were stuck with their 'green mamba' passports. Dinner parties were full of sardonic comments about getting away:

'What's the difference between an emigrant and a refugee? ... Timing.'

'Bloody sanctions. Business is so quiet, you can hear the turnover drop.'

'When the Jews leave you know there's a problem. When the Greeks go it's bad. When the Porks [Portuguese] start to leave, it's too late.'

Rich Johannesburgers suddenly started taking a keen interest in portable art (and gold Krugerrands).

I soon left teaching to move into fulltime journalism, especially documentary filmmaking. I teamed up with the tough-minded and elegant Marie Bruyns, South

Marie Bruyns, South Africa's leading producer; the balding gentleman to her right is the famous comedian, Pieter-Dirk Uys. His alter ego is behind in the large picture: Evita Bezuidenhout. I am the hairy one on the other side.

Africa's best producer. In such a staid and censored society our films were inevitably controversial; a few were banned but, surprisingly, some made the local single-channel TV (set up only in 1976) and even won awards. One of the most contentious was a film on the religious fervour sweeping the country.

Fundamentalists flourish in all societies in turmoil, and born-again brigades were sweeping South Africa. I could see the point of a Second Coming: Jesus might have been the only one capable of resolving the South African conundrum, although I suspect Pretoria would have locked Him up if He had heeded the call. South Africa's new Christians insisted that the wave of faith healing, visions, and glossolalia were proof that Christ was due.

I concentrated on Ray McCauley, a hot gospeller and one of the most unlikely converts since Saul. This once notorious bodybuilder hung up his dumb-bells and reached for the Bible to thump it in real style. I spent much time at his Randburg Lourdes, a store-turned-church run by the ex-bouncer-turned-priest. His happy-clappy audience obviously found him exciting. I cringed in embarrassment, although the services were certainly lively and full compared with the dull and empty pews of conventional Christendom. With all their American razzmatazz the revivalists were obviously filling a gap in the market, giving what the people wanted: an easily digestible showbiz gospel.

Like ex-smokers the urge to proselytise is overwhelming. Ray told me: 'Don't go to heaven alone. Take someone with you.'

The doctrine was simple: everything good is from God and all sickness is from the devil.

As a well-known local actress, Marloe Scott-Wilson, said with fervour: 'There's no grey. There's a wrong or a right. There is no ambiguity. Doubt is sin.'

Because her hair was dyed shocking pink, and she was dressed all in pink and driving a pink jeep at the time, I couldn't quite concentrate on clever theological refutations of the McCauley line.

When I had recovered, I thought, 'Yes, sometimes faith does require a denial of reason, but the mature believer must also face the possibility that he or she could be wrong.' I debated hiring a pink jeep and driving around to tell Marloe just that.

One of the most worrying aspects of McCauley's Rhema church was its concept that material prosperity was a mark of God's favour. The churches were run like big business corporations, dependent upon tithes, plus the large impromptu donations of their ever-growing congregations. They were erecting massive new buildings. Why, if Christ was about to come? I dug into their finances and worried even more about the credit-card theology of the new supermarket churches. What happened to it being as difficult for a rich man to get into the kingdom of God as for a camel to get through the eye of a needle? Sometimes the sermons seemed to be bargaining with God.

If many churches were perhaps preachy cargo cults, what of their political ties? Some did have affiliations with the ruling Afrikaner National Party. When it came to key social matters, such as conscription or the ANC's concept of a just war, the pastors were dumb. They rendered unto Caesar what was Caesar's – fortunately for Pretoria. On the other hand there seemed little debate about multi-racialism, which so exercised the conservative white churches. Whites ran the Rhema show, but lots of black believers mingled happily.

I witnessed thousands of miracles. Cripples walked and spoke in tongues. The deaf heard; the dumb spoke. I questioned some of them closely. They couldn't all have been Oscar-winning actors; they were often very convincing, especially when they threw away their wheelchairs. Marie's bad foot, she said, had been healed. I had been wounded in my right eye and partly blinded so I tried it, but nothing happened. I'm a cynic, however. Doctors I interviewed told me that often new converts dropped their much-needed medicines. Sometimes patients were cured; at other times they regressed and blamed their lack of faith. They lost their faith and sometimes their lives. Were these fast-talking new breed of pastors conmen on the make, or maligned miracle workers? Were they suffering the condemnation that the early disciples of Jesus endured? The ones I met looked genuine, but so did Americans Jim Jones and David Koresh, when they started up.

Ray McCauley was adamant: 'Everything we do in this church has a scriptural foundation.'

That's how they explained the Spanish Inquisition.

I witnessed fervent youngsters burning thousands of rands' worth of pop records 'because they were satanic'. If they had incinerated heavy metal stuff or, please, Cliff Richard, I would have clapped with them, but I was tormented when someone threw a Chuck Berry LP on the fire.

McCauley caught sight of my anguish: 'If you think we're fanatical, we're gonna get more fanatical because Jesus was a fanatic.'

I thought South Africa had more than enough fanatics, but I knew better than to argue when someone had that manic gleam in their eyes. Those glazed looks, the emotionalism, the unquestioning, if honest, fervour. Better Rhema, I supposed, than joining the neo-Nazi Afrikaner *Weerstandsbeweging* (AWB), or going to church just to show off your new hat.

What happened to their faith or mental balance if and when the new converts burned out and left the hothouse atmosphere? The organized authoritarianism of the hothouses bothered me; total rejection of doubt, whether in politics or religion, often leads to extremism. The movements may have been hugely successful, and even God-directed, but they were not my cup of tea. If Christ did die for our sins, dare we make His martyrdom meaningless by not committing them?

The screening of the born-again film led to literally hundreds of rude or pious messages per day to the South African Broadcasting Corporation and my home. The irate pastors had organized a mass phone in: my answering machine was red hot.

Besides churches, Marie and I also made films in other challenging environments. We spent, for example, three months filming gangs, especially in the Cape Flats, outside Cape Town. Over 80,000 really hard gangsters populated the area. They often started very young and graduated to the prison gangs, the university of South African crime.

The captive states

Because of South African censorship, I started to film in the neighbouring states. As a schoolboy philatelist I had been intrigued by stamps from the three former British protectorates that became independent as Lesotho, Botswana and Swaziland.

Lesotho was twinned with Wales and was also proud of its pony-trekking and choirs. Besides being one of the three remaining African kingdoms (with ruling royals), it also had the shortest railway line on the continent; one mile, to be precise. Its most distinctive feature, however, is that it is one of only three countries completely surrounded by another state — the other two, by the way, are the Vatican and San Marino. Unfortunately, Lesotho's encircling neighbour was a bully: South Africa. So, although Lesotho's coat of arms proudly proclaimed its aspirations, *Khotso, Pula*, and *Nala* (peace, rain, and prosperity), sadly it had missed out on all three.

Swaziland was much more lush and rather more peaceful. I contrived to spend a lot of time in Africa's second smallest country. For starters, until 1986 it had the only all-steam railway system in the world. Another anorak fascination was the country's philatelic history. By and large, things worked in Swaziland, although they worked a lot more slowly. And the hotels could be excellent, especially around the capital Mbabane. Henry Rider Haggard loved the surrounding mountains, and a little of the mystery remained, despite the rash of hoardings.

Many people visited Swaziland, however, for earthier delights: it was considered the brothel of Africa, especially when interracial sex was barred in South Africa. The Why Not Club just outside the capital was perhaps the seediest nightspot in the subcontinent. Topless ladies pranced on pedestals while UK soccer videos were projected on to the back walls; over the snooker tables ladies stretched in micro skirts, despite being totally amnesiac in the lower lingerie department. Naturally, all the hacks congregated at the club during the coronation of the new king in 1986.

The previous monarch, Sobhuza, had ruled for sixty-one years, thus establishing the record for being not just the longest reigning but also the most absolute monarch in the world. Unlike Lesotho, there were no political parties for Pretoria to manipulate; the old king had considered them un-African. Technically, Swaziland was not a monarchy, but a dyarchy. All power was supposed to be shared between the hereditary male ruler — called the Son of the She-Elephant — with his mother, yes, the She-Elephant. This created problems with a king in his eighties. A Queen Regent ruled after Sobhuza, but she was deposed and one of the dead king's many wives took over. The regency was riddled by Byzantine intrigue, tales of witchcraft, massive corruption, and various assassination attempts. Eventually the traditionalists triumphed; in April 1986, a 19-year-old youth, educated at a public school in England, became King Mswati III.

Thereupon nearly all the bickering stopped and invitations went out worldwide to presidents and monarchs to attend the coronation. The correspondents poured in; they might not have comprehended the complex succession process, but they did understand that nearly all the country's single women — black and white — would be dancing topless in front of the king at the capital's football stadium.

I was covering some of the ceremonies live on SATV. I was supposed to interview the new king, but it was cancelled at the last minute, which might have been lucky as protocol required one to crawl out backwards after an audience. Unfortunately, though, I was left with half an hour of live prime time to cover, after a long report I had produced on the lead-up to the coronation. No king or relative was available, and Pik Botha, the South African foreign minister, hadn't pitched up at the makeshift studio in an Mbabane hotel.

Marie Bruyns, the producer, told me all this seconds before transmission. She said: 'You'll have to suck it and see.'

'Suck what?' I asked in panic.

I bluffed for about fifteen minutes with the anchorman in Johannesburg — by discoursing on the arcane structure of the royal family. I was getting desperate; I had run through, twice, all the king's titles: the Great Mountain, the Mouth that Tells No Lies, the Sun, and the Milky Way — the last I think I made up. I was just about to launch into all the chocolate bars when the commercial break gave me a brief respite.

Suddenly, I spied the hotel manager. I grabbed him and proceeded to interrogate him about security arrangements for the VIPs and what special diets they had. Somehow this guff filled a whole live programme.

In Botswana I normally relied not on a TV crew but on my own stills camera, a trusty, idiot-proof Pentax K1000. I did very little political reporting in this big, largely desert country, the size of Texas. Instead I concentrated on 'soft' stories, usually basing myself in safari lodges. Botswana was a country of stark, often unspoilt, beauty. Most of the million or so ethnically homogenous inhabitants lived in the south along the South African border. And yet, for all the poor examples set by its black and white neighbours, and South African raids during the 1980s, Botswana survived as one of the handful of functioning democracies on the continent.

Swazi warriors at the coronation, 1986.

Despite occasional South African military incursions, Botswana was politically in a much stronger position than Lesotho or Swaziland — besides owning vast herds of cattle, the country also had lots of diamonds. Like South Africa and its diamonds partner, the USSR, Botswana then produced 30 per cent of the world's supply. Jwaneng, in the southern Kalahari Desert, became the world's most valuable diamond mine. This piece of nature's bounty contributed to an amazing 11 per cent national growth rate in the first half of the 1980s. Botswana's economic success story, due to mineral resources and sound political and financial policies, was almost unique in Africa; it was literally a diamond in a continental desert of mismanagement. In the 1980s my travels in these three Commonwealth countries, where race relations were so much more relaxed, gave me some hope and respite. For a while I could forget the atrocities of South African politics and succumb to the seduction of the region's scenery and its people. That was Africa: generally great people, usually shit-awful governments.

Neighbouring wars

South West Africa (later called Namibia) was arguably the final unresolved legacy of the German defeat in 1918. If any metropolitan country — besides Belgium — deserved to lose its colonies it was the Second Reich. The German settlers switched Reichs after South Africa conquered the country. It became de facto a fifth province of South Africa, set to take the same route as its minder: both black and white nationalists talked past each other and took up arms.

I had covered the war there on and off for years, but I was more interested in 'South West' for its angry, beautiful landscapes. It was the last great wilderness in southern Africa: the same size as France, Belgium, and West Germany combined and, with fewer than 1.5 million inhabitants, it boasted one of the world's lowest population densities. Much of the land was untouched desert. In some places no rain had fallen for a century. The wild symphony of harsh desert, lunar landscapes and pastoral serenity afforded an almost unmolested wildlife.

One camera assistant, overcome by the abundant wildlife, exclaimed: 'Christ, if you look hard enough you'll even see a smurf.'

I went on patrol with South African troops on horses and motorbikes along the South West Africa/Angola border, 1985.

Ovahimba women, with their plaits and red mud for make-up.

We did see everything but a smurf. Above all, I marvelled again at how giraffes always seem to move in slow motion. In Africa, the best of the day is dawn and evening, when the game is most abundant. At the Namutoni fort I watched the thin sliver of the moon hang behind the battlements. Scops owls called, and in the distance I could hear the strangled war-cry of a hyena.

South West was also the reluctant requiem for twenty-five years of bush war, most of it unreported. South Africa had the military power, but the insurgents had the popular support. Battlefield attrition and the convergence of superpower self-interest in Angola eventually levered Pretoria out of the occupied country.

Portuguese Africa

Angola was one of the least reported countries on earth. The struggle against the Portuguese started in 1961 and it became a civil war after independence in 1975. South Africa backed Jonas Savimbi's rebels. Twice the size of France or Texas, Angola was churned into one huge devastated battleground, when its oil and fertility could have made it a second Brazil. I found Savimbi one of the more interesting African leaders: a charismatic political chameleon. The former Maoist trained in China had made friends with Washington and was even dubbed the 'Mrs Thatcher of Africa' – presumably a compliment. The bearded warlord used to swagger with a pearl-handled Colt revolver slung low over his hip. A visit to his isolated capital in Jamba, in south-east Angola was *de rigueur*: he was always promising to defeat the Cuban and Russian troops backing his rivals in the north.

He later became a mad paranoid dictator before he was shot in 2002, but when I visited Savimbi in the mid-1980s he was leading possibly the best trained and most effective guerrilla army in Africa. True, he had a lot of American and South African help, but he did well to survive the massed might of pro-Moscow forces which led to the largest African tank battles since Rommel versus Monty.

My favourite story about Savimbi's war concerned a small, pilotless Seeker drone that the South Africans used for spying. Savimbi's troops observed the plane being shot down. A South African colonel with a sense of humour told a search party to hunt for it, as the matter was politically sensitive: 'The pilot is a very small Japanese man.'

The South Africans needed humour because they were losing their war. They fought, however, with great skill and bravery in Angola, although they were usually outnumbered and outclassed by modern Russian and Cuban technology.

I took this picture of the mural in Jonas Savimbi's HQ in Jamba, southern Angola. It celebrated the cosy relationship between the warlord and President Ronald Reagan.

During a visit to Jamba, I asked Savimbi about his relations with the anti-Marxist Renamo guerrillas in the other big Portuguese-speaking ex-colony, Mozambique. He was dismissive, implying they were in an altogether different junior league. I was not so sure and was on my way to find out for myself.

****

Tim Lambon wanted to make the first documentary on the elusive leader of Renamo, Afonso Dhlakama. Tim and I had worked together before, with my playing Danny DeVito to his Rambo. It would be highly dangerous, but I trusted his military and filmmaking skills. God knows why he asked me to accompany him on the two-man adventure. No one had managed to do it before because Renamo was ranked alongside the Khmer Rouge for hospitality.

Like all communist dictatorships, Frelimo-led Mozambique was efficient in two areas: propaganda and secret police. Around 90 per cent of the whites had fled at independence in 1975. Of the 350 train drivers, only one had been black. South African tourism was extinguished, leaving over 30,000 prostitutes out of work in the capital of Maputo. The anti-Marxist guerrillas, Renamo, were born in double original sin – they were created by the Rhodesian Central Intelligence Organization and nourished by apartheid South Africa, although it soon became a genuine nationalist movement, fired up by the Marxist attacks on Catholicism, traditional chiefs and Islam.

Renamo's alleged passion for cutting off ears, noses and lips had relegated its leader, Afonso Dhlakama, to a horror chamber with a million-dollar price-tag on his head. He was hunted by over 60,000 Frelimo troops backed by Cuban advisers, East German intelligence officers, 2,000 Tanzanian soldiers and over 20,000 reasonably effective Zimbabwean troops whose officers were trained by the British army. Ex-British SAS were sniffing around as well. Dhlakama was a difficult man to pin down for his first TV interview. Frelimo held the cities, but Renamo owned the night and most of the countryside. Some Mozambicans were Frelimo by day and Renamo after dark.

Tim and I smuggled our TV equipment through the officials in Malawi, a country run by a puritanical bigot who hated journalists. The few who were allowed in, perhaps occasionally the BBC, were sometimes forced to endure haircuts at the airport, not an unreasonable nod to personal hack hygiene perhaps. We crossed from Malawi into northern Mozambique by dug-out log canoe and then proceeded with small motorbikes to traverse hundreds of miles of a war zone to reach Gorongosa, the Renamo 'capital'. We crossed the mighty Zambesi in a small inflatable, bikes and all.

The countryside was lush. Towns were deserted, literally picked clean as if by locusts. I had little time to pursue my affection for trains, but I could not resist

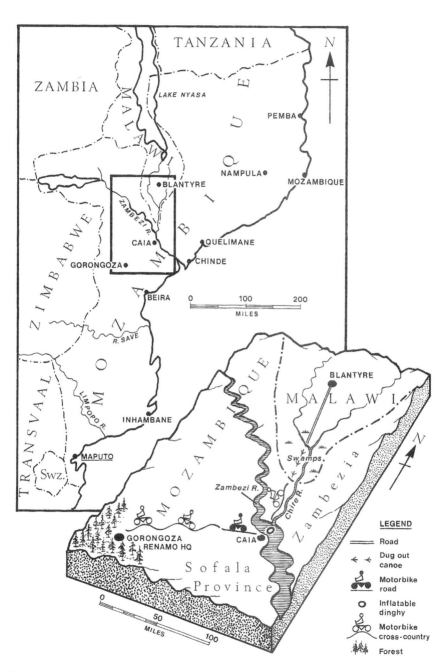

Tim and I travelled through Mozambique on foot, in canoes and on motorbikes to reach the rebel HQ.

exploring an old Orient Express-type train strewn across an embankment almost totally throttled by encroaching bush. It was Mad-Max land where petrol was king. We managed to scrounge some for our three bikes that ferried Tim and me, plus three heavily armed Renamo guides.

After a week's backbreaking travel almost entirely cross-country, sometimes carrying the bikes, Tim had bad news for me. We had kept secret Tim's ability to understand the guides' use of Shona.

'I've been listening to their conversation and something's wrong. I get the impression that they have been ordered not to take us to Dhlakama. We may have to disarm them and make our own way south.'

'What do you mean "disarm them"?'

'Take their guns.'

'And what if they resist?'

'Then we'll have to shoot them.'

I went into some detail about the bad PR, lack of guides and the fact that I had little experience in taking on some of the world's fiercest guerrillas.

Tim countered with the fact that they could easily shoot us.

I had just watched one of the guerrillas fashion a clutch-plate out of an old can. He was a good mechanic as well as a fine soldier who kept his AK in immaculate condition. Removing him might mean that I would have to walk.

Tim on the back of the bikes nursing the camera.

I hated two things in life, walking long distances with heavy kit in arduous terrain, and communal living. They say you are drawn inevitably to the things you hate or fear most. Certainly I spent much of my time with irascible insurgents around the world, both yomping and living with them.

To make matters worse, Tim had a fever. It was the one occasion, despite my being much less physically robust than the special-forces-trained Tim, that I played the role of mentor.

I had learned to transcend fear in war zones. I wasn't suicidal or nonchalant; I had learned that you cannot operate properly in a state of permanent anxiety. You had to live for the moment; Tim was not only ill, but transfixed by domestic problems at home. I have never worked out whether courage is like a well which can dry up, or a muscle which gets stronger the more you use it. In my case, as I got older, I thought it was more like a well which could be emptied.

We stuck with our guides, who took us to the Scarlet Pimpernel of Africa. We met him in a small clearing with two young guards. He appeared an unprepossessing chubby young man, dressed simply in a blue shirt and dark slacks. No posing like Savimbi. Dhlakama looked like a timid bank clerk, although I guess that Genghis Khan had his quiet days. He was 33, and looked a lot like a younger version of his arch nemesis, Robert Mugabe. Unlike most politicians, he seemed keen to listen, perhaps because he had a much exaggerated impression of British influence in Africa. His ambition was to visit London, which I manipulated to help persuade him to release a British hostage held by Renamo.

A picture of Afonso Dhlakama I took later, in 1991.

We talked affably in English and Portuguese for nearly two whole days. We both seemed to enjoy each other's company, though I think he was starved of any foreign non-military company. He appeared neither an African variant of a social democrat, as Renamo propaganda suggested, nor the biggest mass murderer since Hitler, as Frelimo would have it. I was keen to find out, however, whether he was a super-patriot or a crude puppet of Pretoria.

We set up his first TV interview. Most was in a highly lucid Portuguese. We also needed soundbites in English. His aide and translator coached him and suggested a cue board to help the rebel president's faltering English.

Tim referred to the cue as an 'idiot board', common parlance in media circles in London, but not entirely pleasing to an African warlord. Dhlakama understood and showed some displeasure. It was perhaps like mentioning a favourite Jewish grandmother to the Führer. I quickly explained the correct nuance to the translator, who had a sense of humour, both of which were transferred effectively to Dhlakama.

From what I saw in my travels and then the long dialogues with the Renamo chief, it was clear that the rebels had a lot of support among the *povo* – the rural masses. We examined the weaponry, especially signals equipment, surreptitiously, to discover a South African connection. Tim had the technical expertise and we could have made a lot of money if we had deployed a little licence to interpret the kit as apartheid stock. We played it dead straight, however. After travelling for over 300 miles we did see a basic national indigenous organization. We saw food being grown. We witnessed no cruelty to the peasantry, although Renamo was hardly likely to stage a quick atrocity for the benefit of our cameras.

On the long return journey, no sentries were posted; the camps we visited to get fuel lacked even basic perimeter defences.

'The Viet Cong would have made mincemeat of this lot,' said Tim.

We concluded that the Renamo guerrillas were doing so well militarily not because they were any good, but because Frelimo were so bad. The journey to 'Free Mozambique' had been instructive, but we left as sceptics, still wondering about the amazingly coincidental congruence of Renamo's and Pretoria's – let alone Washington's – strategies.

The film was shown in a few places and it covered my expenses. I wasn't sure as to what the experience had done for my academic reputation. At an Oxford University conference soon after, I listened in growing frustration as dons talked in detail about the Renamo bandits. This was still the time of the Cold War and the height of the anti-apartheid crusade. Frelimo was on the side of the angels, *ipso*

A young Renamo soldier in central Mozambique during the 1986 offensive.

facto Renamo had to be crude cutthroats with no organization or goals – mere starving wolfpacks scavenging for food.

The self-righteous omniscience irritated me. Some of the dons assumed to know all about Renamo and even wrote books on their long-distance learning. They refused to visit or at least *try* to visit the areas they described; instead they relied almost entirely on Maputo's government news service. They simply refused to sully their prejudices with experience. A kind of Gresham's Law applied: the farther away you are from experiencing first hand, the greater the sum of intellectual knowledge. Wimp that I am, I came to believe that there is nothing like being shot at occasionally to sharpen your wits, and prose.

The first TV interview and perhaps the release of a British hostage seemed to cement a rapport between the president and this hack, and perhaps also created a (false) impression in Whitehall that I could be a useful point man for the rebel chieftain. I was to meet Dhlakama a few more times, both in Mozambique and finally even on a semi-official visit to London.

I went in again in 1991. No trekking and Mad-Max bikers' world. A missionary took me from Malawi into Gorongosa in a Piper Aztec. It had 'Pilot for Christ' emblazoned on the side. I thought: bugger all the anthropological stuff, this was the way to go. An airstrip had been made between very tall trees to disguise its role. It certainly fooled me.

'That's a footpath, not an airstrip,' I said to the pilot.

As he approached to land, he started to pray – loudly – which did not inspire great confidence, but it was the niftiest bit of bush-flying I had ever seen.

I was to attend a Renamo congress which was preparing for a national peace deal. The independence of Namibia, the winding down of the Angolan war and, above all, the release of Nelson Mandela had transformed southern Africa. With the collapse of its patron, the USSR, Frelimo had nowhere to go but a peace deal with Dhlakama.

This time the cameraman was a bush-hardened South African, 'J. J.' Swart. We filmed Renamo shooting practice, which was useless as ever. And, as on my previous trip, I seemed to be the only fall guy prepared to be polite and sample the local hooch, in this case, *skokian,* which tasted like boot polish, turps and semolina. It kept our headman-host happy, however.

Foreign Renamo delegates were assembled to meet Dhlakama. The men from Kenya were shifty, the man from the USA was brash and wore a baseball hat and the man from Frankfurt acted Germanic. It was interesting to see how exiled Mozambicans had exaggerated the customs of their adopted lands, as with many forced migrants. Perhaps it was better than huddling in ethnic ghettos and celebrating old rituals as the ex-pat Brits tend to do.

Dhlakama greeted me warmly. He had travelled widely and his English had expanded as dramatically as his girth. One of the first questions he asked me was why the then Conservative British government was spending so much money training a still-Marxist Frelimo army in Zimbabwe while London couldn't afford to maintain some of its own famous regiments. A good question, I told him.

We filmed the cabal of Renamo delegates, with Dhlakama dressed in a uniform which made him look like a chief scout. Around him were old clan chiefs in 1930s demob suits, while a white hunter was dressed in smart safari gear, tense academics, some hard-looking hoods, a few *mestiços* … all an attempt, I guessed, to balance the classes and tribes of old Mozambique. I was a rare white face. I didn't know if I was witnessing a historical milestone in southern Africa or a remake of Al Capone.

I did a long TV interview with Dhlakama about atrocities, all but accusing him of being a mass murderer. Asking someone whom 99 per cent of the international media thought was a paranoid and genocidal maniac, in the middle of his army, whether he liked killing people, seems a little bold in retrospect. I didn't think so at the time because he struck me as open-minded.

The Brits must have thought so as well, although it might have been based more on his chances of winning the Mozambican presidency. Dhlakama had eventually got on well with his old enemy Robert Mugabe and both had helped secure a peace deal in Mozambique after decades of war. The Renamo chieftain had become the leader of the opposition and the British Foreign and Commonwealth Office privately thought he had a one-in-three chance of winning a free election. I was asked to go out to see the Renamo boss again.

It was late 1999. I was sitting in an adjunct of Durban airport waiting for a small plane to take me to Maputo, the Mozambican capital. There was only other passenger, a woman who was as nervous as she was pretty. Her eyes grew larger and larger, as I looked around the room for perhaps a huge spider or snake.

She finally spoke, 'I've never flown before and I am *dying* with fear.'

I did a long TV interview with 'President' Dhlakama and all but accused him directly of being a mass murderer and yet he also appreciated my jokes after the interview.

I explained that it was a very short flight.

A well-dressed young man wearing a plain white shirt came in and sat on the other side of her. He looked very much in command of himself and so the young woman fixed on him for support

'Do you fly much?' she asked.

'I hope so,' he said. 'I'm the pilot.'

I travelled from the ramshackle Maputo airport to my over-expensive hotel, circumnavigating the large potholes and the astonishingly garish social-realist murals of Frelimo heroes. The pastel-coloured colonial-era villas on the foreshore looked as if they had not been painted or repaired since their white owners had fled in 1974. Residents seemed to be camping rather than living in buildings.

I had a long chat with the new leader of the parliamentary opposition and Dhlakama assured me, like all African politicians, that he would win if the elections were fair. He didn't because they weren't; but he did pretty well despite the rigging.

Since I was not encumbered with all the paraphernalia of TV equipment, I did a bit of sightseeing, not least satisfying my geeky itch to look at old trains. The main station was resplendent outside in its striking green and white livery. Inside, though, the passenger coaches were more like cattle wagons. Long queues had formed for the slow journey to Johannesburg. Frelimo had not been successful in learning from the good practice of the British army, but their officials had imbibed with alacrity the worst lessons of the UK rail system.

The local diplomats and politicians seemed optimistic about peace. Even the British High Commissioner – strangely, Mozambique had joined the Commonwealth – was more than professionally sunny about the future. We sat talking in the same building where Winston Churchill had sought help after his famous escape during the Boer War. A plaque still commemorated the event, even though the High Commission was adjacent to V.I. Lenin Square and the road running past the US Information Service office was named after Kim Il Sung. The Mozambicans were clearly covering all their bases.

I left Mozambique in a tropical rainstorm. The taxi almost floated to the airport, where the immigration official handed back my passport with little fuss. Only then did he ask me politely for 'something for the weekend'. My memory flitted back to the barbers of my youth, but I pulled myself together and gave him US $2 dollars – a few days' official wages – because the man had been so polite.

****

Angola and Mozambique depressed me because decades of war had devastated potentially rich lands. The poorest African colony of the Portuguese was Guinea-Bissau, another victim of a long colonial war. It was also Africa's most unwelcoming country to foreigners, especially if they happened to be journalists as well. The country was closed, even to the International Monetary Fund-types bearing gifts. It was run by a paranoid military officer who hated all strangers.

Cameraman Tommy Doig and I drove across country to reach Bissau, the derelict capital, after much hard graft. I couldn't believe the state of the harbour – the wrecks looked as though they had been there since the Portuguese had quit nearly twenty years before. I wondered why they had stayed for the previous 500 years – the country didn't have much then, except peanuts. Yet the countryside was unspoiled and beautiful, not that the locals had much except beautiful nuts. The interior comprised a vast plateau covered in almost impenetrable forest. The coast was flat, swampy and very unhealthy. Transportation was difficult because of the many rivers and few surviving bridges.

So why was I again in a god-awful trouble spot? The answer was a fort. I was producing a film on the often imposing old fortifications in West Africa. We drove for four hours from the capital in an impressively new 4x4 hired vehicle to reach Cacheu fort. About 60-feet square and built in 1589, it contained a bizarre tableau of Africa's history: statues of Portuguese colonial heroes such as Vasco da Gama,

The very isolated Portuguese fort of Cacheu in Guinea Bissau. It had all the old gods of colonialism mixed with the recently abandoned communist ones as well.

dumped there after independence, had recently been joined by dethroned Marxist gods – Lenin and Stalin. It was only a short sequence in the documentary so I don't think it was worth it, not least because getting out of the country was even harder than getting in.

The African continent has thousands of fascinating fortifications ranging from the small Beau Geste forts of North Africa to the drystone masterpieces of Great Zimbabwe in the south. In the east, Arab traders had built Islamic citadels. West Africa, however, had the best collection of European stone-erected fortresses. For three centuries nine European countries fought over and ransacked hundreds of forts and castles along the steamy, disease-riddled African coast. Whites originally came to harvest blacks, as well as hunt for gold.

We travelled through the former European colonies of West Africa and found the Francophone areas more congenial, not least the Ivory Coast and Senegal. In the strangest and remotest of places we would find a good restaurant in a hotel which was an oasis of culinary civilization. I had usually regarded myself as a traveller living a day-to-day existence who could forage in local markets. I was a bit sniffy about tourists who would hide away in air-conditioned hotels to avoid stomach upsets. Most tourists I met imagined they were great explorers. The fact that I got the shits in more places than they had should not have made me feel superior. I had to confess to admiring the French in one way, besides food. As one cameraman told me, 'All the colonizers stuffed up the locals, but at least the French called them "Monsieur" when they did it.'

In Anglophone Ghana the food was bad and the castles wonderful, despite their poor maintenance. The country was then ruled by a military strongman, but he was not as obviously bonkers as some of his uniformed peers, not least because he eschewed a personality cult. Still, it wasn't easy getting access to one of his official residences, Christianborg castle. I tried hard to get the castle administrator to let me in. I tried everything including almost resorting to 'Have you seen the film *The Dogs of War,* sir? I have some nice well-behaved mercenary friends who want to come in and take pictures. Is that OK?' I spent hours trying to persuade him and met a brick wall, which I intuited was not connected to any demand for a large bribe. For some reason I went all rustic on him and started talking about my 'village' in Wales. The man's face suddenly lit up. By sheer coincidence he had been treated for a serious complaint in a hospital a mile from my home. The warmth and tenderness of the National Health Service had won his eternal affection. This might come as a surprise to most Britons, but perhaps few of them have been sick in Accra. I secured rare access to the castle.

The other historical wonders required small bribes. For example, Elmina – built by the Portuguese in 1482 with dressed stone brought from Europe – is perhaps the most important and certainly the oldest colonial edifice in sub-Saharan Africa. We approached along a palm-fringed beach full of custom-painted pirogues.

Decaying colonial buildings squatted around the castle. Parts were deteriorating, but it was still imposing. In the morning mist, it looked like an African Camelot.

Unfortunately the warm glow of architectural treasures was dispelled by the exit from Accra airport. The threatening demands for bribes, even to get our passports back, made it my worst airport experience in Africa.

******

Most of my time in Africa was dedicated to covering conflicts, but the documentary on the castles was a pleasant exception. It was not the only one. I produced a glossy documentary on Morocco in 1984, with Henry Bautista, a highly professional cameraman. Nick della Casa was our soundman. Nick was a charming and hardy companion, as he proved later to me in Afghanistan. Morocco was his first assignment. Iraqi Kurdistan was his last. Sadly, he, his new wife and his ex-SAS brother-in-law became posthumously famous for meeting a grisly end at the hands of bandits.

In Morocco Nick was supposed to record my playing 'As Time Goes By' on a piano in a mock-up of Rick's Bar in Casablanca (of course not a frame of the famous movie was shot in North Africa). I didn't play the tune; I was miming to an automatic pianola. A delighted child standing nearby interrupted and asked me to play 'Happy Birthday' for him. Nick broke up laughing and inadvertently erased

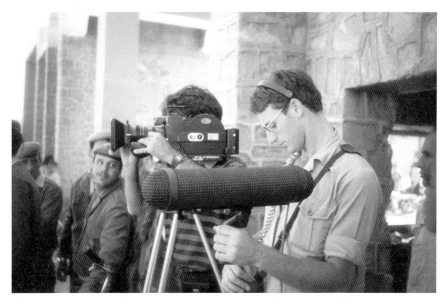

Filming in Morocco in 1984. Henry Bautista on camera (obscured) and Nick della Casa, on sound. Nick was to be killed soon after in Iraq.

the sound on that segment. He managed to get all the rest of the sound right for the film, including my disastrous attempts to perform to-camera pieces while riding a camel. Old film lore relearned: never work alongside kids or animals.

We enjoyed our trip together and bonded well. We had made the 40-minute film relatively cheaply and quickly, although we knew that Morocco was not a typical Arab state. We had enjoyed the richness of the country's history, although the ghosts of the past rich heritage were being shooed away by package tours and hamfisted local bureaucracy. We wandered in the cities' endless souks and ventured deep into the deserts where rain hadn't fallen for a decade. I found Morocco a land of extremes: ancient and brashly modern, simultaneously both dazzling and seedy.

Shortly afterwards we three went to the East African island of Réunion to film another documentary in the same series as Morocco. Nick's French was much better than mine and that helped a lot. Réunion's booze, and especially the local rum, was excellent. The melange of races had produced a unique combination of naturally elegant golden-skinned women who could cook, and converse like Parisiennes, only much more politely. We loved the island as much as the locals loved France. It was effectively a colony that wanted to remain an integral part of France, not least because the health, education and welfare benefits were the same as the metropole.

Réunion was probably the highpoint of my more relaxed journalism. We all soon returned to Johannesburg, the centre of the political revolution that was sweeping South Africa. That was where the action was, so that's where we hacks had to be.

Endgame in South Africa

In 1984 the Orwellian nightmare began to assume a tangible form in South Africa: from the blasphemy of the 'necklace' (a burning, petrol-filled tyre around the neck of an alleged collaborator) to the frenzied doublespeak of government propaganda. At the beginning of that ominous year the armed struggle was just over twenty-two years old. ANC guerrillas had proved remarkably inept, even by African standards. White power looked more entrenched than ever. From the Sharpeville massacre to the June Soweto uprising sixteen years had elapsed. On the cusp of each crisis capital and whites had fled. They had panicked, but the security forces had not. Each wave of resistance was absorbed, diluted, pushed back and pumped underground. From Soweto the cycle of revolt had been reduced to eight years. But no African National Congress master plan existed: the exiled leadership in Lusaka was always slow in keeping up with, let alone controlling, events forged in the crucible of black anger in the townships. From 1984 to 1986 blacks in both urban areas and countryside would rise up once more, hyped by foreign media as the beginning of another 1917. It was not to be.

I had written a book on the South African military (*Africa's Superpower*) suggesting that while holding the ring some military reformists might encourage a moderation of apartheid. This was parodied in the *Star*, even though I also wrote a political column for the same paper. (Abe Berry, courtesy of the *Star*)

The vicious pantomime of death was endlessly recycled — boycotts, stay-aways, rent strikes, demonstrations, riots, police retaliation or provocation, single shots, tear-gas, panic, confusion, concentrated automatic fire … funerals and more funerals. At the burial services — one of the few legal outlets for the outpouring of political and personal grief (before funerals were also restricted) — ANC and Soviet flags were openly displayed, along with wooden replicas of AKs. The cutting edge of the insurrection was arson and murder of suspected informers, black councillors, and policemen, perceived to be the main, and available, local representatives of apartheid. The 'necklace' became a trade mark of the young comrades in their war on collaborators. In the compressed, often breathless, reportage on TV screens in Europe and America, South Africa was going up in flames. In contrast, little of the violence, except the occasional necklacing to emphasize black barbarity, was shown on South African televisions.

The whites were digging in. As one Afrikaner farmer's wife told me, 'We will never give up. We will fight to the last Afrikaner. We did not accept English rule and we will never accept Bantu rule. We don't mind sanctions. We will go back to ox-wagons if they cut off our petrol.'

Another woman, from a Jewish, liberal, business background, was ruthlessly candid, 'Let's be completely logical. We can hand over peacefully now, fight and lose, or we kill the lot of them.'

The comrades struggled to make South Africa ungovernable. 'People's courts' were set up to establish their often arbitrary rule. Sometimes adults were terrorized by bands of feral youngsters, especially for breaking consumer boycotts. Often victims were forced to consume all their 'illegal' purchases on the spot, sometimes fatally in the case of cooking oil, washing powder, soap, and paraffin. Parents grew frustrated with the long school boycotts and self-defeating demands for 'liberation before education'. During 1986 the liberation mania began to dissipate. After two years the severity of the repression, sheer physical exhaustion, and frustration with the excesses of both disciplined comrades and roving bands of *tsotsis* and psychopathic elements had taken their toll. Chaos in the townships was not the same as people's power.

In June 1986 George De'Ath, a friend who worked as a freelance cameraman for the BBC, died from head wounds received from axes and pangas deployed in the fighting between pro-government *witdoeke* vigilantes, the police, and the comrades in Cape Town. He was the first foreign correspondent to be killed while covering the civil war.

The AWB claimed it had no connections with the Nazis.

The ANC kept up its bombing campaign. In July 1987 sixty-eight people were injured in a bomb attack in central Johannesburg. As long as the ANC waged war and the white right wing bayed for tougher action, the Afrikaner government found it difficult to move ahead with its stalled, if not moribund, reform programme. The rise of the Afrikaner Resistance Movement, the AWB, mesmerized Pretoria. The South African government hoped that given enough rope the AWB leader Eugene Terreblanche, a spell-binding orator, might hang himself.

In April 1987 I attended an AWB mass rally in Jo'burg city hall. I was chilled to my marrow … and, sitting at the front-row press table, sprinkled by Terreblanche's spittle. In an action replay of 1930s Germany, long swastika banners adorned the hall, jackbooted stormtroopers raised a Hitler salute, little blond children waved flags, and powerful rhetoric raged against liberals and communists, anyone who questioned the Afrikaners' divine right to rule. The gleam in the eyes of the wildly enthusiastic audience bode ill for the future. After a series of antics, including a well-publicized dalliance with an English-speaking liberal ex-beauty-queen-turned-journalist and the habit of falling off his horse in public, Terreblanche became a music-hall Hitler for some. The conspicuously armed right wing grew; so did underground cells. Terreblanche, the dark messiah, bided his time.

On 2 February 1990 the new South African president, F.W. de Klerk finally dragged his party out of the bunker and across the Rubicon. The ANC and the Pan-Africanist Congress were unbanned. On 11 February Nelson Mandela was finally freed after twenty-seven years in jail. De Klerk and Mandela haggled long and dangerously over the details of a transitional government and the elections scheduled for April 1994.

I didn't see the whole endgame. I had become aggressively argumentative at dinner parties, wanting to shake people warmly by the throat and make them see sense. It was bad journalism. I had become a talker not a listener. Some of my films were banned and I found it increasingly difficult to report. In mid-1987 I moved my base from Johannesburg to write in Spain, though I would continue to return to South Africa for short reporting trips.

South Africa had been a difficult conflict to cover. Some journalists felt it was a special case, apartheid a special evil. After witnessing a massacre or two it was easy to take sides. No wonder Pretoria accused foreign journalists of incitement. Afrikaners said that many overseas hacks had a Jericho complex: one more blow or one more trumpet and the whole edifice would implode. Most journalists did not crusade against Pretoria. Nevertheless, the vast majority, even the crusty old Africa hands, were frequently appalled by Pretoria's hamfisted manipulation of the media. It was always difficult in Africa to balance moral convictions with professional standards. Just giving a rough balance, say 50 per cent blame to Mugabe and 50 per cent to Smith, sometimes created a legitimacy by default. Maybe neither man deserved 50 per cent of the moral argument. Yet it was better to make this kind of mistake than give in to advocacy journalism and crusade against apartheid.

I don't want to appear too pious about my reporting of South Africa. It was not all moral indignation. After all, I had my second-best job in my career there. I was a judge in the Miss South Africa competition and the winners over three consecutive years moved in next door to my mock Cape Dutch cottage in trendy Melville, Johannesburg. It was less to do with my personal charms, and more about the fact that the official competition chaperone shared my cottage (platonically). My glamorous neighbours weren't all airheads. The 1984 winner, Tish Snyman, was not only beautiful but smart, and kind. I dedicated my book about South Africa's Robin Hood, *Stander,* to her, and to our friendship.

Mostly, however, I felt ill at ease in South Africa, despite my commercial success. I had loved Rhodesia/Zimbabwe, but I felt angry in South Africa. Some of my films were banned; most of my weekly national

Leticia Snyman, Miss South Africa 1984, with author. We were good friends and neighbours in Melville, Johannesburg.

newspaper columns in *The Star* and the *Sunday Express* appeared, although sometimes only after long meetings with in-house media lawyers. Political journalists could bark, but not bite. As I had become a resident, infringements could lead to jail, as opposed to non-resident hacks who were often simply deported. When I returned to Europe, it was refreshing to use a phone and know that you weren't being monitored. Trouble was I moved to Spain and couldn't get a phone installed – for nearly three years. And that was in the days before mobile phones. I had swapped one version of media hobbling with another.

Chapter 2

European Interlude

Spain

Paper clips can be more injurious to your health than bullets. That was my experience of Spain's bureaucratic Leviathan. Give me Russian gunships any day rather than a semi-literate Spaniard on the make. For three years I lived near Altea, on the Costa Blanca. The colours and light in the old town could produce an instant orgasm for artists and photographers. But nearby loomed the breeze-block paradises of expatriate ghettos where Scousers and Brummies pursued the English dream — a house with more bathrooms than people, or at least *a* bathroom. Altea was beautifully old and shockingly new. That was Spain all over; so many different styles, peoples, and languages. To define Spain as one country is to call the Equator a town.

Why was it that Spanish airports were always under construction? Indeed, the whole country appeared to be under construction. The greedy building booms which did so much environmental damage to the coastal regions played no small part in the economic collapse after 2008. The European Union pumped in funds, or bribes perhaps, whereby money was taken from poor people in rich countries (northern Europe) and doled out to rich people in poor countries (southern Europe).

When I lived in Spain, from 1987 to 1990, much of the talk was of 1992, especially full membership of the European Community. Personally, I think Spain should have joined not the EC but the Organization of African Unity. That year was billed as a triumphal symbol of the end of centuries of Spain being cold-shouldered by the rest of Europe. There was always potential for mayhem, however, induced by the volatile Iberian mix of incompetence and overconfidence.

Spain's dark history intruded upon the glitzy dash for modernity; 1992 was also the 500th anniversary of the expulsion of the Jews and Arabs from a country which launched the terrors of the Inquisition. Similar terrors were inflicted in the 1980s on European foreigners, who queued for years for endless permits. There was a technical requirement, presumably never observed, for permits to wallpaper your own house. Beleaguered foreign residents hoped 1992 would be the beginning of the end of a system which seemed to regulate everything except flatulence.

Altea was one of the last areas to fall to Franco in the civil war, so the local council had a strange complexion: 1930s Popular Front socialists, anarcho-syndicalists, peasant Marxists with a soft spot for Stalin, and a sprinkling of Valenciano nationalists. The council decreed that the union leader who ran the main post office should refuse to sell stamps. He despised foreigners anyway, especially the 99 per cent who couldn't speak fluent Valenciano, and he used an electronic random selector to calculate prices for those who couldn't count in his native tongue. Tobacconists were given the monopoly on selling stamps, although they had trouble prising any out of Madrid. I suppose the millions of tourists were expected to take their postcards home with them.

I must confess to having a bit of a negative attitude to Spain. Perhaps it was my refusal to pay a large bribe to get a phone – for most of the time I did not have a conventional landline phone (in the era before mobile phones). For a hack that is like losing a limb. Also, my mother-in-law moved in next door and, although I liked her company, she comprised 99 per cent of all visits to my house.

I was surprised at how many unreconstructed Nazis I met in Spain. One or two were old SS men in retirement, but even younger Germans seemed reluctant to accept any responsibility for the Holocaust. Nearly every German I met said the genocide of the Jews had been grossly exaggerated or completely invented. As both my then wife, Sue, and I spoke German we were sometimes invited to German dinner parties. Sue always gave me the Basil Fawlty line, 'Don't mention the war', but it inevitably came up when people asked about my war reporting. At one party two serving West German army officers treated me to a highly intelligent if historically bogus version of the extermination of the Jews. The one German I met who was politically correct on the genocide issue was a doctor. I asked him what his speciality was.

'I am medical doctor, but working in research.'

'What research?'

'On pain thresholds.'

With all the British crooks, Spanish red tape, and roaring Nazis, I wondered about the 'new' democracy, thinking Spain was not ready for Europe *sans*

Altea: the charming old town. I lived in the hills above the town for three years.

frontières. Some parts of the country were on the move, however. *La movida* was true of Madrid, where everything except traffic moved quickly. It was an elegant, sophisticated city, but its outskirts were afflicted by shanty towns. Spain was full of such contradictions, always ready to confirm or confound every cliché. It was third and first world at the same time, both a 'fragment nipped off hot Africa', as Auden called it, and the most European of all EC states. It was collectivist, yet attractively individualistic. Even anarchy was too organized for most Spaniards. You could see that in their homicidal driving, madcap parking, compulsive littering, and sheer delight in chain smoking in very confined public space, such as lifts. Tax evasion was a national passion, along with gambling. *Mañana* sleepiness held everything up, but visitors always asked, paradoxically, 'When do Spaniards sleep?', because they caroused so late, so often, and so noisily. It was a country dedicated to the worship of the Virgin Mary, but whores outnumbered nuns by six to one.

The contradictions inherited from an often humiliating past were reinforced by sudden, recent democratization and the resulting swings of the moral pendulum. Spain revelled in, or raged against, the new-found freedoms. It became legal to smoke dope. Almost-naked Spanish girls relaxed on the beaches where their mothers would have walked well covered, accompanied perhaps by chaperones. Imperial isolationism was also to blame. Like Britain, the Spanish often referred to 'Europe' as though it were somewhere else. Both nations once ran empires in which they expected everyone else to learn their language.

Barcelona: The fairytale masterpiece of Antoni Gaudí's Casa Batlló.

In Spain it was also a case of the plural: *languages.* I had a historic interest in the Basque language and made some clumsy stabs at getting my head around Catalan and Valenciano. The most centralized state in Europe mushroomed into a quasi-federation of seventeen autonomous regions, each with its own flag and capital, and in some cases its own language. The most bloody- and independently-minded were the unruly Basques, my favourite 'Spaniards'. I also liked Barcelona, capital of Catalonia. Ever since the wonderfully named William the Shaggy made the title Count of Barcelona hereditary in the ninth century, Catalans had exhibited a fierce sense of independence.

Barcelona was the most fashionable and go-ahead city in Spain. Even the phones and lifts worked. Barcelona was an arty place, forever associated with such names as Picasso, Salvador Dalí, and, above all, Antoni Gaudí, whose brooding genius is best exemplified by the unfinished *Sagrada Familia* Cathedral.

Spaniards wore or drove their new-found wealth. As José Ortega y Gasset, the country's greatest modern philosopher, noted, 'Spain has an absolute genius for art and absolutely no talent for economics.' From my perspective, Spain was committing economic suicide in keeping out foreign professionals who could help to rationalize the cumbersome systems in preparation for the big bang of 1992 and 1993. Part of the problem was the *gestors*, legal middlemen unique to Spain and her corrupt ex-dominions in South America. They were a throwback to the days when illiterate peasants had to employ educated professionals to deal with the state. This applied even to driving licences late into the 1980s. The *gestors* had a vested interest in keeping the bureaucracy as complicated and corrupt as possible. And everyone from sanitary inspectors to estate agents formed guilds to use the permit system to keep out foreign competition. Spain had become one huge closed-shop union, even more bloody-minded than the most predatory of print unions in the old Fleet Street.

In the three years I lived in Spain I failed to get a permit to reside, work, or even legally import furniture into the house I shared with Susan and her daughter Laura. Gelert, my dog, managed to avoid the paper *blitzkrieg*. Susan, a fluent Spanish speaker and erstwhile Hispanophile, was threatened with deportation on several occasions. The family was genuinely European. We spoke the major European languages and had between us German, Dutch, and British passports … but apparently no rights in Spain.

My wife tried to run a farm and a business and pay tax. I helped to edit a small English-language magazine. But we were threatened, usually by fellow expats, with a quaint form of social revenge — being 'denounced' to the authorities for having inadequate permits. (Technically, the denouncers would get 10 per cent of fines imposed on the denounced. Spaniards, who also had to live with the permit mania, usually disdained the *denuncia*.) We employed three or four Spaniards part-time and would have employed more if we could have secured permits to run a business. But no, we spent much of the first year in queues and going back and forth out of the country to get fresh visas. We spent a small fortune on lawyers.

In the end we gave up, and begged to be allowed to take our furniture out of Spain.

Standing in one of the endless queues, treated regularly like cattle, Susan said, 'Now I know what it's like to be a black in South Africa.'

'The difference is,' I replied, 'our maids have the vote but the madam doesn't.'

One bureaucrat was honest enough to admit, 'We do everything we can to keep foreigners out, especially those with skills or who want to run businesses.'

Inspectors would fan out from the *comisario* trying to catch people working, even professional, middle-aged expats who might own a farm and a large villa. One Dutch woman in her sixties was almost deported for helping a colleague with some bookkeeping on an informal basis.

'I went through the war,' she told me. 'It reminds me of the feeling of terror when the Nazis were rounding up Jews.'

Vanloads of young EC foreigners doing casual jobs were herded together, taken to the border, and dumped. I was incensed by articles in the Spanish press about how wonderfully European Spain was. I even nagged a friendly British MEP to help me by taking my case to the European Commission on Human Rights. That too led to more inconsequential bureaucracy…

Passport to Pimlico

So you will understand what prompted me to take refuge from the modern-day inquisition in a little piece of England in Iberia — Gibraltar. It was a day's drive from Altea to Gib, but there were some wonderful pit stops. Old Granada, especially the Alhambra, has to be one of the glories of Islamic civilization. I would dally for a day or two with unreformed criminals on the Costa del Sol. Occasionally I stayed with a retired conman in Fuengirola, which local expats wittily called 'funny guerrilla'. My appetite for big dollops of sleaze and plastic opulence in places such as Marbella was limited, but inland were the Hemingwayesque bridges of Ronda, one of the oldest of Spanish towns.

I also liked Mijas, not for its over-visited prettiness, but for the magazine its massive Mafia palace of a town hall published. Its Spanglish and discordant detail made it much funnier than *Private Eye*, partly because it took itself so seriously. It published, for example, information about how many contraceptive coils had been fitted in local clinics. Good taste prevents me from going into further detail. The glossy municipal mag played up two things: the town's unique square bullring and its even more unique, and round, mayor, who appeared on every page. The mayor's own publication described him as a 'fox-like man' who had very rarely been 'left with his behind uncovered'. He was also said to be an 'octopus that still hasn't even felt the need to use his ink'. I shared some of this unintentional humour with John Gordon Davis, one of my favourite novelists. His *Hold My Hand I'm Dying* was the quintessential novel of the Rhodesian bush war, even though it was written right at the start of the conflict. John lived in the hills above Coín, and put me up provided we could swap African stories in his sauna over endless bottles of wine.

Then I would tumble down the steep Andalusian hills and slide into Gibraltar to revel in the red post-boxes, efficient phones that rang, not burbled, Marks and Spencer, post offices that sold stamps, bank tellers who did not spend an hour reading your passport, Marmite … all the little English things to cheer up the jaded expat, right down to the stale sandwiches in the (over 100) pubs.

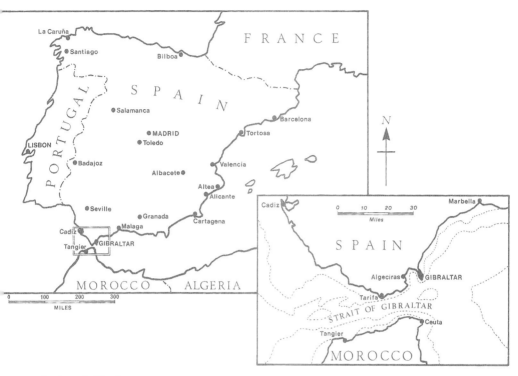

Spain and Gibraltar.

Gib, or 'the Rock', as it's often called, is just that: a big rock which forms a tiny peninsula jutting out from southern Spain. The 30,000 inhabitants were packed into an area of 2.5 square miles. I liked Gib a lot, despite its claustrophobia. The streets were clogged with traffic — which unusually for a Brit colony drove on the right — but the climate was sub-tropical and the crime rate very low. It was a historical and sociological curiosity, rather like a small English town frozen in the 1950s. And it was unusual: a colony that wanted to stay that way. It had an attachment to Britain and traditional hostility to Spain. Always essentially a garrison town, a military Butlins for troops' R and R, its Britishness and martial past gave the statelet its special charm.

For anyone who liked militaria, the Rock was heaven. Its wars went back to Roman times, although Gibraltar is said to take its name from Tarik ibn Zeyad, a Moor who conquered the area in AD 711. Gibraltar is a corruption of Gibel Tarik (Tarik's Hill). Frequent sieges spawned the numerous fortifications and cannon. Nelson's body, apparently pickled in a barrel of rum, was taken there after the Battle of Trafalgar. The *Mary Celeste* was towed there in 1872.

With the run-down of British forces on the Rock, Ministry of Defence land was handed over to commercial and residential development. Some new buildings were strikingly modern. But, for me, the Rock's appeal was its traditional architecture. Gib was truly a jigsaw of history: an eighteenth-century British Regency town built on a fifteenth-century Spanish town, itself constructed over a twelfth-century Moorish settlement. A tour of the churches clearly illustrated the different types of religious architecture. Under the Gibraltar museum, for example, stood a well-preserved Moorish bathhouse dating from the fourteenth century. Gib's inhabitants have mainly been Catholics, with substantial minorities of Muslims and Jews. During the wars with Spain, however, the Rock was always portrayed by the British parliament as a bastion of Protestantism in Iberia.

The Rock itself could be climbed on foot, or by cable car for the less energetic (like myself). Near the top was the den of the famous Barbary apes. During the Second World War, Winston Churchill ordered that the apes be secretly replenished. They had begun to die out and local superstition held that if the apes left so would the British. The apes are in fact tailless macaque monkeys; Gib is the only place they are found in Europe, supposedly having used an undiscovered tunnel that ran under the Mediterranean from their natural habitat in the Atlas mountains. The story goes that no one has ever seen an ape die or found an ape's skeleton.

The Convent, the name of the British governor's residence. I took many pictures of the imperial military presence on the Rock.

Perhaps more interesting, though, was the Barbary partridge, also unique in Europe on Gibraltar. Their natural habitat was Africa. They couldn't fly across the straits; either they were better fliers centuries ago, or the Moors introduced them. That they have remained naturalized in such a small area is unusual. For such a crowded place, there was a lot to engage the naturalist, especially in spring and autumn when Gib became a staging post for migrating birds flying between their breeding grounds in northern Europe and wintering areas in Africa.

The Rock also contained numerous caves and miles of tunnels. St Michael's Cave was the most interesting. Most tunnels were still MoD property and off limits, but the 'galleries' — gun emplacements blasted out of solid rock in 1782 — could be explored. Gib had dramatically improved its harbour facilities, especially for leisure craft. The new marina was one of the best in the Mediterranean, not least because of its good medical services, often deficient in other places. The Rock bristled with hotels, some of them rather seedy. On the other hand, many ex-military types had settled there and operated excellent restaurants with military precision. 'Main-streeting', walking down the narrow thoroughfares, was the major outdoor occupation for locals: the opportunity to show off new babies or beaux. Gibraltarian women, often astoundingly beautiful, wore their wealth, just like the *Madrileños*. The shops offered a wide variety of British goods, especially electrical equipment, at slightly above British prices (even though no VAT was imposed); that meant way below Spanish prices for the expats on the Costas.

The unarmed, smart, and helpful Bobbies, who switched effortlessly from English to Spanish in mid-sentence, were a comforting contrast with the monoglot Spanish *Guardia*, often unshaven Tonton Macoutes with Ray-Bans flashing and guns swinging on the hip. This was the border for Europhobes who relish the old-fashioned sense of occasion when crossing a border in Europe. It could take up to three hours on a good day, with the Spanish police helpfully reminding you that every car needed a first-aid kit and a fire extinguisher. I was once hauled over the coals for not having a spare pair of spectacles. (I kept a spare pair in my glove compartment thereafter.)

For me the Rock was a friendly and efficient colonial relic, a welcome island of sanity when I edited a Spanish magazine there. I made a point of talking to the local political leaders. On my first visit in 1984 I was introduced to the luminaries by Henry Bautista, one of my favourite cameramen. His uncle was the equivalent of the local chancellor of the exchequer.

The chief minister was then Sir Joshua Hassan, the Jewish leader of an essentially Catholic electorate, who told me, 'Like the Welsh, small people have their rights, despite their size.' I wasn't sure whether he was being personal or philosophical.

Although the Moroccan workers felt hard done by, the colony evinced a cosmopolitan and tolerant sense of harmony (except towards Spain): I later discovered that the kosher restaurant had a Muslim head waiter.

Nearly all the population was fanatically pro-British. As the editor of one of the Rock's three weekly newspapers explained, 'We may not be English, but we're certainly British.' He spoke with a heavy Spanish accent, yet he was sure London would not do a Hong Kong on him. Indeed, when the Iron Lady's empire struck back in the Falklands, jingoism of a positively nineteenth-century flavour swept the Rock. Waving the flag was not just a phrase: Union Jacks sprouted everywhere.

After years of one-man conservative rule under Sir Joshua, in March 1988 Joe Bossano led his Socialist Labour Party to power in a colony which had its own parliament, flag, and currency. Joe had his critics. To them, he was the 'Joe Bananas' who would disrupt the fragile economy with dogmatic socialism. And always the eternal quarrel with Spain, the core of Gib politics.

The Rock of Gibraltar from the Spanish side.

I interviewed Joe — as everyone called him — regularly, finding him a highly intelligent, approachable man, even though he did look like Groucho Marx on an off day. I asked about his relationship with his counterparts, led by Felipe González, the fellow socialist prime minister in Madrid:

'They still feel that Gibraltar is politically too hot a potato for them to start behaving as socialists and stop behaving as Spaniards. The national question transcends the ideological question .... They still tend to look at Gibraltar as Spaniards, independently of whether they are fascists or communists.'

'So there's no relationship at all?'

'None.'

I recalled my friend Henry's comment: 'Because of the siege, I didn't leave the Rock until I was eighteen. I saw my first cow then.'

That insight into Gib's collective house arrest inspired my continuing interest in the colony's staunch hostility to any takeover by Spain. Britain had maintained sovereignty of this tiny piece of real estate since 1713. The inhabitants had resisted regular Spanish attacks during the eighteenth century, Italian naval assaults, and Nazi conspiracies. The perpetual enemy was Spain, however. Gibraltarians might occasionally talk of UDI and conjure *Passport to Pimlico* fantasies, but all the bravado relied upon British military and diplomatic protection. I could hardly blame the Gibraltarians for developing a siege mentality. In 1969, after the colony was granted full internal self-government, Franco imposed a blockade of the Rock which lasted until 1985. At least there were no traffic jams; the locals just drove around and around, prompting Spanish wags to dub the place 'the Scalextric'. Under the 1969 constitution, Britain said it would respect the wishes of the Rock's inhabitants regarding any transfer of sovereignty. In referenda and elections, 95 per cent of Gibraltarians made it clear that they wanted the *status quo*.

My new friend Joe pooh-poohed hints that Spain might ask for joint rule of the colony, just as Andorra was administered by Spain and France. The King of Spain and Queen of England would become Gib's dual heads of state. The Rock's future, Joe insisted, rested upon tourism and its role as a financial centre, developed according to Community and British, not Spanish, rules. He attacked the Spanish for using bullying tactics to slow down tourist and business traffic at the border, saying that Spanish truculence over landing rights had caused a delay in sending vital American equipment to US forces during the first Gulf War.

Madrid counter-argued that Gib was turning a blind eye to smuggling in the area, alleging that its financial centre had become a haven for Spanish tax dodgers and money launderers. Spain, though, had to tread carefully. It had two Gibraltar-style, smuggling-prone colonies of its own in Morocco — Ceuta and Melilla.

To the outsider, the squabbling seemed more than absurd because local tourist and business interests dictated that Madrid and Gib should co-operate. Despite its tiny beaches, nearly four million visitors squeezed onto the Rock annually. It was the gateway to the Costa del Sol. But the bitterness ran too deep. Joe, an affable visionary and workaholic, was determined to build a rich mini-state, a second Monaco. His rocky fiefdom's economy would be plastered with brass plates. He was an ex-trade union leader heading a belated Thatcherite revolution. Everything depended upon British steadfastness.

'Colonialism isn't a word that stinks here. We want to remain a British colony,' a top Gib civil servant told me passionately.

Gibraltarians swore by the Falklands factor: Britain had defended far fewer colonial dependants who also refused to be 'integrated' into their big Hispanic neighbour. Thatcher was forced to lay down her sword, however, and Britain was reducing its military subsidies and garrison. It was no longer just a strategic but also a moral question. Anglo-Spanish trade was becoming increasingly important. Gib's stonewalling relied ultimately upon Britannia keeping faith with her loyal colonists.

*****

I moved from Spain in 1990 and never returned, although I did visit the Iberian peninsula, especially Gib, quite often, and also Lisbon. I much preferred the friendlier manner — and the food — of the Portuguese. I will admit that my somewhat personalized pessimism about Spain was not entirely justified. Full membership of the European Union did lead to many improvements, not least in their pettifogging rules for foreigners.

Gibraltar still disturbed Anglo-Spanish relations, despite the good chemistry between Tony Blair and the Conservative premier who replaced González. Spain did threaten to disrupt EU business over the landing rights in Gib's airport. The isthmus upon which the airport was constructed is claimed as Spanish territory, as distinct from the treaty agreements on the Rock itself. When a UK nuclear-powered submarine, HMS *Tireless,* was forced to berth in Gib to undergo lengthy repairs, Madrid used the incident to put the boot in.

The sub eventually moved out in May 2001, and the UK government decided that it was time to wave the flag a little. The Secretary of State for Defence, Geoff Hoon, dropped in on the overseas territory in July, the first such visit for five years. I happened to be attached to the small ministerial party which travelled in the Queen's Flight to the Rock, and observed that the plane diplomatically avoided overflying Spanish air space.

Despite the many new buildings, the Moorish charm of the older areas still survived. Joe Bossano, back in opposition, still appeared to be wearing the same demob suit. This time I got to see the inside of the Convent, the governor's residence, and was duly impressed by the restored ballroom. And finally I travelled through some of the MoD tunnels which are normally off limits. There are more miles of road *inside* the Rock than there are on its exterior. They contained lots of spare ammo, but my signature on the Official Secrets Act form forbids further disclosure. Travel writer Harry Ritchie, however, claimed that the tunnels contained 'a mocked-up Northern Irish village (with pub, church and fish-and-chip shop), and a thermonuclear arsenal'. I won't comment on those details except to say I would have noticed the smell of fish frying.

The UK defence minister confirmed that millions of pounds were to be spent on upgrading military accommodation on Gibraltar. And Joe's successor, Peter Caruana, was just as keen to keep the Spaniards out. Moreover, Gib had recently been used as a staging post for all sorts of British military adventures in the Balkans and Africa.

The Gib saga heated up in summer 2013. Spanish pressure on the borders in retaliation about fishing rights led to a major row between London and Madrid. The then Gib chief minister talked about the Spanish behaving 'like North Koreans'. Britain sent warships, apparently in a long-planned exercise, when Madrid suggested teaming up with the ex-colony Argentina to exert joint pressure on both Gib *and* the Falklands. No British prime minister, especially a Conservative one, could survive in office if he or she were seen to surrender on the two overseas territories. David Cameron risked being tested in a colonial war in the same fashion as Mrs Thatcher.

Gibraltar is technically a 'pene-exclave' of British territory. The Spanish critics of British sovereignty still conveniently forget that Madrid also controls two pene-exclaves on the Moroccan coast. They are the last vestiges of European territorial imperialism in Africa.

No doubt the Rock is an anachronism. Imagine how the Brits would feel if the French held a small enclave — outside of Arsenal FC — in the UK? Nevertheless, despite Brexit, this former bit of Spain looks as though it will remain a colony; maybe the last bit of pink on the imperial map.

Relics of empire

It's often forgotten that Britain still has the largest empire in the world — over 1,000 territories, many of them uninhabited rocks, although only thirteen of these colonies (or 'Overseas Territories') are significant. Literally, the sun never sets on these last imperial relics; they can be found in the Caribbean, and in the Indian, Atlantic, and Pacific Oceans. And, despite the official end of colonialism, in most cases these colonies want to remain under the British flag. Why should British taxpayers still fund this far-flung imperium in the new millennium? They are often politically, militarily, and ecologically controversial — Britain paid a high price in blood and treasure in the Falklands, for example. And Gib is still a diplomatic thorn in the side of the EU.

There are many reasons beyond kith and kin and imperial nostalgia. The British Indian Ocean Territory, for instance, is crucial to American intelligence operations throughout the world, and British naval patrols in the Caribbean assist the US crusade to counter drug smuggling and money laundering in the area. Many of the British islands, especially in the Atlantic Ocean as well as British Antarctic, contain vital ecological sites. Some of the territories are very wealthy — Bermuda and the Cayman Islands — while others are small and poor. All of them boast stunning scenery on land and under the sea.

I spent a lot of time researching a projected TV documentary on these pink leftovers, which unfortunately was never completed despite Foreign Office encouragement. The popular impression was that empire finally ended with the transfer of Hong Kong's six million citizens. Although individual events in the territories — the volcano in Montserrat, for example — had been covered in news reports, no one had made an up-to-date TV documentary on the so-called 'permanent empire'. *Inter alia*, I wanted to find out whether British forces were sufficient to protect these far-flung possessions, which usually face threats from international criminals rather than conventional enemies.

Much debate had been generated about legislation giving the citizens of these colonies reciprocal residence rights with mainland Britons. The British West Indies, Bermuda, the Cayman Islands and the British Virgin Islands supported rich brass-plate economies and flourishing tourism. These islanders boasted very high standards of living, and didn't want every Tom, Dick, and Harry living there. In particular, they didn't enthuse about giving the entire UK population the right of residence, while some of the inhabitants of the less affluent islands, such as Anguilla, Turks and Caicos, and volcano-ravaged Montserrat, were keener on full rights to live in the UK. Since corruption in some of these small paradises was endemic, the islanders could have done rather well in Britain.

In the deep south, the colonists in the Falklands warily tried but failed to improve relations with Argentina and looked forward to an oil bonanza, still protected by thousands of British servicemen. South Georgia and the South Sandwich Islands are still dependencies. Other imperial outposts in the Atlantic are Tristan da Cunha and St Helena, where Napoleon spent his last years of exile. Ascension Island is a military and communications base. The RAF and Royal Navy are still vital to the survival of these out-stations. The British Indian Ocean Territory is an archipelago dedicated to British and US defence purposes. Despite the beautiful lagoons, and the publicity given to the original islanders, who were shamefully dumped on Mauritius, US intelligence stations ensured that the area was out of bounds to everybody not in uniform, or civilian contractors working for the Americans.

The loneliest outpost is Pitcairn Island in the Pacific. It is home to around fifty people, descendants of Fletcher Christian, leader of the mutiny on the *Bounty* and presumably forever imprinted on the imagination as looking just like the thin Marlon Brando. Nearly all the islanders are Seventh Day Adventists, and make a living from scraps of agriculture and fishing and selling postage stamps. Until

The remaining pink on the map.

fairly recently, the shipping schedule to the island was so awkward that a visit entailed a stay of either two hours or six months. Denied the glories of package tourists and the possibilities of an enhanced gene pool, the colony assumed a reputation for inbreeding, a sort of tropical *Deliverance* without the banjos. Once formerly governed by a strict moral code, including a very early grant of the female vote, the island's menfolk degenerated into under-age sex with local girls. Police action brought Pitcairn much morbid news curiosity in 2004.

Recent British governments have tended to downplay the surviving colonies, not least because they annoy the UN, the Argentinians and, of course, the Spanish. And, for starters, that's good enough reason to keep them.

The lost legion

After Spain, I returned to my native Cardiff in 1990. I dabbled in Welsh politics while teaching at Cardiff University's journalism school, probably the best in the UK, if not Europe. I thought it important that journalism teachers should provide practical leadership to their students, so I was allowed to travel abroad to make films provided I used them to pedagogic effect when I returned home. I also kept up a flow of print journalism.

Soon after I arrived back in Wales, I was summoned back to old memories of Africa. It was July 1990 and I was covering the 100th anniversary of the foundation of Rhodesia for the *Guardian*. Some of the lost legion were celebrating with beer, troopie songs, and a few words from Ian Smith. West Lavington, a peaceful, pretty, Wiltshire village, was an unlikely place to celebrate a conflict in far-off Africa. Hundreds of ex-Rhodesians — they would never call themselves Zimbabweans — converged there to commemorate the pioneer column's erection of a flag in what became Salisbury. They also came to worship their old hero, Smithy. The event was sponsored by Rhodesians Worldwide, an organization that supported the white diaspora in fifty countries. Peter Hagelthorn, an administrator at a private school in West Lavington and editor of *Rhodesians Worldwide* magazine, supervised the gathering. Hagelthorn, a patently decent man, insisted that the organization was for charity and not politics, aiming to help Rhodesians settle in their new countries. Strict government controls meant many refugees left Zimbabwe with very little money; some were civilians, others soldiers wounded in the bush war. This weekend was not a wake, it was to celebrate the good old days.

It was hot, as though the Zambezi sun was broiling the Wiltshire hayfields. Initially the strangers looked like ordinary Englishmen. Soon, though, the colonial garb emerged — shorts, *veldskoens* without socks, T-shirts, and (apparently) wartime Crimplene for the older women. As they greeted old friends in their peculiar clipped accents, memories tumbled out of wild, wide spaces of Africa, Kariba, and Inyanga. It was long gone, but one colonial type commented to a man struggling to unload his car, 'Better get the boy to help you'. Life was easier with servants.

The school was bedecked with the green and white flags of the rebel republic. In essence, perhaps, the ex-Rhodies were celebrating their UDI against Britain, not the foundation of the colonial state. They had come from at least eleven countries but here, for one weekend, they could all be Rhodesians again. As one observer noted cynically, 'It's like being at a gay club outing with everyone rushing to leave the closet.'

That was unfair: a macho, heterosexual culture so typical of war veterans and also the normality of colonial family life, with kids galore, were more evident. The men drank Castles and Lions, South African beers brought in specially, while the women gossiped about life without maids and gardeners.

Although the men embroidered on their war stories or, more often, understated them, some of the memorabilia on sale provided a less heroic view of the fighting. The slogans on the T-shirts read 'Rhodesians — an endangered species?' and 'We didn't make it'. The most plaintive said 'Rhodesian war 1965/1980 — we came second'. A few diehards still sported T-shirts about 'slotting gooks'. Only one black attended this hooley (party).

The Saturday night dinner-dance was attended by about 500 people. John Edmonds flew from South Africa to sing troopie songs in Rhodesian English, Chilapalapa, and Shona. His ditties were given a rapturous reception by the exiles as they recalled the flat dogs (crocodiles), chasing *gandangas* (terrorists) while drinking *shumbas* (beers), and taking *muti* (medicine) for hangovers.

Smithy's short speech got an even better reception, bordering on adulation. The irreconcilable old prophet was once more among his own people. He hadn't changed a jot; the same phrases as in 1965, but his audience hung on every word. Instead of deceased Rhodesia, South Africa was now the 'last bastion of Western civilization on the African continent …. You may not agree with everything they do, but at least you know where you stand with them.'

The 71-year-old ex-premier, now grey and stooping, spoke about Zimbabwe with some caution. He had often been rapped over the knuckles by Mugabe's men for speaking out of turn while travelling abroad. Smith had always said what he thought. Few doubted his courage, even while damning his bigotry.

'Things are not so good back home now, I must tell you … when you scratch beneath the surface.' He cited the Willowgate government corruption scandal. 'Many black people have had enough,' he claimed. 'They say it was better in the old days and that "this is not what we fought the war for".' This was an interesting variation on Smithy's evergreen of 'We have the happiest Africans in the world.'

Smith told his adoring audience that the anniversary celebrations in South Africa were being organized around a Rhodesian flag-raising ceremony north of Messina, overlooking the border with Zimbabwe. This taunt brought a volcano of applause.

'You can't keep Rhodesians down wherever they are,' their leader concluded.

Amid the triumphalism no mention was made of the tens of thousands who were killed in the war. Yet I could see, but not understand, why 75 per cent of the whites kept backing Smith. Like Margaret Thatcher, he was a conviction politician. Charismatic without a discernible trace of personal charisma, yet people believed what he said because he was so patently sincere.

The evening ended with the most painful rendition of 'God Save the Queen' in the history of the empire. 'What do you expect from the rebels against the Crown?' muttered my cynical companion.

On Sunday the inevitable *braai* was conjured up. The sun shone again as in the 'old country'. The pinched, sundried, prune faces of the older women contrasted with the healthy, tattooed, tanned bodies of the young ex-warriors, who performed various eccentric regimental rites. Edmonds sang again.

Ian Douglas Smith, an old prophet among his people once more but in Wiltshire, England.

Smith told his people that they should not mind being called 'When wes' (When we were in Rhodesia … or Kenya). 'We should be proud of being this small group of people with the finest spirit this world has ever known.'

Rhodesians managed to defy the world partly because they were so well organized. Ladies rushed around with black plastic bags clearing up the rubbish of more than a thousand people at the *braai*.

'Rhodesians are a tidy people,' one said.

A people? The last white tribe? A nation? Or a racist suburb masquerading as a country? The (fortunately) inimitable Rhodesian foreign minister, P.K. van der Byl, once said that the Battle of Britain spirit had not evaporated; it had migrated to Rhodesia. All that remained of Rhodesia were memories, a large supply of crippled ex-soldiers, and a breed of dog, the Rhodesian Ridgeback, many of which were in evidence in West Lavington that sad, sunny weekend.

The Gulf War

Ever since God gave Charlton Heston the Ten Commandments Israel has been in the news. The media, however, have usually expected Israelis to behave better than other tribes in the region. That's what you get for having a hot line to God.

Precisely because nearly all Western journalists believe they are above and beyond ideology, they are most susceptible to its effects. I did not believe there was a wide-ranging media conspiracy to sanitize — to Americanize — the 1991 Gulf War, but many Western correspondents switched off their brains as they put on desert camouflage. From the numbers of Iraqi troops to the percentage of smart bombs, the official line was swallowed. It was later realized that only 7 per cent of the bombs were smart, laser-guided weapons; the vast majority were free-fall, old-fashioned gravity bombs. And they usually missed. The carnage of the Iraqi retreat was severely sanitized on Western screens. Gory footage and splatter shots had no place in TV spectaculars that looked more like arcade games than military massacres.

I had a terrible war: I had to watch the build-up on TV. It took so long. And I thought Saddam would back down, not believing it would come to the crunch. When it did I tried to scramble out of my lecturing schedule at Cardiff University and persuade TV stations to buy my promised film in advance. My longtime cameraman friend, Tim Lambon, was already in Saudi Arabia, hired by a British network. And you needed big network muscle to get a TV team through the very restrictive Saudi authorities. J.J. Swart, my old South African cameraman-colleague, joined me on a plane to Israel; Tim said it might be possible to cross from Jordan into Saudi and come across the desert. The trouble was J.J. had a South African passport, then unacceptable in most Arab countries.

With my usual immaculate timing, I arrived in Jerusalem the day the war ended. To be fair, it had lasted only 100 hours and I had moved fast. There was no point in trying to join the thousands of hacks in Kuwait. I had to do something different and I had to make some kind of film. I couldn't rely upon the standard phrase — 'calm but tense' — used by war correspondents who had arrived just after the fighting and needed to justify their expenses.

J.J. had organized for us to stay at the Tel Aviv Hilton — fortunately, because the Israelis had set up the major press centre there. Compared with the bribe-burdened, paranoid Arab states, Israel's smooth PR made life easy for foreign journalists. The high literacy rate, an urbanized, multilingual population, often fluent in English, a democratic government, and a vigorous press — plus the influence of the US Jewish lobby — had prompted many news organizations to set up bureaux in Israel. At the press centre I bumped into a CNN cameraman who knew me from South Africa. He was friendly with the Israeli officials and told them I was a very distinguished journalist — it's nice when friends are prepared to lie for you. In less than fifteen minutes we obtained our work permits: more than I got in three years in Spain.

Ramming my brain into overdrive, I checked into the hotel at 7 pm, fixed up accreditation, attended and filmed a press conference, and did a one-on-one TV interview with the charismatic deputy foreign (and later prime) minister, Bibi Netanyahu, and another with Ra'anan Gissin, the equally telegenic army spokesman. I sorted out editing facilities, did a brief voice report for the BBC, then walked around Tel Aviv for two hours to film the ceasefire celebrations. Most people were not sure that the war had ended, but Israelis were jubilant that their greatest enemy, Saddam Hussein, had been defeated.

I had forgotten how scruffy Tel Aviv was; one suburb gave the impression of a seedy oriental bazaar filled with dusky Israelis. As we filmed in (Ze'ev) Jabotinsky Square, I recalled the words of the old Zionist in the 1920s: 'We won't really be a country until we have Jewish policemen and Jewish prostitutes.' I saw lots of both. J.J. and I returned to the hotel to attend a press party, where we bumped into a Dutch army captain manning a Patriot missile system. The Patriots hadn't knocked out any Scud missiles — or not more than one or two — but had played a vital part in the propaganda war. The captain said we could film the battery the next morning during the visit of Teddy Kollek, the celebrity mayor of Jerusalem. After viewing some of the footage on our monitor, we crawled into bed about 2.30 am. We had done an awful lot in less than eight hours.

Early the next morning we filmed the Patriots and did an interview with an irascible Kollek. He went straight into a tourist pitch with the ambiguous line: 'Why is it that every time someone gets killed in Jerusalem it's blamed on politics? There's a hell of a lot of "ordinary" crime.'

Right on, Teddy, that's sure gonna make people rush out and buy an airline ticket to Jerusalem.

We filmed some of the damage done by Scuds in Tel Aviv. The Israeli government claimed 20,000 homes damaged, but this seemed a tremendous exaggeration.

I bumped again into my CNN mate, who said that Shimon Peres, the leader of the opposition, was attending a wedding at our hotel. I had a soft spot for Shimon and risked the intrusion of grabbing him as he kissed the bride. The old pro gave me ten minutes of canned wisdom.

I always liked his ponderous Kissinger-style delivery, oozing gravitas: 'History is like a galloping horse. When it passes near your home you must mount it or miss it. Now is the time to negotiate with the Palestinians.'

I had assumed that the war would spread to Israel as Saddam Hussein had promised. Apart from a few Scuds, it didn't, but I had to make a film and find some 'bang bang' to satisfy the film companies that had put up the money.

I used old contacts to get in with the UN troops in southern Lebanon. In the UN office a sign read: 'If you think you understand Lebanon, you've not been properly briefed.'

We had to attach ourselves to various UN contingents to get around. Thus we persuaded some very reluctant Fijians to take us into Tyre where J.J., a shopaholic, indulged in some compulsive purchases. Since tourists were an endangered species there, he managed to haggle some real bargains, the only time and place in the Middle East where I saw a foreigner get the better of an Arab trader.

J.J., a compulsive shopaholic, with our Fijian escort officer, southern Lebanon.

Zia, our burly Fijian escort, was very uncomfortable in Tyre as the Syrian army had more than encouraged us to get out quickly. Zia said by way of compensation that he would take us to an interesting place. J.J. was wary until Zia said it was a shopping trip.

About ten miles from Tyre, way up in the hills, was one of the world's greatest army surplus stores. The Lebanese owner had spent years amassing stolen weapons and equipment. J.J. was in seventh heaven, and we immediately bought two UN caps.

Suddenly Zia started shouting and raving, clutching a flak-jacket with the name of a close friend on it, stolen a few weeks before from the Fijian HQ, he explained. This was a massive affront to the honour of his country, his army, and himself.

The shopkeeper said he could have it for $20.

Zia said he would take it for free. It belonged to him.

Zia drew his pistol.

The shopkeeper, with great speed, pulled out a brand new AK-74, cocked it, and aimed it at Zia's chest.

In Lebanon the customer is not always right.

While they cursed at each other J.J. took cover. I sneaked out to tell the Fijian private guarding the Land Rover outside to get in there with his rifle.

The two Fijians, with rifle and pistol, faced the determined shopkeeper, who had been joined by another man armed with an AK-47. Four weapons a few feet apart and lots of angry words. What would all those shots going off do in a shop full of ammunition?

Luckily, I spotted an Amal militia officer sitting in a jeep across the road, and quickly explained the situation. He rushed in to defuse what was about to become, literally, an international incident. The guns were lowered and half an hour later Zia came out with the flak-jacket. He didn't pay anything. He had made his point.

The Fijian mess was dry so we thanked Zia for his excursions and decamped to the more bibulous hospitality of Finnish troops.

We eventually crossed back into Israel to explore conditions in Gaza and speak to Palestinian Liberation Organization officials on the West Bank. We had many tight scrapes trying to evade Israeli troops, including using J.J.'s purchase of two

UN caps to make a quick escape. We had a PLO female translator in the car so we had to hightail it for her sake as she dropped down in the back seat. After pausing at the sight of UN caps, the patrol fired warning shots in the air as they may have realized we were the Western hacks they had been looking for. Most other Middle Eastern armies would have immediately riddled our car with bullets.

We dumped the car quickly and laid low for a while in old Jerusalem. We took one or two days off to film the ancient city of Jerusalem, which enchanted me no matter how often I visited. You could see, smell, touch history here. In many streets you could pretend to be in any time of the last two millennia. Many shops were still closed and few tourists were evident because of the Gulf war and PLO-ordained shutdown. Nonetheless, storekeepers whispered to us to come in and buy behind closed shutters. Business was business, and J.J. was still a shopaholic. Again, he managed to beat down the best hagglers in the world.

We wandered for hours through narrow medieval streets, full of twisting lanes, oriental souks, steep stairways, and dark, covered passages. We felt no threat, just wonderment. I could almost understand the Jerusalem Syndrome, which hospitalizes forty or fifty visitors each year. The spiritual overload of the old city causes people suddenly to think they are the messiah or his mum, with the odd sprinkling of John the Baptists and the occasional King David. Most of the

The Dome of the Rock, Jerusalem. The city of three great world religions had a profound spiritual impact on many visitors.

nutters come from Europe or America, and they are usually Protestants rather than Catholics or Jews. The psychiatric literature abounds with analysis of the syndrome which is divided into various stages. Stage four, for example, involves preparation of a long, ankle-length, white, toga-like gown, often, I presume, with the aid of hotel bed-linen. Then sufferers march about and sing (popular in the locality anyway, though not in togas) and one of the final stages is preaching a sermon.

An Israeli hospital psychiatrist told me that he once had two Jewish messiahs in his care at the same time. Apparently they got on very well with each other, even though they both told the psychiatrist it was a pity they had to chat to an impostor.

Most patients recover after four or five days and recall their crisis as a pleasant experience before flying off home to resume their normal lives. Going back to, say, selling insurance – after being the Son of God – must be tough, however.

Jerusalem must have affected J.J. and me because we ended up in the desert filming and visiting St George's Monastery. Both of us were attracted to the place and the long walk there, though neither of us succumbed to wearing togas.

Israel/Palestine.

I left the Middle East feeling again just a little optimistic (though that feeling was always soon shattered). Saddam had been kicked out of Kuwait, but not defeated, and it soon became apparent, at least in Washington, that another round was required. Saddam had won his propaganda war by accident; he had claimed he wanted to put the Palestinian rising, the *intifada*, centre stage, and he had.

The proverbial window of opportunity was opening just a mite, perhaps. The basic issue was still straightforward: land for peace. Jewish survival versus rights for the Palestinians. Cynics would say swapping Jews for oil. Nevertheless, the Palestinians had lost everything, and had turned to Saddam Hussein in utter despair.

I often thought that much could be agreed, given goodwill. Call me an old-fashioned liberal. And Jerusalem? How do you divide that ancient and holy citadel? Perhaps, just perhaps, the city should be shared under UN supervision. Jerusalem is the toughest nut to crack, but nobody said a Middle East solution was going to be easy. Maybe Steven Spielberg could make a film called *The Jerusalem Syndrome*. In it Charlton Heston Mark 2 would star as a deranged messiah who comes up with an answer to the city of three great world religions. But Spielberg knows that his co-religionists would be unlikely – willingly – to deliver Jerusalem to the UN or anybody else.

Balkans

Marxism's downfall brought many changes, not least in language. From A to Z, from *apparatchik* to Zhivago, the 'evil empire' had popularized numerous concepts and phrases; now Orwell's Big Brother and the gulag became less fearsome terms. Novelists had to invent alternatives to James Bond, moles, and KGB honey-traps. The biggest change was that Marxists no longer set the intellectual agenda.

I had been watching the collapse of the Soviet Union from afar. I was fascinated, but twitchy about being stuck in Cardiff. A friend of mine, Peter, was involved in sending aid to Romanian orphanages. In July 1991 he invited me to see what he was doing. We travelled to Bucharest on the same day. He was a charity worker, so he flew classy Swissair; I risked economy class on TAROM, the Romanian airline. The aircraft, of obscure origins and past its sell-by date, looked likely to fall from the sky. But at least I was without a film team. Travelling the world with full video gear is like running a marathon strapped to a bulky vacuum cleaner.

Bucharest international airport was a fair reflection of the whole country— post-revolutionary Romania was in the grip of a post-Orwellian nightmare. After queuing for an hour for my baggage, I was swamped by taxi drivers drooling for payment in real currency. I found a man who looked and sounded like the idiot in Eco's *The Name of the Rose*. He spoke a smattering of all European languages in a way that suggested he had no native tongue. In a torrential downpour he had to find and then attach his windscreen wipers — such capitalist trimmings were far too valuable to be left on a car. On our way through the flooded streets to the city centre I could see remnants — a few villas here and there — of the old grandeur of the 1930s. Bucharest once called itself the 'Paris of the East'. Unfortunately most of it had been demolished by the dictator Nicolae Ceausescu and replaced by appalling concrete towers dedicated to the socialist utopia.

Ceausescu had spared the old hotel I stayed in, but it had seen better days – maybe better centuries. My room was a decayed masterpiece of Art Deco. You could see it had been nice once, but many of the important bits, such as the shower head and light bulbs, were missing. Peter and his Romanian girlfriend, Diana, arrived to help me negotiate room service. It was just that: I had to go to a tiny room marked 'Service', discover what was available, and then haggle on the price, amount of food, and timing. Prices were cheap. The £700 monthly rent on my house in Wales could have bought Diana's flat outright. She paid less than a pound a month in rent.

I asked her about local politics, life, and booze, but I could never get a straight answer on anything. She was like a chameleon on a tartan rug. Most Romanians were evasive on most topics … except the possibility of getting out of Romania. Perhaps it was because they had spent a lifetime being threatened with jail for unauthorized conversations with foreigners. Bucharest reflected a weird, shabby, sad, disorganized society.

I spent the next few days driving around Bucharest in a white coat in a brand-new ambulance donated by a British charity. It was sticky hot and we stopped to buy drinks from a roadside vendor. We wanted to take the bottles away with us. This was impossible, explained Diana. To do so we had to give the vendor the equivalent number of empty bottles of the same size. But how do you start off your bottle collection if you are new to the country? We offered to pay extra for the privilege of taking a drink plus bottle; but no, we needed our own bottles. I began to understand why Romania had one of the world's highest suicide rates.

I was just beginning to comprehend Eastern Europe's transition to capitalism. The first advertising billboards had just appeared in the city — praising Panasonic and Xerox. The city had a currency black market, but very little in the shops. Once Eastern Europe had socialism without social justice, now it had capitalism with very little capital.

Only in Romania was military force used extensively in an attempt to save the regime from the revolutionary fervour that swept Eastern Europe. The entirely out-of-touch Ceausescu was overthrown by a combination of popular insurrection and a local communist party coup, encouraged by Moscow. Romania was the most backward state in Europe, except for Albania. The economy was pitiful. The workers and the population in general seemed utterly demoralized. Little foreign investment ventured in — and for good reasons. Elements in the government were paranoid about Romania being 'taken over' by foreigners.

The atmosphere of fear and deprivation created a society with degraded values. Misha Glenny, when he was the BBC's Central European correspondent, used the phrase 'psychotic proletariat'. Hence the horror tales of dumping and trading in babies. Ceausescu's rundown of the medical services had led to half of Europe's child AIDS victims subsisting in Romania, according to official figures. And Romania was also milking the AIDS and orphanage stories for all they were worth.

I saw some aid enterprises in Bucharest, but I wanted to get out into the countryside, away from PR exercises — not that Romanians were capable of understanding modern PR, though they'd had decades of training in public lying. Peter drove me to Slatina, about three-and-a-half hours from the capital. I had heard of massive industrial pollution in Romania, but I didn't see much evidence of it, just drab peasant country with ribbon developments of roadside shacks. One or two shacks were elaborately decorated in the Eastern style; most were breeze-block, wooden, or occasionally square mud huts. Donkey carts were everywhere. So were soldiers. I wondered where the war was.

Slatina seemed more cheerful than grey, ill-lit Bucharest. It had a main street with recognizable shops. The orphanage had been given a few hours' notice of our visit. The children's home, in a normal apartment block, was also a home for senile adults. It stank of must and urine. Peopled with swivel-eyed cripples and toothless dribbling crones, it was straight out of Dickens.

Then we had an inspection. Toys donated by British charities were taken out of a large box: the kids obviously hadn't seen them for a long time, if ever. The children went mad for a while, but soon seemed more interested in the attention that Peter, Diana, and I were giving them. They appeared utterly starved of affection. Although they didn't look unfed and were vaguely clean, they lived in stark, primitive surroundings. Their rooms — with open windows on the fourth floor — had just a few playpens and dirty mattresses. There were no pictures and nothing else, once the toys were returned to the big box. All the children were mentally handicapped. One had just pulled his own eye out. As they clambered all over us, I had to leave with tears streaming down my face.

When I recovered, I asked Diana why unskilled volunteers had to come all the way from England. Peter had brought four sixth-form volunteers to spend their summer helping in the orphanage. Why couldn't some of the many unemployed locals, who spoke the language, help out? I was treated to a classic piece of Romanian evasion in response.

Diana negotiated a hotel in Slatina for our volunteer do-gooders. It took less than half an hour. The place didn't have working toilets, but it did have some food. The cabbage was OK and the rye bread and tomatoes were excellent. Tomatoes, I noticed, were always available in Romania. Even beer and Coke were on sale. In the bar a group played a terrible mix of folk music and Turkish rock 'n' roll. The male singer sang in falsetto; the most moving thing about his performance was his hairpiece. It sounded like Nana Mouskouri played at very high speed.

Peter commented, 'You've got me into some bad things, but this is the worst.'

Then and there I decided to nip over the border into Yugoslavia.

'I'd prefer to get shot at than listen to this. I'm going to Yugoslavia tomorrow. At least it'll be quieter there.'

Peter laughed. He understood my impulsiveness.

Until the break-up of the Yugoslav federation newspaper editors tended to avoid political stories on the country because it was so bloody complicated. But in recent weeks the world's media had been full of little lectures on, and maps of,

Yugoslavia's six republics and two autonomous regions, as well as its different languages, religions, and various *isms*.

Straddling east and west, Yugoslavia once had everything, from picture-book Alpine villages, ancient Roman ruins, and glorious coastline to reasonably efficient hotels, phones, and transport. The abundance of splendid cathedrals, monasteries, and mosques echoed the fact that, although most Yugoslavs were Catholic or Orthodox Christians, the federation also had Europe's largest Muslim community. Scarcely larger than Britain, the country ranged in the north from Slovenia, a little Austria, to the Albanians in the south, one of the most backward regions of Europe. Many of the 24 million inhabitants spoke some English, especially in the main cities and on the hot, dry Adriatic.

****

After a difficult and long journey in train carriages which seemed of Second World War German-army vintage, I reached Belgrade which was the federal capital and one of Europe's oldest cities. Because of its strategic position on the Danube it had been conquered and rebuilt thirty-eight times. I went to the local press club to get up to date, as I wanted to move closer to the fighting in the West.

I caught a train from Belgrade to Zagreb, the capital of Croatia. The Serbs in my compartment warned me to stop talking politics when we reached the Croatian border. They were visibly angry, but also tense when Croatia's new defence force stopped the train and demanded identity documents.

An old Croat woman, dressed all in black, started to cry. 'All my family was killed in the fighting between Serbs and Croats during the Hitler war. I don't want it to happen all over again.'

Once the Croat soldiers had left, a young Serb said, 'Those fascist Croats killed tens of thousands of Serbs in camps during the last war.'

The bitterness ran deep … and the new war was only just beginning.

In Zagreb independence flags were as commonplace as the rumours that federal tanks were about to seize the city centre. Croatia seemed more efficient, but not necessarily more democratic, than Serbia. The country was ruled by a single party, the Croatian Democratic Union, which owed more than a few debts to its fascist predecessor. The break-up of Yugoslavia was not simply a question of brave little democracies challenging a communist centralism.

Since no tanks had appeared I decided to explore Zagreb. It seemed a wonderful city, a little Vienna, clean and quiet except for the immaculate trams. In the plush piano bar of the best hotel in town I fell in with some foreign journalists. I wanted to go to Osijek, the scene of fierce fighting, so I needed some instant knowledge. If I had been filming I would have felt obliged to leave immediately for the front.

The Balkan wars.

But I was half on holiday, so I decided to roam around Zagreb persuading myself that the tanks would come to me.

The medieval part of town was dominated by the twin towers of the cathedral, first consecrated in 1217. Two other churches interested me: St Mark's, the roof of which displayed the coats of arms of Croatia and Zagreb in enamel tiles; and St Catherine's, built by Jesuits in the seventeenth century. I was entranced by the baroque detail. Outside the main government building, multi-coloured Toytown soldiers paraded up and down in an amazing march, part goose-step and part ballet. Zagreb took its cultural role seriously, with numerous theatres and museums. The town's classical architecture was well proportioned, Austro-Hungarian style, rococo in parts, but not over-dressy.

Zagreb was not all art, architecture, and piety. I would argue that it was perhaps the best place in Europe to sample outdoor café life. Winding through the old town were streets full of open-air restaurants buzzing with vitality. Perhaps because foreign visitors were thin on the ground, people often came up to talk to me.

I hired a car to drive to Ljubljana, the capital of Slovenia, normally an hour's journey. It took me considerably longer as some main roads were blocked or damaged by recent fighting. This was my good fortune because the side roads yielded scenery that was idyllic in its rustic charm: utterly tidy villages with spotless Alpine-style houses, perfect little guesthouses, and everywhere little churches with onion-domed spires. War in Europe seemed even more preposterous in this setting. I had seen the occasional burnt-out tank and armoured vehicle on the way into Ljubljana. The city itself, however, seemed unscathed. The River Ljubljana ambled peacefully beneath an array of over-decorous little bridges. The small city was dominated by a twelfth-century castle and, below it, the cathedral next to a daily open market full of produce, flowers, and apparently relaxed people.

In spite of the war, I really liked ex-Yugoslavia. The occasional bursts of old-style communist bureaucracy aside, the mood of Oriental decadence, Balkan intrigue, ubiquitous courtesy, and European sanitation was very appealing. In early 1991 it was obvious even to me that nobody could put Yugoslavia's Humpty-Dumpty back together again. I wrote at the time that the problems of dividing up that Rubik's Cube of mini-nationalities would probably not be accompanied without major population movements. I had not anticipated the future horrors of ethnic cleansing, and naively believed that the EC could be a peace broker.

I had got a taste for the Balkans and was to return again frequently over the following decade of war, but more immediately I had to get back to my teaching in Wales. Soon I was on the move again, however. I had been awarded a visiting professorship in Waco, Texas, at Baylor University. It had a good reputation for journalism scholarship, especially under the leadership of the eminent correspondent, Loyal Gould. What I didn't know was that the Baptist college did not allow drinking, dancing, smoking or music on the campus. Of course I indulged in all of them in exaggerated proportions and was joyfully forgiven as a foreign eccentric. It was my first, very belated, encounter with the US and, except for irksome airport entries, I must admit I've never had a bad experience in America.

It was June 1992 and I was happy to be back home. My dog, Gelert, was very pleased to see me, but my wife could perhaps tolerate Wales but not the Welsh. She no longer rejoiced in the title Mrs Moorcraft. She drifted back to southern Africa and I went to Australia, very reluctantly, because I had to leave my dog.

Chapter 3

Australasia

Way up woop woop

I was offered a job teaching journalism at Deakin University, in Geelong, about fifty miles from Melbourne. I discovered later that some locals called it 'way up woop woop' – out in the sticks. The university, spread over five campuses, was the equivalent of the Open University in the UK. Deakin said I could bring my dog as a dependent instead of my wife, which was kind, but the quarantine issues were too strict; so Gelert went to stay with good friends who had a big garden and even bigger hearts. I really didn't want to leave Gelert, but I thought that going to Oz would clear my head after a messy divorce.

Although I was headhunted and was told no one else could fill the job in Oz, the bureaucracy was mind-boggling. The work permit took a year and included numerous repetitive demands. Health and AIDS procedures were expensive, though understandable. The detailed enquiries about my travels, however, particularly in former communist countries, prompted me to explain regularly that the Cold War was over. Eventually, I thought they might be recruiting me to set up a new intelligence agency, not a film school.

In high summer 1993, I had all the necessary papers and my old college friend Gareth drove me to Heathrow. He tried to cheer me up because he knew I was rather sad at leaving my native Wales, after recently returning there after so many travels.

'Cheer up,' he said, 'It's not the other side of the world.' Then he realized what he'd said.

He saw me instinctively patting my pockets to check for my keys – but I had none – the house, office and car keys had gone. I was a vagabond once more.

On long journeys into new adventures I always take the wrong book. This time the twenty-four-hour flight was eased by *A Prayer for Owen Meany* – the story of a little guy obsessed by writing who knew he was destined to meet a grisly fate.

I walked out of Melbourne international airport not knowing a soul in the great big state of Victoria. Despite being exhausted I couldn't risk looking sorry for myself. From long practice at third-world airports I had learned to look as if I were the personal guest of the president, knew the country backwards and could speak in five local dialects. Otherwise you get ripped off immediately, especially by taxi drivers and porters. Unfortunately, my experienced traveller act fooled Murray, the generous Deakin lecturer who had arranged to meet me at what was an allegedly a first-world airport.

When he and his wife finally located me, Murray explained, 'I said you looked like a journalist when you walked out. You know, worldly-wise. But you seemed to know where you were going and that you knew the place, so it couldn't be you.'

After feeding me, Murray took me on a tour of Deakin University's Geelong campus. My first impression was of half-finished isolation. It seemed rather like a well-tended crematorium. It was obviously quite new, founded in the late 1970s. The stark bare brick design was partly alleviated by the trees, similar to the flora I had enjoyed in South Africa. In the centre, a muddy lake brooded alongside the Deakin Club, the local variant of a senior common room, where I was soon to learn about Oz culture.

My office had been kept for me over five months, despite frequent raids by other departments. It was in a brand new wing of the Arts building, which also overlooked the lake and a little stone chapel. A path led from my office, past the chapel, and over a small Chinese bridge, right to the senior common room bar. Thoughtful positioning I reckoned. Strangely positioned beneath the desk in my office was a lamp, securely fixed *under* the desk top.

'Why is that light fixed there?' I asked. I imagined some pervert obsessed with examining his piles or other varicose veins in seclusion. That could be the only logical explanation for the very unusual position.

Murray didn't know. I asked the very nice departmental secretary. She said they were 'chook lamps'. 'They keep your knees warm in cold weather.'

I asked what 'chook' meant.

'Little chicken,' she said.

Ok, I thought, I've got a little chicken lamp under my desk. No phone or filing cabinet. Incommunicado, my knees were going be warm. But I wasn't ever going to complain in Oz, and play to the local stereotype of whinging Poms.

I soon became fascinated by the Oz variant of English. I had been in the country before and had learned some Strine when I lived for two years with an Australian girlfriend in Johannesburg.

My first real induction into Strine was when I had laryngitis and I couldn't make a rehearsal for a TV programme I was due to record at the nearby Auckland Park studios of the South African TV service.

'Please ring and make my apologies,' I croaked.

Jenny, sweetly innocent, despite being a fiercely intelligent lawyer, lifted up the phone to speak, probably to some racist white Afrikaner – this was the height of apartheid – 'Sorry, Paul can't make it today. He's crook and in bed with a wog.'

She meant I was ill and had the flu, I think, but the recipient may have decoded it as I was a criminal homosexual fornicating across the colour bar. That one sentence broke a string of apartheid laws.

Thanks, Jenny, for ruining my TV career and teaching me Strine in one sentence. It was to be the start of a beautiful friendship, and endeared me to Aussies and their patois for ever.

In Deakin, I struggled hard to acculturize, though I kicked out against the bureaucracy and political correctness that swamped the college. Unhelpfully, I reminded my new colleagues of Henry Kissinger's famous quip about universities: 'The politics are so bitter because the stakes are usually so low.'

Although some of my colleagues welcomed my attempts to shake things up, I soon realized that I'd made a mistake with this job, or it had made a mistake with me. I was offered rapid promotion to shut me up, so I kept my head down and concentrated on my writing and preparing new courses. I also had to find accommodation and a car. Except for Murray, Deakin was most unhelpful on these matters.

'Victoria is a state which doesn't have an immigrant culture,' I was told, accurately.

Houses and food were half British prices, but cars cost double.

In my cheap hired car (officially – and accurately – called 'Rent a Wreck') I hunted around second-hand car 'yards'. I first came across the perverse logic I was to meet all over Oz.

'Why are cars so damn expensive here?' I asked an over-friendly, but not too bright car salesman.

'There's a recession on,' he replied with definitive tone that implied an irrefutable statement.

'But prices come down in a recession.'

'No, we need to sell more cars.'

'But you would sell more if you dropped the prices.'

'Nope, car prices are pretty much fixed.'

'By whom?'

'Car yards. We're down on customers – got to make some money where we can.'

I gave up.

I managed to get a car, (awful) temporary accommodation and to put in a phone and electricity with no problems. After years of trying to get a phone in Spain, I was pleasantly surprised when Australian Telecom said 'Today or tomorrow?'

'Today,' I replied nervously.

'No worries.'

That, I soon discovered, was a catch-phrase almost as ubiquitously annoying as 'Have a nice day' in the US.

On my second day at the university I was asked to join the 'Metaphysicians', supposedly a literary club, but in fact a weekly booze-up. Damien, a journalism colleague with a sparkly earring, was the ringleader. Kay was a born comedienne. She had a sense of humour and wore provocative split skirts despite being a feminist. Hazel Rowley was another very bright feminist who taught English literature and went on to become one of the country's foremost literary critics and writers.

Initially, the feminists gave me a hard time, insisting I was a racist because I had worked in South Africa and a fascist because I had been to Sandhurst. They also assaulted my ears with lots of high-falutin' nonsense about 'post-modernist structuralism'. The forced intellectualism seemed strained and defensive, a sort of 'cultural cringe' in relation to England's Oxbridge. My experiences of working in first-rate universities elsewhere suggested an inverse ratio between intellectual debate and being down to earth. But Hazel and some of the others were possessed of a very high intellect; once we became friends the conversations descended to normal university gossip. Hazel even became my protector against the miasma of feminist dogma that swamped the arts faculty.

Previous visits to Oz had taught me that it was a robust place. I understood that the 'Ocker' – the beer-swilling foul-mouthed, Sheila-baiting backwoodsman – was largely a myth, especially among the urban intelligentsia. The culture had outgrown the crude stereotypes of Crocodile Dundee and Dame Edna Everage. I wasn't prepared, however, for the powerful and well-funded women's studies' group which conducted a McCarthyite witch hunt against male unbelievers in general and me in particular.

One senior feminist, a diesel-dyke professor, invited me to her barbie. She fired a half-joking warning shot on my arrival, 'You must eat the sausages sideways to avoid phallic misinterpretation.' So immediately I mastered the fine art of sideways sausage-eating.

Hazel Rowley was a member of the Metaphysicians' club. She became my friend and advisor on how to deal with the feminist onslaught. She also became a famous biographer.

Not all or even the majority of the 'wimmin' were bearded vegetarians with luxuriant armpits campaigning to kill every lipstick in sight. Some looked vaguely normal and were polite to me.

Nevertheless, I shared some of my concerns about the women's crusade with Magnus 'Nuke Em' Clarke. As his nickname implied, he taught defence studies. He was also a crusading naturist, a trait not normally associated with militarism. I mooted the formation of a men's studies' group. Magnus agreed, but he was just stirring, whereas in my naiveté I was half-serious. Hazel, though, issued a serious health warning. 'The feminists rule the roost here, so why inflict unnecessary pain on yourself?'

I took her advice and joined the Women's Studies' Group. I explained honestly that I was not a fullblooded convert, but did want to learn, and I did say I might write about my experiences as their apprentice. The feminists had already started to vet my student handouts for non-PC language, but nearly all this stopped when I signed up to the cause. One of the most ardent feminists, as it happened the prettiest and the only one who wore make-up and mini-skirts – I would never have risked describing her thus at the time – took me under her wing and made life so much better for me. Her name was Karen.

I duly attended all sorts of seminars, including topics such as birthing and tubal ligation. I did learn a lot especially when I went on outings with the group. On one occasion I was handed a Tampax on entering a music event.

I did demur and say, 'Thank you but obviously I don't menstruate.'

'No,' they replied tartly, 'You must say "*femstruate*".'

I am not making this up, by the way. I was about to share the benefits of my classical education by explaining what the Latin word for month was, but I had learned by now to shut up. Actually, I enjoyed the evening. The lesbian pop group, dressed in denim boiler suits, was called the 'Pap Smears' and they were quite good.

I did open doors, stand up when women entered the room and occasionally sent flowers so sometimes I was criticized for my old-fashioned habits. But my membership of the elite ladies' group by and large meant a trouble-free ride for the rest of my stay at the university. I soon conceded, however, to the Oz habit of calling everyone by their first names on first meeting, though I didn't do that to students. I stuck to the UK tradition of expecting undergraduates to call me by my title of 'Doctor' which might be modified, eventually, at post-graduate level.

Despite being a short, portly, middle-aged bloke, I was surprisingly often directly propositioned by attractive young Oz women (though the feminists never did it front of other feminists). I was two or three times punched hard on the back even if I *politely* declined such offers. I was beginning to see why Oz males had a reputation for crowding together on their own in one corner of a party. It was not machismo, it was more a protective scrum.

Feminists on the pill in Britain in the 1960s argued for the right to say yes to men. The current heterosexual Oz variants, I feared, were keener on making *men* say yes.

Like all newcomers I tried hard to blend in. I didn't wear a hat indoors, though I did jettison my tie. I had to be careful to avoid being dubbed a 'tall poppy' who needed cutting down to size. One way to mix with the locals was to go to an Australian Rules footy match.

Bruce – that really was his name – was a kindly lecturer in English, and also a footy fan. Since I was struggling to understand Oz women, I needed more time in male company. Bruce picked me up in his ancient 'ute', the all-purpose Oz utility vehicle, and wearing a sort of Stetson called an Akubra.

'Are hats compulsory?' I asked.

'No, but beers are.'

Inside the grounds, the home of the famed 'Geelong Cats', I queued at a kiosk for beers. I thought I'd better show willing and buy six cans – 'tinnies'– for my host and myself.

'You can only have two tinnies, mate.'

'Why?'

'It's the rules.'

Alright, another dent in the myth: Aussies are restricting booze at a sports event. Sensible, I thought, in the light of UK soccer hooliganism.

'Is that one drink per person?'

'No, two.'

'OK, four cans, please.'

'But you're on your own.'

I summoned Bruce and got my four beers.

Australian Rules football is waged on a large oval and it struck me as very American. Cheerleaders waved big pom-poms. Then supporter clubs erected large plastic banners, with inspirational messages for their teams. Then the eighteen players on each team run through the banners and rip them up. The game is supposed to be derived from Gaelic football, although others claim it originated from an Aboriginal pastime. It has far fewer infringements than the UK variants of soccer and the two codes of rugby. I enjoyed it because it was so fast, though the rules were hard to decipher.

I kept pestering Bruce. 'Why are they kicking into their own goal? With cricket or soccer, you must defend a wicket or goal.'

With just a slight touch of testiness, Bruce eventually tried to shut me up by saying. 'You've got to forget other kinds of football.'

I continued to be perplexed by the four referees or umpires, plus the fact that that so many team managers and advisors ran back and forth on the pitch. Some appeared to bring tactical instructions while others gave pep-talks or supplied drinks.

Footy was a local passion, enjoyed by young and old, male and female. It all seemed goodhearted with none of the menace and primitive tribal passions that had done so much harm to British soccer. I thanked Bruce for my introduction to the state religion.

By this stage I was getting the hang of the small town of Geelong and so accepted a dinner invitation in Melbourne. Riding across the immense sweep of the West Gate Bridge over the Yarra River, my first sight of the city was exhilarating: a mini-Manhattan in sleek steel and blue glass rose up to meet me. The watery late sun silhouetted the skyline and I was reminded of the square block of skyscrapers in central Johannesburg.

Murray had taken me to central Melbourne and then I caught a cab to a friend's house in the suburb of Surrey Hills. The Greek driver dropped me outside a large spooky mansion.

The cabbie asked: 'Who lives here? The Addams Family?'

'Yes, as a matter of fact.'

Rob and Rose Adams were old friends from Africa. Rob was now the city architect, just the man to teach me about Melbourne. After a bout of African 'when-we-ism', I asked about the city and in particular where I could get a bottle to take to the nearby dinner party. I was living in a part of Geelong where no booze could be sold, and I'd heard the expression 'booze bus'. When I explained that perhaps they were mobile liquor stores where I could purchase alcohol it amused my hosts.

Melbourne. Normally I was fascinated by stream trains but the Melbourne trams were also charming to this geek.

'Booze buses are police vans. They don't sell booze, they test booze levels.'

Mary-Anne, who had joined me as a blind date for the evening, thought me mad. Josie, an old friend in Sydney, had rung her up and told her to look after me. Mary-Anne, a beautiful former ballet dancer, provided excellent street cred for my first dinner party in the city, arranged by my new university friends.

Mary-Anne picked up immediately on my reluctance to engage in polite university conversation – and she commented on this as we were the only smokers keenly talking *a deux* in the garden. The only time I talked 'students' – the occupational hazard of all teachers – was to recall a particularly difficult schizophrenic (that was the term used then) in the UK. Damien had prompted the discussion by talking about one of his current students who attended lectures in his pyjamas. After a few days in Oz, that no longer struck me as strange.

'Tell us about your schizophrenic,' Damien insisted.

'It was in Cardiff, when I taught at the Open University. He had two distinct personalities and voices – his own and his mother's. It was a touch of *Psycho*: he lived a rather isolated life with his aged mother. It was macabre when he rang up, which he did regularly. I would never know which voice he would use.'

Damien asked: 'Which personality got the best grades, his or his mother's?'

Mary-Anne and I retreated relatively early to the Adams family mansion almost next door to the dinner party. My hosts had left a blazing log fire and champagne in a bucket. I had told them of my total incomprehension of Oz women. They were trying to give me a head start.

I tried to impress Mary Anne with my war stories, but this was marred by the fact that I lost a contact lens and had to bribe her with more champagne to find it for me.

The mood deflated, I walked Mary-Anne to her car parked outside the mansion and very correctly went to shake her hand.

'Aw, shit, yeah. You could knock a sailor off my sister,' she said in surprise. She almost manhandled me and kissed me properly.

In the morning, Rob took me on a tour of the city he managed. It was clean, well-organized and full of marvellous Victorian buildings. I liked Melbourne.

A few days later I was glad to see Melbourne and Mary-Anne again. It was a glitzy book launch for Hazel's new book on Christina Stead, the famous Oz novelist. The event was full of scruffy academics, brightly dressed socialites and a sprinkling of top Labor politicians.

After the launch was over, Hazel, Mary-Anne and a few drunken Deakin friends gathered around a small table for dinner. It had been a good evening, except when it came to paying the bill. Then the haggling started. I was probably the poorest person in the room, but I ended up paying for a number of people rather than suffer the full induction to the great Australian bill-paying ritual. This is how it worked.

The waiter/waitress brings the bill. All conversation stops. Even the most carefree and garrulous member of the company goes into a silent, fixed-stare accountant mode. Sometimes calculators are produced, and the bill is forensically examined.

'I had the steak but no coffee.'

'But you also had the salad.'

'Then there was the garlic bread.'

'But I didn't touch it.'

After a few minutes of such quibbles, the sullen members of the table put down what they think is fair, while trying to find the – *precise* – change. The most innumerate member then will add the pile of cash. It is inevitably short and so everyone is asked to add, say, two dollars more.

The company gets really grumpy now. They all contribute, very reluctantly, exactly two dollars. No tip is considered.

'Australians don't tip,' I was told. 'It offends their egalitarian spirit.'

I paid for Hazel, Mary-Anne and no doubt a few others.

(To be fair, not all Aussies did this – many were very generous. When I recounted this story to non-Deakin friends later, they suggested it was perhaps more a trait of stingy intellectuals and anal academics. Maybe that's true, as I have come across the embarrassing ritual in other countries and universities as well.)

I retreated to Mary-Anne's house by tram. The city lights twinkled like a fairyland as she pointed out the sights. When we arrived at her home, a red-bricked former worker's cottage in trendy St Kilda, I asked if she had read any novels by Christina Stead. I had bought Hazel's weighty, expensive and signed book and wanted to know more about Christina. I retired almost immediately to Mary-Anne's spare bedroom to explore Australian literature.

The next morning, Mary-Anne set off early for work. I said goodbye and never saw her again. I did send her flowers to thank her for her hospitality, but my feminist friends told me it was a huge mistake. 'Sending flowers to women can be interpreted as unbelievably patronizing,' I was told.

I also sent flowers to Hazel and she loved them.

I had been in Oz just a few weeks and I had learned a lot, though I was also even more confused.

******

I was living in a broom cupboard until I met Trish, a sporty brunette with a very large and obsessively protective Dutch boyfriend. Trish saw my broom cupboard and immediately insisted that I share her large six-bedroom house. She lived there alone and was off soon to Adelaide to study for six months and I was asked to house-sit thereafter. This is where Pickfords delivered my life packed up in brown boxes.

I offered the two tough Ockers a midday beer which they accepted with alacrity after off-loading all my boxes.

'Best country in the world, this is.'

'I agree entirely. Have you been overseas?'

'Yeah, Tasmania.'

'What it's like there?'

'Beaut, mate. But no Abos.'

'Why?'

'They killed all the bastards.'

'Don't you like "Abos"?' (Although I had learned to call the indigenous peoples 'Kooris' on my very first day at Deakin, I didn't want to argue with these hard men.)

'I love 'em…not that I know many. But I don't like all the foreigners who are taking our jobs. Especially the Poms. They don't stop complaining …. Where are you from? South Africa?'

It was best to be compliant. 'Well, I lived there for a long time. Journalist there … now I'm teaching at Deakin.'

'Yeah, we just moved some Indian fellows into Deakin. We don't do many South Africans now. I refused to unload for a South African woman. She was ordering me around – "Do this and do that" – just like I was some bloody black servant. I just packed up and drove back to the depot. I went back the next day and she was as nice as pie. That should teach her something about Australia.'

Australian nationalists liked to argue that social hierarchy broke down in Oz because English gentlemen beset by flies could no longer stand on their dignity, although probably it was more the historical shortage of labour.

The removal men were not historians, but they were keen sociologists. They regaled me with a litany of all sort of foreigners' faults until he foreman said. 'We gotta go. It's poet's day.'

'You interested in poetry?' I asked even more politely.

'Nah, mate. It's poet's day – don't 'cha know? – Piss Off Early Tomorrow's Saturday. Spells poets.'

Despite frequent warnings that tips were un-Australian, I gave the men some money, suggesting they celebrate poet's day by having a few drinks on me. They accepted with good grace. Maybe because we were now drinking mates and we had established a social parity. No condescension was involved.

I needed to dump my Rent a Wreck and contacted Helen who was leaving Deakin to return to the UK. Her overpriced banger was possibly the best deal on offer. Helen told me that she had taught at the Open University. Before we settled on a price, I mentioned I had also taught a social science course there.

'It was full of Marxist twaddle, riddled with inaccuracies. Crap, in short,' I declared.

Helen looked at me coldly. 'I devised that course.'

That probably bumped up her asking price on the car. She gave me a hard time and then the keys of her car.

Helen was teetotal, vegetarian and a hyperactive member of the smoke police. She dripped righteous angst. But she was a Pom, and I had no excuse not to understand her. Aussies were different. I sped-read some of the classics, such as Robert Hughes's brilliant book, *The Fatal Shore,* about the convict system. And I hung out with a wise man called Patrick. He had been an electrician before he taught psychology at Deakin. He was normal, and liked a beer or two after our regular squash sessions. Our boozy seminars helped me to explore Oz myths. And Oz misses. Patrick introduced me to all sorts of eccentric females.

The first was Frances who immediately invited me to a quiz night. I didn't know it was a fundraiser for the Labor party. The local MP gave me a rousing welcome from the stage. I had incautiously mentioned to Frances that I had formerly been a Plaid Cymru local councillor.

'We are very happy to have a fellow socialist republican with us, comrades,' he said loudly and then repeated it.

I pondered my politics over the excellent local beer. I was certainly no socialist. I was a capitalist with bugger-all capital. I was not even a convinced republican, despite some bad experiences with Princess Anne when I worked with her unhappy first husband at Sandhurst. (Ironically I was to work later with her much happier second husband and learned to respect HRH's hard work.) So I was a very tepid monarchist, though most of my Deakin colleagues were avowed republicans. I was also a lousy Welsh nationalist as I spent most of my time travelling a long way from my Welsh valleys.

I did not entirely endear myself to my hosts that night by asking not to be addressed as 'comrade'. I very succinctly outlined my experiences in socialist states, not least in Eastern Europe. Nor did I excel in the quiz which involved knowing some very real trivia about obscure socialist mayors of West Geelong in the 1950s. Frances soon learned I was hopelessly politically incorrect but – 'Good on her', to use my favourite Aussie phrase – she continued with my induction into what passed for polite political society.

She next invited me to a 'tuxedo and eskie' event.

I had fleeting thoughts of the new Labor multi-racialism, inspired by the recent Mabo court judgement that conceded that native people did actually live in Australia before whites arrived. Eskie? Native eskimo? Was I supposed to ask along an Aboriginal as a rite of passage for me and as a gesture towards the local variant of paternalism? As I said, I had learned that 'Koori' was the required term.

'Do Kooris have to wear black ties too?'

She gave me one of her half-knowing, half-sideways looks that I grew accustomed to in Oz. It said, 'Is this guy nuts, yanking my chain or trying to start a fight?'

'I don't expect any Kooris will be there,' she said very suspiciously. 'But bring an eskie.' She sensed my genuine confusion. 'A cool bag for the food, and drinks and knives and forks and plates.'

'If it's a formal occasion, why must we bring all those sorts of things?'

'It saves money.'

'But what is the $20 ticket for?'

'The jazz band.'

Trish – now dubbed my 'glamorous landlady'– came along and provided all the eskie equipment. We both dressed up, but she refused to drink in a nearby pub before the main event in the town hall. She said it was full of women of low repute. She explained that the pub was officially called The Saint George, but the locals always added 'And the Dragons'.

'I didn't know it was a parachute club.' I was deciding to get my own back.

'What does that mean?'

I refused to tell her because it was rather crude.

'I insist,' she said.

'Parachute – every time guaranteed a jump.'

She gave me a disgusted look. I constantly observed the paradox. I was often accused of being too prissy and proper. On a number of occasions Trish called me a 'piker' – 'a Pom with no balls'. Trish was a staunch Catholic and quite reserved, though most Aussie women, of all classes, swore like troopers and were usually sexually direct, but an occasional smutty joke could provoke real or pretended rebuke.

It didn't help that when Frances arrived she picked up on the fact that Trish was a recent divorcee. 'I am writing a book on newly independent divorcees,' she proudly announced.

I inadvertently fed her the required line: 'What's the title?'

'"Orgasms on a shoe-string" … and I've got a publisher.'

I think she was genuinely working on such a book. And all the women in the group rushed at once to provide anecdotes.

The ball was like a tea dance in Norwich in the 1950s (I supposed). It was a blue-rinse hop. The jazz was good, but no one danced. I asked Cindy – a wild blonde who had invited me on a number of occasions to rock 'n' roll on the large, low, solid table in the august Deakin staff club – why everything seemed to be slow and formal. Since I had actually acceded to her Deakin club dance requests a few times and earned a minor reputation, she gave an honest answer to my question.

'Is it the tuxedoes?'

'No, daahling,' she said in her very broad Oz drawl. 'We are all here with our spouses.'

QED, I suppose.

I was always happy to play the naïve anthropologist at strange Oz rituals even when I didn't actually enjoy myself. But this 'ball' was the pits so Trish and I decided to leave early. Though I had drunk just one beer, we decided to grab a cab. Trish spotted her very large boyfriend's taxi nearby, before he saw us. Trish had said she was indoors studying, not out at a dance. She assured me that he was a gentle giant. I was unconvinced and sneaked around the back of the Town Hall to catch an out-of-sight taxi. We went home to play pool.

We were up early for a visit by Trish's sister. All I had been told was that she had been a nun who had left the convent to marry an Anglican priest. For some reason I was left alone for a long time with the ex-nun and struggled to make polite conversation. Desperate, I started talking about Catholicism which didn't appear to interest the visitor. Then the ex-nun started talking about breasts. She kept up the topic for some hours. I listened intently. Trish later enlightened me. Her sister had an obsessive interest in breastfeeding and had written books on the subject. Trish had been caught in her obsessive breastfeeding headlight before and left me to be the dazzled victim this time.

Trish soon left for her Adelaide trip and I was alone in the big house. The pool table in particular was to prove popular with the Metaphysicians who moved the weekly booze-up to my temporary home. Sometimes it got out of hand. Damien invited the Dean's wife – the same Karen who was my saviour in the Women's Group – to come along. He plied her with drinks and persuaded her to rock 'n' roll. She fell awkwardly over a table and later did a dramatic back somersault over a chair because of Damien's enthusiastic if inexpert dance moves. People were smoking joints, although I disapproved, and everybody was drinking too much. At two o'clock in the morning I suggested to the bruised and tipsy Karen that she should not drive. Damien wanted to ring her husband, our Dean, to

The ironing ritual in Trish's house. This was a spectacle enjoyed by my feminist friends who liked to see a Pom male working. The famous pool table is in the background.

say she was staying. Since Damien was about to be interviewed by the Dean to try to turn his temporary job into a permanent one, I persuaded my colleague that it would be more diplomatic if he and I chipped in for a cab for the lengthy ride home. It may not have been the sight of his bruised, inebriated and late-arriving wife that inspired the Dean's failure to grant the permanent job.

I started to explore more of the area. Geelong was once a formidable industrial centre with a number of car plants. De-industrialization, however, had left many shops empty in the town. The central part still maintained a number of attractive colonial buildings, especially the post office. On nearly every street enough architectural gems survived to dispel the gloom of the neon signs.

The university, ten miles out of town, was an important part of the local economy. Deakin had five campuses spread across the state which made the usual departmental bickering even more tiresome. As the administrative centre, Geelong was the core of the system. I tried hard to get the so-called Communications Committee to work. In theory the university had a sophisticated audio and video conferencing system. I was no techie and had to rely on engineers to get the system working – it never did. We never managed to get more than one campus to link up with Geelong to even start talking about improving communications. It was a farce. Perhaps a deliberate one. Even if I had got all five campuses on line, the hostility towards Geelong's perceived central dictatorship would have scuttled any reforms. So the tyranny of distance triumphed again. I was always told – 'Australia is a big country, you know.' And it was a long way from anywhere else, I would mutter *sotto voce.*

Most universities attract a stock of eccentrics. Deakin seemed infested with them. Some of the eccentricities were a contrived substitute for intellect, though others genuinely had kangaroos living in their top paddock, to use the vernacular. Murray, my initial host, was genial and gentle, but his eccentricities earned him the university-wide epithet of 'Man from Mars'. Denis was a Kiwi philosopher who had been to (maybe even read something at) Oxford, and never let anyone forget it. He epitomized yet again the cultural cringe, the term used to describe the historical inferiority that Australians felt towards the allegedly more sophisticated Europeans. Denis performed obscure Hindu dances in the corridor while always wearing a natty little scarf. He was also a one-man slum in dress and in his office. He had been moved three times in a vain attempt to reduce the fire risk clutter, but the dust, debris and piles of books were lovingly and precisely recreated each time. He lived in Melbourne and regarded all those who lived in 'Sleepy Hollow' – Geelong – as real hicks.

Much bizarre behaviour was exhibited during the lunchtime seminars for visiting academics. I understood why people brought packed lunches, but not why the messiest eaters, with vast hampers, sat right next to the guest speakers, often drowning out their words with frenzied feeding noises. I'd seen better food behaviour among monkeys in the wild.

A few of the seminars were stimulating, though the zoo-time feeding frenzies deterred me. I collected a few of the portentous lecture titles – 'Moral vegetarianism and Indian thought', 'Deconstruction and Madhyamika Studies', and 'When my body turns nasty on me: women negotiating parenthood'. The most intriguing was 'Feminism without women: A Lesbian reassurance'. This was supposed to be about the so-called 'Lesbian man'. This one might have been worth a spin, but I was busy, not least with attending other feminist events.

I tried to find out if any practical and serious research was being done. A few years before, a large grant had been given to a researcher to work on cancer. A major part of the costs was for laboratory animals, especially beagles. Some time later, with the media agitated, animal liberationists decided to free the dogs. Not one could be found. The research was bogus. Twelve thousand dollars were also donated to the women's group to produce a 'feminist surfboard'. The research was genuine, but I could never find out what design fault was discovered in the 'male' board.

A glaring example of male chauvinism was to be found in the journalism department: it was all male. The Dean suggested that his latest wife – the dance-battered Karen – should teach journalism part-time. Like all latecomers to academia – she had risen through the ranks from being a secretary – she was very earnest. Karen was also very bright and had a good doctorate, although she claimed that her best qualifications were 'giving birth to beautiful babies'. She also asserted that she had been a Marxist 'until the Berlin Wall came down'. I didn't like her politics, but I thought she should be allowed to teach because she was well-qualified, charming and we needed female teachers. The radical Damien, who always disagreed with me, and chided me for cracking jokes in staff meetings, was surprised when I supported the feminist entryism. My other colleagues accused me of brown-nosing the Dean, though with Damien on my side we got our way. And the students benefited.

The dance-battered Dr Karen Lane was a member of the feminist group who tried to protect me from the extremists.

Damien also started being extra friendly. He was an ardent biker and began to invite me on rides, and even suggested I buy a Harley-Davidson. I wore my hair longish (as I had an ample supply and all my own teeth), but my extended mid-life crisis did not extend to a Harley.

I used to ask what the students thought of the madhouse they were in. As in many universities at the time, their views seemed to matter the least. They dubbed the place 'apathy city'. The students had campaigned halfheartedly for a student bar in the isolated campus, but to no avail. On National Condom Day, a part of the anti-AIDS campaign, the college nurse set up a stall to give away free condoms. She had hardly any takers at all from the students, even when she approached them and thrust them in their hands. If you could not get students excited about beer and sex, you could hardly expect political activism.

I tried to interest them in politics during my lectures. I showed my young Einsteins some of the films I had made on South Africa.

The first question was: 'Why don't the whites go home?'

I couldn't help myself: 'Some Afrikaner families have been there since 1652. All of your families have been here less than 200 years so why don't *you* go home?'

That got them debating, and perhaps even thinking.

Geelong reminded me of the Texan college I had taught at. The students were friendly, direct, poorly motivated and largely apathetic. Most academics will confess that colleges would be better without students; this view seemed to be taken to extremes in Deakin. Some lecturers were extremely disparaging about the intellectual qualities of their charges. I felt that this might be self-fulfilling and that it also reflected subconscious doubts about their own intellectual strengths perhaps. Deakin was self-conscious about its newness and fairly low status in the Oz university hierarchy. Despite its claims to classlessness, Oz was as obsessive about pecking orders as England.

It has to be said that some aspects of the university, especially the study guides for off-campus students, were very good. This provided a second chance for many older students as they worked or brought up families. One student who was bed-ridden rang me regularly. The university courses, she told me, were her *raison d'être*.

Australians have a reputation abroad as hard workers. I didn't always get that impression in their homeland. So that might explain why many students were not that diligent – they joined in the rather socialist suckling-at-the-public-teat sense of entitlement that permeated the college.

Still, I had to join in the Oz culture of being a 'battler', one who gives it a go and who deserves a fair chance. But I couldn't greet my colleagues properly no matter how hard I tried. I couldn't get my nose around 'G'day'. My attempts to replicate the nasal twang met with universal derision.

I continued to be a battler in the women's studies group. Some were hostile harpies, though the majority took an increasing interest in this strange new specimen: me. Increasingly paranoid, I began to assume a Clausewitzian theory of

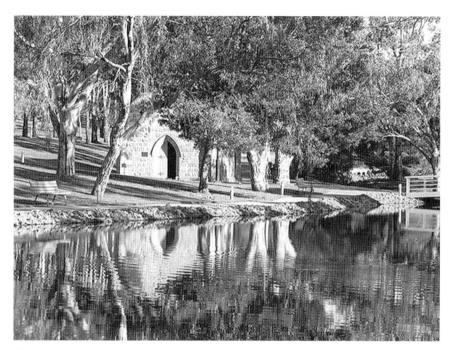

The chapel in the Waurn Ponds campus of Deakin University in Geelong. I had to walk past the chapel to reach the bar at the Senior Common room.

sexual harassment. Having failed to convert me intellectually, were they ganging up to seduce me by other means? I had to jump out of a (first-floor) window to escape one particularly predatory female. I felt I was in a David Lodge novel or was it really Tom Sharpe? Or possibly the *Goon Show* meets *Valley of the Dolls*? My experiences of bad-tempered Afghan warlords or assegai-wielding Zulu chieftains were mere examples of friendly fire compared with Oz termagants in full battle cry.

****

Luckily, in the nick of time, a young Croat-Australian journalist called Slavka took on the role of guardian angel. She was great fun and stimulating, despite being half my age; our mutual interest in the Balkans and her command of Serbo-Croat were to prove useful later in real war zones as opposed to Deakin's battles of the sexes.

Slavka was combative. On our first night out we went to one of Frances's bashes. They clashed head on.

Frances said: 'Slavka, I read your feature today in the *Geelong Advertiser.* Is English your second language?'

Slavka, the Balkan spitfire (on my left), at a hacks' 'ball'.

I had to physically restrain Slavka, who had a fiery Balkan temperament.

I plied them both with drink and directed Frances onto her favourite subject, orgasms – an understandable obsession with a first-time author. Frances soon launched into a detailed account of her vibrator. A circle soon formed around us.

'I call my vibrator Trevor,' she said possessively.

'I don't believe in vibrators,' Slavka retorted. She'd had a very strict Catholic upbringing, though she was no spoilsport. 'But if I did have one, I'd call him Eric.'

I shut up, as did the outer circle, as both women fought for possession of the lewdest stories. Slavka won a knockout blow with the story of her investigation of the local 'Faggots Boys Club'. She explained it was like the Freemasons except that the initiation rites involved sticking a lit, rolled copy of the *Melbourne Age* up the bottom and walking in a circle.

I hadn't spoken for an hour, entranced and also too nervous to interrupt the duelling Amazons.

I couldn't help but insert a technicality about the *Melbourne Age*. 'Was it the thick Saturday edition?'

This ended the Frances-Slavka bout, as I'd hoped. The feisty raven-haired hack had got her revenge for the older woman's opening jab.

Desultory dancing followed until Slavka, who had over-celebrated her victory with champagne, livened up proceedings with a heavy metal interpretation of

Croat folk dancing. Intrigued, one of the most senior academic members of the party started to half-paw, half-dance with her. Slavka immediately pulled him off the dance floor and dressed him down.

'You dirty-danced with me. In fact you slimed me.'

I don't think the deputy Vice Chancellor had ever been spoken to like that before.

It was time to go as some of the hangers-on were preparing to share a spa, led by the ever-campaigning naturist, Magnus Clarke. Neither Slavka nor I fancied infringing our modesty. And, anyway, this was my first date with the Balkan spitfire who had the innocent aura of a young Madonna (the Catholic icon not the singer).

On the way home, my car was stopped by a forest of blue wands ….

'Have you had anything to drink, sir?' It was two o'clock in the morning, Buddy Holly was playing full volume in the car, and Slavka was singing at the top of her voice, a wild look in her eyes. I didn't look entirely respectable.

As it was a first date, and I felt protective towards my young companion, I had drunk orange juice all evening, except for one small beer at the end. After blowing twice in the bags, I was told I could carry on.

At least I now knew what a booze bus actually did.

******

Victoria is dubbed the Garden State – I needed to get out of Geelong and see more of the countryside. A fellow Welshman, Frank, invited me to his small farm in Moriac, not too far from what he called the 'looneversity'. A Red Dragon fluttered over his isolated farmhouse. The 47-year-old possessed the endearing aura of a man who didn't care about his appearance, yet his innate charisma made him look like a rustic Eric Clapton.

Frank rushed me to meet his aged mother who came from Barry, South Wales; she looked like she had just quit the International Brigade of the Spanish Civil War. Her long hair and beret added to the effect. She greeted me warmly and pulled out the family Welsh-language Bible, insisting that she wanted to hear the language of heaven one more time. I did my best to read a short extract aloud from the *Psalms*. The difficult script and my poor Welsh fell far short of the Richard Burton delivery that was expected.

Frank had an endearing passion for old houses; he had fashioned a museum of a dozen old historic buildings at the university. He also planted indigenous trees all over his property and had developed an overriding hatred of rabbits which were destroying his saplings.

As he was showing me his rabbit traps, I risked asking: 'Have you ever seen *Watership Down*?'

'Nah, I hate the bastards. I sit on my veranda at night with a spotlight and a rifle. I usually manage to shoot a few.'

Frank had an equally gung-ho attitude to the university bureaucrats. He was one of a very few academics who used their tenure properly: to say what he really thought. His collected e-mails and letters were sometimes read aloud in the Metaphysicians' Club. He addressed his bosses as 'low-grade fuckwits'– to their faces. He was also a prominent member of the teachers' union. Unsurprisingly, the mandarins offered him a large lump sum to retire early.

My friendship with Frank ended abruptly when I refused to heed his call for a university strike (over a very trivial dispute). I drove right through the picket lines at the university entrance, scattering the *bien-pensants* – without touching them. Nearly all my students did the same as the strike was called just before prep periods for the exams. Frank claimed I betrayed both my Welsh roots and my working-class origins. I received one of his famously abusive e-mails. The university needed lots of reforms, yet I didn't think striking would help one iota.

I had a more successful visit to the Mornington Peninsula, which hugged the Port Phillip Bay, a massive lagoon for Melbourne and Geelong harbours. Early settlers had erected attractive homesteads. The Peninsula also boasted over thirty vineyards. I drove to Queenscliff to catch the ferry after a quick exploration of the late Victorian seaside town. Much of the period architecture was well preserved, especially the old fort, still a military HQ where I was later asked to lecture on guerrilla warfare. Another attractive feature was the steam-train station.

I left my car and went across on the ferry to Sorrento, to stay at the Sorrento Hotel. Another Mary-Ann, whom I hadn't met before, had arranged for me to attend a posh event for Melbourne socialites. I was beginning to feel like a permanent blind date. I was picked up at the hotel and driven to Redhill, where the occasional stretch limo hinted at what I was to encounter. Mary-Ann introduced me to her friends, pretty wasted souls with empty eyes. I was reminded of the line from Australian poet James McAuley, who described the local women as 'hard-eyed, kindly, with nothing inside them'. A bit harsh perhaps.

I was introduced to the doyenne of Melbourne society, Primrose Dunlop, who had come in one of the limos. She was a bit down, I was told. She was recovering from being left at the altar by her ultra-handsome bridegroom who had eloped instead with his boyfriend. A stunning air hostess, with equally stunningly superficial conversation, took me on a tour of the grand beach houses. She could dance better than she could talk and so, anaesthetized by the good-quality champagne, I survived the evening.

Better was my morning walk around my hotel environs. Like many country towns, especially the Chelseafied resorts, the streets were friendly, spacious and graced with real or mock Victorian architecture. Things fitted together pretty well, perhaps because nearly all the buildings were one- or two-storey. The style was designed with humans in mind. *Homo Australiensis* seemed to respond by not dropping litter or defacing buildings with graffiti. It was a very litter-conscious society. Maybe it was the space that Australia had to play with, unlike cramped, dirty old Europe.

My next outing was to Daylesford, an hour's drive inland from Geelong. The small township, spawned by the area's gold boom, was surveyed and laid out in 1854. Maybe that was another explanation for a sense of peace in many country towns in Oz. Not only was there space (and apparently money), but the towns were *planned.* My companion – let's call her Mary-Ann to avoid confusion – suggested we stop at the Convent Gallery. This elegant mock-Gothic building was originally built as the private residence of the gold commissioner. Then Mammon succumbed to the Mass when it became a convent. More recently, it had been transformed into an art gallery with a Mediterranean-style restaurant. Many Australian restaurants and hotels looked splendid on the outside, but this was first one I had visited where the interior matched the quality of the façade. Most Australians seemed to enjoy eating and drinking in cattle barns.

After lunch, Mary-Ann suggested a visit to the nearby Hepburn Springs, a health resort modelled on the old European spas. Normally spas don't appeal to me. It had nothing to do with my being a Brit. I bathed or showered at least once a day, despite the Oz saying – 'As dry as a Pom's towel'. It had everything to do with my preference for showering or bathing *alone.* I didn't realize that I was about to encounter another elaborate ceremony akin to the Oz bill-paying ritual.

I had in mind to try a solitary spin in a flotation tank.

They were booked out for two hours, we found out, as a queue of ten people formed behind us.

'Why not try an aerospa bath?' suggested the receptionist.

'Sure, why not? I said boldly, not knowing what I was volunteering for.

The receptionist saw the two of us standing there and she simply said 'A double?' with hardly a question in her voice.

Mary-Ann looked at me slightly aghast, slightly bemused. The queue was beginning to take an unhealthy interest in our proceedings so I didn't think it was appropriate to discuss the parameters of our very recent friendship.

'OK, I'll take the double spa,' I said.

'What!' said Mary-Ann. 'I'm not going in there with *you*.'

'We might as well share the damn thing.'

The queue was now thoroughly enjoying my embarrassment. The receptionist handed me the key.

We had to wait for a few minutes. I wandered off and left Mary-Ann talking to a male attendant who was handing out towels etc.

'Did you ask him for bathing costumes?' I said perhaps a little naively.

'No, I did *not*,' she replied with a mix of determination, and resignation. I had impinged on the macho Aussie psyche there. Mary-Ann displayed a touching glimpse of shyness. I certainly felt awkward.

The spa room was more spartan and certainly smaller, more *intimate,* than I had anticipated. It was so basic, obviously run by the local council. There was not even any piped music as I had imagined. As the green water bubbled away, I slipped off my clothes and gingerly hopped in. With just my neck above the water, I told her I was closing my eyes and suggested she got undressed. When I opened them, she was opposite with her head just above the cloudy – concealing – water.

We both relaxed and started to chat amiably in the soothing water. This was possibly a prelude to a later sexual situation. Even I realized that. I was immediately jerked out of such reveries, however, when Mary-Ann said sweetly: 'Can I pee in here?'

'You certainly cannot,' I said, hardly stifling the alarm in my voice.

Mary-Ann was probably joking, but she surely dispelled any amorous thoughts. Perhaps that was her intention. Or it might have been good old Aussie Rules foreplay. I shall never know.

I got out, towelled quickly and left her to dress on her own.

Sovereign Hill museum, near Ballarat.

Not surprisingly, Mary-Ann chose not to accompany me on my next outing to an interesting country town called Ballarat. This fascinating town is one big Victorian monument to adventurers from all over the world who sought fame and fortune in the gold rush of the 1850s. The best way to appreciate the history was to tour Sovereign Hill, a 'living museum' on the outskirts of Ballarat (although it was also good to walk around the main town and to let the buildings tell their own story). I did both with the help of Mary, a friend from South Africa, who was now the local marketing officer. She emphasized that 'It's not a theme park. It's a historical park. Everything has been replicated as accurately as possible.' It was indeed an excellent replica of life that followed the discovery of gold in 1851. A 64kg nugget was found in this goldfield.

Sovereign Hill was no Disneyland, despite the stagecoaches and characters dressed in period costumes – they were all unpaid volunteers, who clearly cared about their history. I was impressed by the attention to detail, especially in the bars. What interested me even more was the Eureka uprising, which was restaged nightly in a fancy sound and light show. The miners – the diggers – were upset by the way the colonial authorities operated the licencing system for the right to dig. Everybody accepted that the system was badly run and reforms had been promised … though delayed. The murder of a digger sparked a rebellion. The miners built the Eureka stockade and flew their own flag representing the Southern Cross. At dawn on 3 December 1854 government troops attacked and overwhelmed the rebels, killing twenty-four of the diggers. The battle was lost. Nevertheless, the miners' conditions were improved as a result of the brief rebellion.

I researched the subject because it played such a role in the country's self-image. The revolt was said to depict 'Australian mateship', early republicanism, embryonic socialism, ties with Irish resentment of English authority, even the first rejection of Yankee imperialism, and so much more. A lot of this was bunkum. It was the defeat of small capitalists who had jumped the gun on inevitable reforms.

The mythmaking said a lot even where it was patently inaccurate. The country of battlers had few great legends of freedoms gained by struggle. Ned Kelly, the ironclad bushranger, struggled and was killed. That is a great Oz legend, despite the film role assumed by the clanking performance of a strangely-cast Mick Jagger. It was the seventh film made on the Australian iron man, and one of the most badly received. Jagger himself claimed that he had not even bothered to see it. The other celebrations – Eureka and Gallipoli – were also defeats for the Oz 'battlers'. The Brits also had a habit of celebrating noble defeats, although in the long imperial saga defeats were always redeemed by final victories. Dunkirk led to D-Day. Australians have suffered constant military setbacks, from the fall of Singapore to Vietnam, despite the undoubted gutsiness of diggers in battle. Defeats without redemption, except on the back of Brits and Americans (or despite them, as in the excellent contribution of Oz special forces in Iraq and Afghanistan):

perhaps this explains partly the chippy nationalism without a nation that is peculiarly Australian.

I grew fascinated with the depths of historical mythification that Australians revelled in. Maybe it was the legacy of the Irish, the world's greatest self-deceiving storytellers. No wonder it took 200 years for the Aussie settlers to admit their country wasn't empty when they arrived. The rejection of *terra nullius* – that aboriginal peoples didn't have their own laws and land customs let alone rights to the land – came as something of a national shock in the Mabo decision of the early 1990s, even though nobody expected the indigenous people to get back much land.

And if you believed the local amateur genealogists, the First Fleet that brought the first convicts must have had more officers than the Starship *Enterprise*. Aussies liked to exaggerate the impact of the Eureka stockade, but tended to ignore the much greater disorder inspired by racist attacks on Chinese workers in both Victoria and New South Wales. Much of the early and current racism was swept under the polite multicultural carpet.

I travelled next to the South Australian border area, the rich farming lands of the Western Districts. This time my travel guide was Anne-Marie. (This is true – I did not place regular lonely hearts columns in the local papers asking for single adventurous women called Mary-Ann or similar.) The four-hour drive took us through rolling fields, parts of which were like Wiltshire, but with exotic trees and far fewer fences and buildings. My farmer host, Reg, was an ardent conservationist and he bemoaned the destruction of indigenous trees to make way for pine plantations. He did his best to maintain the original flora and fauna, including rare cranes. Emus darted around in the open country. I also came across my first koala, which treated me with shy disdain, though perhaps uniquely did not urinate on me. We encountered mobs of kangaroos. They were a big problem on country roads, especially at night. Hence the big roo-bars around Reg's ute, although other deterrents were high-pitched alarms such as the 'shoo-shoo' and the 'hopper-stopper'.

Reg and his brother were surprised when I volunteered for some 'hard yakka' – tough work mulesing sheep. They assumed I was a piker, but I was determined to stick to the gory physical effort of carrying sheep into cradles, cutting off their tails with a gas knife and castrating them. Because I stuck to the bloody smelly work and had not been squeamish I was heartily welcomed at the evening dinner.

Next morning Reg took me to a neighbouring farm 'to meet the 'girls'. The farmhouse was of rough wood, stone and mud construction, oozing bucolic charm. The girls were three middle-aged flabby lesbians. They were very friendly, not just to me, but to all animals. The large lounge was full of beasts. A small kangaroo jumped in front of me, then another limped past. They were completely tame. From the back of the sofa and armchairs dangled small round bags, which moved occasionally. A small furry head emerged from one, then another from an adjacent bag. One held a tiny possum, the others orphaned joeys. I was given one joey to hold in my lap and feed with a bottle.

'Is this cow's milk?' I asked ignorantly.

'No, that would blind them. We feed them a special milk compound which costs a dollar a day.'

'How long do you look after them for?'

'About a year to eighteen months.'

They were just really caring, and not remotely trying to incite donations from a soft-hearted visitor.

Reg took me around the goats, sheep, ducks, dogs, llamas and alpacas which populated the farmyard. Over tea, the three ladies talked animal conservation. As a bonus it was a rare smoking household.

The three women were excellent company. They had to be, because they had lived together in a small farmhouse without electricity for eight years. When we left, I asked Reg the obvious question. He explained that two were a couple and the third was, so to speak, the odd man out. 'She's looking for a man,' said Reg. 'She has a bob each way.'

'They're doing a great job running an unofficial sanctuary, but does their lifestyle fit in well with a conservative farming community?'

'Yeah, they're totally accepted and very popular.'

'I can't imagine the same response in the English countryside.'

In the evening Reg took me to meet his father, who came from Pontypridd. I was presented with a book about a Welsh swagman. From 1869 to 1894 Joseph Jenkins had kept an intriguing diary of colonial life, his involvement in local Welsh-language *eisteddfodau* and his success even in the most complex form of Welsh poetry, the *englyn*. I wondered why so many people wanted to leave Wales, though in Joseph Jenkins's case, overcome with *hiraeth* – homesickness – he returned to his prosperous Welsh farm in his mid-80s. I presume he must have had a good story to tell his long-suffering wife.

On the long journey back Anne-Marie and I discussed the nature of Oz rural life. I had also engaged recently in a rabbit-skinning festival and a camel-racing derby. I wanted to see what the bush was really like. My urban friends were always burbling on about the glories of 'Black Stump' or going 'way out woop woop' to search for their rustic idyll. In a country where 80 per cent of the population live near the sea, nearly all the literature (and humour) was about the bush. In one sense the climate makes even pale suburbanites into leathery larrikins every time they light a barbie or launch a surfboard. I suspected much of it was idealistic obeisance to an arid, largely monotonous desert terrain ill-suited to European settlement. Much of the land was red baked desert. The countryside was being depopulated in the lemming rush to the thin green fringe of the coastal plains. Most Aussies were in reality in thrall to the malls of the sprawling suburbs. Bournemouth was easier than Mars.

To be fair, Aussie suburbia was not a replay of Milton Keynes. Space, sun, big barbie sets, nature strips, largish plots and lots of southern European immigration added a Mediterranean flavour. The plaster lions and ornate ironwork distinguished the villas of southern European newcomers. Perhaps California was a better model for comparison than Milton Keynes or Bournemouth.

I learned that few farmers and graziers *enjoyed* the outback. It was a job, and a hard one. Too many floods, fires and droughts undermined any complacent romanticism. To sing of the wide open sunsets, billabongs and kookaburras was all very well. In those days, most Aussies were too addicted to surf, video shops and pizza parlours.

My trips to the country made me realize how suburban my own life had become. I took long walks around my house and counted the gnomes in the gardens. I even read the Neighbourhood Watch newsletter avidly. It detailed a law-and-order panic about missing garden hoses, as well as the bizarre juvenile crime of hedge burning. I wondered whether the plastic bottles of water standing on many lawns had something to do with the arsonists. I asked a neighbour about this.

'No, it stops dogs crapping on the lawns.'

'So is there some chemical in the water?'

'No, just plain water.'

'But why should that deter the dogs?'

'I dunno, mate. It just does.'

A more street-savvy Geelong friend explained that there was a possible connection between the missing hoses and the popularity of water bottles: 'Kids steal the hoses to make bongs.'

'Ok, what's a bong?'

'Well, the kids use short strips of hose-pipe and water bottles to make a kind of hookah pipe to smoke marijuana.'

'Does that keep the dogs away?'

Apart from minor issues with gardens, the 'City of Geelong West' where I lived was well run. Geelong itself, a city of 200,000 souls and the tenth largest in Oz, had just scrapped its town councillors and appointed commissioners. It seemed to work. The city was orderly, and a large majority owned their own houses. The municipal (and state) services worked efficiently, including the garbo, ambo and rego. Aussies shortened everything – this translated as garbage, ambulances and car registration. The central library functioned well too. The polite assistants knew their way around the Croat, Serb, Italian, Spanish and Dutch collections that catered for the town's many European minorities. Surrounding the library were solid, ornate Victorian buildings which I grew to appreciate more and more. Geelong was also blessed with marvellously solid Art Deco structures. Near the library stood the impressive Wool Museum. The city had been founded on gold, shipping and, above all, wool.

With the decline of traditional industries, the city tried to enhance its reputation for inventiveness. The first commercial use of refrigeration was developed in Geelong, as well as the invention of the ute. In the 1960s the locals started making plastic bags with taps for storing wines. This coincided with the rebirth of the local wine industry. The Geelongites took to the new Oz cultural icon – Château Cardboard – with missionary zeal.

Russians play chess, Hungarians eat goulash, Aussies drink. Boozing appeared to be the major local cultural activity. Geelong once prided itself on being a working-class town with strong unions and close ties with the ruling Labor Party. Bob Hawke, a previous Labor prime minister, had earned himself a place in the *Guinness Book of Records* for his drinking prowess. He had gone on the wagon, however. Perhaps that partly explained the dramatic drop in support for Labor in the area in the 1992 state elections.

Booze, not politics, was the major issue in the pubs in Geelong, especially the Criterion which housed the press bar. Like most press bars it was seedy. I've never worked out whether it's regular patronage by journalists that makes bars seedy, or whether hacks are instinctively drawn to pubs where the carpets are sticky, the food soggy and staff surly. I liked the Criterion. It was a place to escape Deakin and dancing on academic eggshells.

The Balkan spitfire, Slavka, chose the press bar as the venue to announce her departure for Croatia and its war for survival. Her assembled colleagues, full of champagne valour and keyboard courage, dispensed their collective wisdom on designer flak jackets, bulletproof laptops and shrapnel-resistant hairspray. One thoughtful sub-editor suggested she wrote her own obituary before she left.

Slavka had been spending a lot of time with me, not least because I had actually been recently to Croatia. Slavka used to visit me regularly when I was ironing my shirts and then bring friends to drink and watch this eccentric foreigner perform. My shirt-ironing speed became a topic of popular enquiry. On principle none of the visiting ladies would offer to help (even after I deliberately burnt a shirt I was going to throw away). I asked my bachelor friends what they did. The universal answer was that they didn't bother. And it showed.

I was trying hard to resist the sloppy local dress code; not very successfully because one of Slavka's friends described me as a 'wrinkly in cardies and cords'. Being half my age, Slavka thought it was hugely funny. She said, 'You dress too old, too English. I'm gonna "re-image" you.'

In the first boutique, Slavka pulled out an expensive check shirt. The very attentive shop owner was trying too hard. She said, 'Your daughter has excellent taste.'

Slavka exploded into laughter.

I said nothing, but obviously I did need a makeover.

Slavka was good at spending other people's money and I was kitted out with new glasses, a suit and lots of check shirts. Luckily, Slavka decided that an earring suited Damien, though not me. She thought I now looked 'cool', but silently I thought I looked like I was going through the longest mid-life crisis in history.

Newly attired, I took Slavka to the Empire Grill, one of the very few establishments that modelled itself successfully on good-quality European restaurants. I had kangaroo for the first time. I was told it would taste rather like strong game, but mine tasted like bland mutton. At the next-door rowdy table, Betty, an elderly lady, recognized me from a Jewish gathering I had recently attended to give a short talk on Israel. We had no choice but to join their table – Aussies are very sociable. Betty gave me the Jewish grandmother routine and invited me to the *Royal* Geelong Yacht Club where she was a *prominent* member. I should have seen it coming. I was duly introduced to Sandra, a fuzzy-haired harridan pretending to be a bimbo.

When Slavka and I left, she said, 'They gave me such a hard time. They asked what a young girl like me was doing with you when there are so few eligible bachelors in town. Sandra hasn't dated anyone since her divorce.'

'I'm not surprised,' I said a little unkindly.

'Do you know she kept shouting "incest" across the table?'

'Sorry, I didn't notice anything.' (I was too busy thinking of my promotion from permanent blind date to eligible Jewish bachelor.)

'You wouldn't, you're a bloody journalist. Look, Paul, let's not argue, I want you to come to a wog barbie on Sunday.'

'What's a wog barbie?'

'We second-generation Aussies from southern Europe call ourselves "wogs". You know, it takes the sting out of things. Just like blacks call themselves "niggers" in America.'

She offered me her patented provocative smile.

'And don't worry, wog barbies have excellent food, and you're not expected to bring anything. That's taken as an insult.'

The food was indeed excellent. And I was on my best behaviour. I had gained an insight into the mores of the large Croat community from my friendship with Slavka. Except for big events, non-related men were taken to the house only if they were Catholics, single, young and had honest intentions. And divorced men didn't count as single.

Some of Slavka's friends had teased me that I could receive the gift of a 'Croatian necktie' – an adjustment to my throat with a sharp knife – if I mucked around with a Croat girl. Many of the local Croats were nationalists who had lingering affections for the fascist Ustasha of the 1930s and 1940s. The rumours of pictures of Adolf Hitler on some of their walls were unfounded (though there were definitely photos of the local Croat führer, Ante Pavelić). Moreover, many of the current generation of nationalists had sent their sons to fight in the Balkan wars of the 1990s against the old Serb enemy.

Slavka and her cousins regaled me with stories about difficulties with their families who in exile had become even more conservative than in the home country.

Slavka said, 'My mother has been pestering me to marry Teo for years. She says, "He's a good Catholic boy. Why you not marry him?" Finally, I'd had enough. I told my mother that he tried to sleep with me. That stopped her in her tracks. Trouble is, she now cuts his whole family dead, even in church.'

One cousin had to trump her story: 'My mother accused my sister of being on drugs. She told me, "Your sister Elena is doin' bad tinks. She do drugs. I find them in her cupboard … . She take them every day. The drugs say Monday, Tuesday, Wednesday …. What do I do?"'

They could imitate to perfection the heavy accents of their parents. Slavka observed: 'My mother once said, "You can warm food quickly, sweetie. Put it in the microphone oven. I'm going to bed with a terrible migrant."'

I didn't drink much because I was very nervously watching my rear, guarding against protective male Croats and a relative who was reputedly nicknamed Vlad the Impaler.

Slavka was dangerously flirtatious, I thought, especially after she confessed she was really a 'two-pot screamer' – drink went to her head straightaway. She lamented that she could not invite me to stay at her home and cook me a hearty breakfast in the morning. Even mentioning such an invitation was a potentially fatal anti-Catholic and anti-family apostasy. I made a polite but quick getaway.

At 8 o'clock on the next morning, a large unshaven man with a big moustache and a heavy Southern European accent, knocked at my door. I was instantly alert and ready to run. He was carrying a large silver salver.

'What is it?' I asked nervously.

'Dunno. I jus told to bring dis. I am jus taxi-driver.'

'No message?'

'No, but it to do with Croat girl.'

He left me holding the heavy silver platter. I carried it carefully inside and put it on the table. I stood back at a safe-ish distance and stared at it. It looked too small to contain a horse's head. I leaned closer and put my ear to the silver orb. No sound. No ticking. I stood back and waited. Was this from Vlad? If it were, it would not be pleasant.

Curiosity got the better of me. With my head averted, I slowly lifted the lid off.

I burst out laughing. Inside were two boiled eggs, with little covers, plus a small army of toast soldiers.

Later that day, Slavka rang. The present was from her. She had sent the breakfast around in a cab.

After the gift of a meal on wheels, I did see a lot of Slavka. She still had some months to go before her trip to the Balkan war zones. We decided to enjoy it, even though I suffered even more teasing from her friends that I was being lined up for the 'Croat neck-tie'. At least, I assumed it was mere teasing ….

Slavka invited me to the annual media ball in Bendigo; a bunch of hacks from the Criterion were descending on the old town rich in buildings associated with the goldmining era. We all checked in to the Shamrock Hotel, a fine example of nineteenth-century baroque architecture with the peculiar Aussie twist: a wide encircling veranda. Despite the shabby hamburger signs and other detritus of American influence, central Bendigo's main drag – Pall Mall – exhibited a quiet colonial harmony.

I had the flu and Slavka nursed me with decongestant remedies that indirectly caused the disaster. I was sleeping badly because I was so dehydrated. Half-asleep I flushed out a glass with some water and drank tap water and vitamins.

I was woken up by a shriek. 'My lenses – they've gone. I can't see anything.' She was in a state of panic. Either I had drunk them or flushed them away. Not a good way to cement our relationship. Slavka had persuaded me to buy a new suit and now I might have to stump up for new contact lenses as well.

I spent much of the day finding tools to strip down the sink to see if the lenses could be found in the U-bend. They weren't there.

'How can I go to the ball almost blind?' Slavka asked accusingly.

As it happened, I had some lenses with me, which I used for squash. Her myopic left eye matched my right, roughly. I suggested an eyepatch and parrot as a substitute for the other lens, but it was quite clear that Slavka didn't always relish my humour.

Slavka was always very direct. Any altercation might inspire: 'Now don't get blokey on me – your job is to make me happy.'

The formal ball was a misnomer. It was rather informal and little food was provided. For the 300 or so journalists the free bar was more than enough. I enjoyed myself and I think Slavka would have too if she could have seen what she was doing.

And the fall didn't help. The wrongly-prescribed lens and a glass of champagne had caused her some disorientation. As we tried to make a grand entry down a sweeping staircase, she fell the last six or seven steps. I think it was more a case of bruised pride than bruised knees, and the new dress could easily be repaired.

Most of our mutual friends at the ball were journalists who would never allow facts to stand in the way of a fancy story. The glamorous young Croat and the middle-aged arriviste were already something of a minor scandal. Now I had swallowed her lenses deliberately so I could go off and flirt unseen and she had stamped on my glasses in retaliation, and then I had pushed her down the stairs…

The next day Slavka sat in myopic gloom as I drove her back to Geelong. I nursed a hangover and flu. It had not been the most successful weekend, though strangely we were even better friends for it and confirmed that we shared the same sense of humour … mostly.

******

I worked hard as well as exploring émigré Croat culture. My university office was always full of students. Statistically most of the students were female, so proportionately most of my visitors were also female. I made a point of always leaving my door open, not least to protect my sense of propriety. An open-door policy also signalled my professional availability. I liked the students' informality and friendliness, but I didn't want to appear a soft touch. The mature students, a few my own age, met their deadlines. The majority, in their early twenties, came up with every excuse imaginable. I started keeping a record. Within a month the list covered everything except my 'My nanna's been abducted by the IRA'. One student did venture to say that his granny had been shot. It was original and possibly true, so I gave him an extra week. Deadlines are vital in journalism so I eventually put a notice on the door that read: 'Even if your leg is hanging off, unless a doctor's certificate says it is, don't ask for an extension.' So I usually got the certificates, some excellent forgeries included. I didn't often question them; forgery is arguably a stepchild of journalism.

Many students had part-time jobs, some two or three jobs. A large number came just one day a week from Melbourne. Perhaps they took their cue from the absentee lecturers. Even in the final year, students kept up their jobs. I failed to see how part-time students could earn full-time degrees in three years. Either they were very clever or Oz had very slack degree standards.

I was a tough marker, which didn't always make me popular. But most weaker students appreciated the extra time I was prepared to put in to help them. Better students thanked me for keeping them on their toes. I also encouraged the keener ones to do work experience at newspapers and local TV stations, which I (and my colleagues) spent a lot of time organizing. I always emphasized practical talent, not academic theory.

Sometimes I would give them TV exercises. They had to make short news items about events around the campus, real or imagined. One was a light-hearted topic: an alleged monster in the college lake. I asked one of my Metaphysician pals, Kay, to act as an interviewee. She hammed it up beautifully when she claimed that the monster had stolen her Vegemite sandwich. Kay was known for her passionate interest in food.

Damien, another Metaphysician, walked by and commented slyly, 'It must have been one hell of a monster to steal food from you, Kay.'

I enjoyed the camaraderie of our drinking club even though the hacks in the Criterion insisted on calling Deakin people 'anaemics'. My friends were fun and smart, though obviously small-town Geelong could not compare with the metropolitan centres such as Sydney. Except for the Metaphysicians I didn't find much stimulation at Deakin. The university did run a popular belly-dancing club, with the 'irrepressible Betty Castro instructing how to stretch, sway, and shimmy the winter-body blues into oblivion'. The local Geelong theatre was sometimes worth patronizing, although the audiences seemed unable to decide whether they were dressing for a wedding or a picnic. Personally, I would never wear trainers with a suit.

Melbourne, being bigger, had more to offer. The state theatre complex was very impressive and so were many of the events. Alongside the theatre and the Yarra river stood a bunch of plastic cafés trying hard to appear bohemian. Loudspeakers played recorded birdsong and frog croaks for some unfathomable reason.

Melburnians liked to talk arty. Their cultural obsession was part of their search for national identity. Once, it had been easy. First, the adoption of British culture, then a love affair with Americana and now it was 'Australianism'. But what was that? The Anglo-Celtic ties, once loosened, created the mental space for 'multiculturalism' and republicanism. But if Oz became a republic, it would consist of many tribes, each with their own different foreign cultures, often more traditional and fiercely defended than in their former homelands. So what was definable as purely Oz culture?

Aussies claimed that some mysterious core, a secret essence, of Australianism did exist. But people like Clive James, Germaine Greer or Barry Humphries and certainly Les Patterson could not find it at home. They sought it in the UK or US. Intellectuals who left were considered traitors, but if they came back they were failures. If they didn't go at all, they were never any good in the first place. The exception – in those days – was Rupert Murdoch who became an American, but every Australian secretly regarded him as a dinkum Aussie, so therefore he was allowed to buy up nearly all the Australian newspapers and TV stations.

When I occasionally and reluctantly mentioned that I was writing a memoir about Oz, even my friends would attack me for being a 'superficial Pom having another go at us'. But many Aussie intellectuals – those who actually returned from Britain – would often pronounce the UK to be 'totally fucked' after the briefest of visits. It is true that a Brit might need years to understand a foreign culture, even if they sort of speak English. No Aussie writer, however, has ever captured Oz scenery in the way that D.H. Lawrence did in *Kangaroo*, though at least Australian writers had the grace to admit it.

It is natural for Australians to resent being defined as marsupialized Englishmen, but their cultural and intellectual insecurity hid a national paranoia about lack of identity. The historic stain of a convict past (though some Aussies revelled in it) was bound to forge – for some – a national sense of oblivion and a compulsion to mythologize. That was the main point of Hughes's *The Fatal Shore*. All Australians I met wanted to be seen as relaxed and self-assured. It was part of the national myth. They also fancied themselves as very approachable; the affability was often skin deep, though. They did indulge – like the Irish – in frequent wisecracks and that was endearing and even sometimes quotable. But they also fancied themselves as racially enlightened when in fact I found most Australians, despite the veneer of multiculturalism, more racist than whites I encountered in southern Africa. Inside, Australians were often very uptight, both on a personal and intellectual level. Perhaps that explained the Oz passion for perpetually marking themselves (and not just for sporting achievements) and giving themselves glowing reports. In my travels I was always suspicious of people who wanted to mark their own homework.

Part of the problem was the distance from other English-speaking cultures. After 200 years of being tied to the 'West', Oz was trying to re-invent itself by looking towards Asia, not least for sound economic reasons. Yet the Queen is still head of state, not because insufficient Australians had extinguished smouldering Irish resentments, but because they could not agree on a suitable replacement. A distant sovereign is arguably better than a slimy politician turned nearby president.

Writing from the perspective of 2018, when Oz seemed to have bucked the economic travails of the 2007-08 crash, it might seem a little unfair to knock Oz politics. But when I was investigating the country in the early 1990s, the political system seemed dysfunctional. Even one of the founding fathers of the Oz Commonwealth, Alfred Deakin – after whom my university was named – foresaw the problem of a centralized federal government controlling the tax money, while the states had all the expensive obligations of schools, roads and hospitals. Oz seemed both over governed and misgoverned at the same time. On the other hand, I found the verbal knockabouts in the Oz federal parliament refreshingly robust, not cloaked in the hypocritical language of Westminster.

Yet I felt Australians were hypocritical about their relations with the Kooris – they were often patronizing or quietly abusive. In the first article I wrote about Oz, after my initial visit in 1982, I said in my regular column in the South African *Star* newspaper:

In a society obsessed with counting things in extraordinary detail – votes, scores, TV ratings and especially the temperature – Australians are remarkably imprecise about counting their blacks. When Captain Cook's tour first arrived an estimated 300,000 natives thrived in primitive freedom. By 1930, after massacres, alcohol and white civilization, the

> black population was about 63,000. Today the official census guesstimates 160,000, but the number of 'full-blooded' Aborigines is unknown ….
>
> The Australians can become sanctimonious about how others treat blacks while forgetting the sordid treatment of their own blacks. Today many rural Aborigines live in scrubland reserves – saves them worrying about plumbing or mowing the lawn. They're paid so little it saves them worrying about income tax. But white Australians – if they're politicians – have a bad conscience about land rights so they posture periodically on the Commonwealth stage…
>
> Australia is a genuine democracy. Everybody has to vote or get fined. That's the difference [with South Africa].

I was being unfair and deliberately provocative, partly because Australian leaders and observer missions had bashed South Africa, but ten years later I was astounded by Oz racial views. Even at the height of apartheid in South Africa viciously funny jokes could be made about bad white attitudes to blacks. This seemed a no-no in Oz. The one occasion I heard a racist joke in public was in the hit *Wogarama.* The stage show was mainly about new immigrants but the Koori member of the cast made one joke about Koori-white relations. She said, 'I've been up here for a minute and I've not had a drink yet.'

In the ten years since my first visit, the Australian High Court had finally recognized 'native title', Aboriginal land rights that existed before British settlement. But the payment for land rights – not least in rich rural mining areas or central zones in the cities – was likely to prove lengthy and excited much redneck resentment. Racism is rooted in Oz history. In the long frontier wars, about 2,000 to 2,500 whites were killed compared with 20,000 Aborigines. Sometimes they were hunted like animals. Often they fought back hard, but they were always outgunned. In the nineteenth century, Aboriginals were referred to as a 'dark cloud', precisely because of the whites' belief in the inevitable passing of the indigenous peoples. Eventually, the guilty 'whispering in their hearts' forced Australians to review their history: white settlement had been based upon naked theft and oppression. By the 1980s most of the legal restraints were removed: Kooris could drink alcohol and vote; their culture, languages and traditions, however, had all but been destroyed, except in remote areas. Whites chose to commemorate the past world wars by erecting memorials in nearly every small town and village, yet the history of the indigenous people was subjected to selective amnesia.

Nevertheless, Aborigines did have a role to play in the settler mythology. As in the settler myths of southern Africa, the image of a tough capable colonizer developed – the only mention of indigenous peoples was as savage marauders. As the Wild Colonial Boy became Crocodile Dundee, the Aborigines were transformed from pests, like dingoes or kangaroos, to a crucial element of the outdoor, survivalist, mateship bonding that was integral to both urban and rural Oz male psyche. The barbie and tinnie might be the only tangible evidence of outdoor life; that didn't matter. Aussies might decry the lifestyle, land-claims and habits of the Kooris, but some of their customs, especially the 'dreamtime', were revered. The *idea* of Aboriginals was preferable to the reality.

I used to play a game with liberal, concerned whites at dinner parties in South Africa at the height of apartheid. They would bang on and on about the inequities of apartheid. Then I would ask, with faux innocence: 'Have you ever been to the black "location" [nearby areas reserved for blacks]? And what is the surname of your maid?'

The white family members might have lived next door to the black township for all their lives, although they almost certainly had never been inside it, except as policemen or soldiers. And most whites did not know the correct surname of a maid who may have worked for them for many years.

My Australian variant was: 'Can you name any of the 500 Aboriginal tribes? Do you know any Koori words? Do you know what happened to the Koori families who used to live where your house is now?' It would have been too obvious to ask if they had any Koori friends.

Most of the intellectuals at Deakin could stumble out a reply to most of the above. That was to be expected as a Koori institute was next to my office. A red, gold and black Koori flag fluttered on a pole alongside an open air eating area for Kooris; I rarely saw any whites sitting there. I did once for a quick 'smoko' (smoke break), but some of the Kooris started muttering about 'white bastards'. I couldn't be sure whether they were talking about me, probably because I hadn't asked their permission to sit in their reserved area.

I had Kooris to my right and women's studies to my left so you will understand if Deakin provided me with perhaps, initially, a lopsided view of Oz.

Some of the politically correct feminism still got up my nose, despite my apprenticeship in the women's studies group. One ex-Catholic lesbian used to rant about the injury she felt that she could never become Pope. 'I can never forgive the pale patriarchal penis people,' she declared. Another feminist said plainly, 'I never wear knickers … stops me getting them in a twist.' I realized that bras were not PC, but knickers? Oz weather could be very hot at times, I suppose.

Some feminists obviously loathed nearly all men, but even the declared heterosexual feminists appeared ambiguous, at least to this male. They could be very bitchy about each other, out of earshot: 'She would fancy anyone who can keep his dick up long enough … so would I for that matter.'

Some of the feminists' more academic comments about men were more on target, I thought. One complained to me about Oz males' lack of emotionalism, which seemed true. 'It was rooted in defective relationships of men with other men. Sly disloyalty masked by superficial friendliness, homophobic suspicion reinforced by ineffectual fathering.' Quite so.

Many male academics were ultra-nervous about the fatal charge of alleged sexual harassment at work. Even on a date, feminists might discuss the US model where positive verbal assent had to be given to each sexual advance.

'May I undo the top button on your blouse? Please?'

'Yes.'

'Thank you. Now what about that second button? Please.'

Any verbal assent given under the influence of alcohol could be equated with rape.

I was still battling with gender-conscious fanatics, when a 'newsflash' from a women's collective on another Deakin campus reached me:

> Attention has recently been focused on the lack of safety precautions in the car parks. Five male students, two senior lecturers and two members of the Administration have been brutally attacked in the last two weeks and fears are held for the safety of others on the campus.
>
> Men's groups on campus are very concerned. A spokesperson said, 'These crimes reflect the oppressed status of men in society. They are by their very nature political attacks. Men must unite against oppression.'
>
> In one particularly brutal case, a man was savagely attacked and forced to remove his trousers at knife point. A woman faces charges of offensive behaviour and indecent language, offences which carry fines of up to $200. She explained that she had been driven to commit the assault by an uncontrollable passion for his body. She said that at the time of the alleged assault he was wearing nothing but a very tight pair of footy shorts and an Adidas singlet. She stated that he smiled at her and, being dressed so provocatively, she assumed that he was a willing party. 'Why was he walking around the car park anyway?' she asked. 'It was obvious that he was asking for it.'
>
> An Administration spokesperson said today that there was no cause for alarm as long as men take simple precautions: they should never go out without a female escort and they should keep their car doors securely locked…

That was a joke, but I also had to consult a genuine edict called *Non-Sexist Language for the Film, Television, Radio and Video Industries.* It ordered me to never use 'she' when referring to inanimate objects such as countries, ships, cars and aircraft and in particular disaster nouns such as hurricanes, tidal waves and fires. Any gratuitous gender references should be replaced with 'it'. The edict also told me to avoid 'master the art' and instead say 'become skilled'. The manual, I am pleased to say, struggled with traditional titles used in the film industry such as 'Best Boy'.

I was still battling with the accent – I was halfway to wrapping my nose around 'G'day', though not achieving much more because Oz English has little music in it. It is a tuneless monotone, except for the inflection at the end and sometimes at the beginning of each sentence. In the land of the rising interrogative, every statement becomes a question. Perhaps the best way to punctuate Strine is to use the Spanish double question mark: '¿Some people are going where?' It is important for Aussies to deliver these unmusical sounds through an almost closed mouth, with a compulsory slurring of consonants and a drawl or rounding of the vowels. In the towns it must be delivered as rapidly as possible; in the countryside as slowly as possible. Slow or fast, the words should come from the nose when the mouth is shut tight.

The best way to transliterate the accent in received English is to add spread-eagled vowels. For example, 'delightful' becomes 'deloightful' and 'nightmare' can be transcribed as 'noightmare'. Then you have to learn to shorten everything. 'Tickets' become 'tix', 'wetsuits' become 'wetis', 'criminals' become 'crims' and 'tarpaulin' transmutes to 'tarp'. Even the Sally Army is not immune, that becomes 'Salvo'. The first time I heard the word used, I listened for mortar fire but I've had an eccentric past.

When I first arrived, some words caused genuine confusion. People constantly talked about going 'interstate'. To my ears, it sounded as if Aussies had a kamikaze desire to die without a will. Word truncation and slurring troubled me a lot in the first month or so, because I was living in an area which did not allow pubs because a wide swathe of local land had been granted in trust from the Methodist church with the proviso of strict temperance. I would be told in shops that I couldn't find booze. I would thank the shopkeepers and they would say 'No Ice'. Hell, man, no booze and then they rub it in by forbidding ice as well. After a while I realised that 'No ice' was Strine for 'No worries'.

I was told by a visiting British heart specialist that he was surprised to learn that 'aorta' was the most commonly used Strine word.

'How come?' I asked naively.

'Aorta do sumpin' about those bloody flies.'

Wrong – or should I say different – emphasis threw me too. 'Meeemo' for 'memo' and 'larse cheer' for 'last year'. I hope I never catch the strangled 'a' as in 'de-MAND' (rhyming with 'band' not 'darned').

Such Anglo-Welsh pickiness on my part was transcended, however, by the sheer inventiveness and humour of the slang, although some phrases claimed by Strine nationalists are derived from US and British lexicons. Only an Oz politician, however, could have come out with 'The Victorian Country Party is now furiously trying to pick the maggots off its bum'. The classic was the note passed by a colleague to a longwinded parliamentarian: 'Pull out, digger, the dogs are pissing on your swag.'

Barry Humphries and *Private Eye* made famous the dozens of ways of asking for directions to the 'snakes' (rhymes with snake's hiss). Humphries was equally famous for his variations on 'chundering': perhaps 'speaking on the white telephone' was one of his best. Such phrases did not manifest themselves in the august *Melbourne Age* which I read avidly, although also stifling yawns. I did have to ask friends what some editorials meant. 'Rort' was a misdeed; 'shonky' meant dubious, and 'dole bludger' had to be explained (skiver).

'Well, youse should all be cluey now about my deloightful attempts to learn Strine. I may be a flaming galah, but I haven't told any furphies, mate.' That was my first written attempt at Oz English. It was met by the oldest Oz insult: 'May all your chooks turn into emus and kick your dunny door down.' I suppose I deserved that.

I may have knocked Oz dialect sometimes, but I tended to respect the wine. The food and wine in Australia tended to be much better than in Britain, perhaps a poor yardstick then. And there were still the wonderful comments: 'I am so hungry I could chew the bum off a low-flying duck.' The meals in restaurants were usually cheap and the service was good, despite the alleged hostility to tips. It was often very fresh: the burgers would almost start eating the lettuce.

Everyone had opinions on the quality of Oz viticulture. For some reason, I was invited to various formal wine tastings, including a very snobby offshoot of the Geelong Wine Club. The all-male affair of local worthies was luckily experimenting with an American assessment technique. This was an elaborate moving cardboard circle which listed over 100 characteristics. As the custom was to drink rather than spit out the blind samples, the descriptions of the wine started to flow, well, like the wine. We began with chocolate, butterscotch, vanilla ... . Some of the participants seemed articulate and knowledgeable, but some of it may have been waffle. I didn't know as I was out of my league, knowing little about Oz wines. I resorted desperately to imagination: 'This is the kind of powerful red wine I would take to seduce Madonna (the singer was in vogue then).' I seemed to get away with it; maybe they were being polite to such an ignorant parvenu.

Out of frustration and boredom, I started using the bottom of the scale. I slipped into 'diesel', 'kerosene', 'cabbage' and 'skunk'. I kid ye not: they were all on the American list. Perhaps I had opened the floodgates of repressed imagination. Soon the others were using 'rising damp' and 'fresh rabbit's guts'. Above all, I liked 'wet wool' and 'wet dog'. I decided to challenge that last opinion.

'How would you define that?'

'Oh, it's an Americanism for bad.'

Not very convincing, but at this stage everyone was half-cut. I must have been too because I heard myself expounding to these wine wallahs on the alleged virtues of Welsh vineyards, and – to a Scottish immigrant – the refined qualities of Welsh whisky (sic). Thankfully, the cavalry arrived in the form of Slavka to save me from a lynching. She drove me home, by now a gibbering oenophile.

****

Slavka had become a constant companion. She fretted (slightly) that I would fall into bad company when eventually I had to wave her goodbye as she flew off to Croatia. I promised I would come to see her in Zagreb. I also needed to get out of Geelong – I was feeling stir-crazy. I knew how big and how wonderful other parts of the continent could be. Ten years before, I had enjoyed Western Australia and Perth, the most isolated capital in the world. In Adelaide, I had revelled in the colonial architecture and the delights of the vineyards in the Barossa Valley.

First I planned to return to Sydney. I stayed with my journalism colleague from Johannesburg, Josie, who had fixed up my brief liaison with Mary-Ann in my first week at Deakin. She was a good host, although for a hack she made a strange complaint: 'You keep me out late, and make me smoke and drink.' I revisited the most wonderful harbour in the world, and of course the stunning Opera House. I marvelled too at the clean and efficient underground as well as the ferry-boat system. I wasn't really a tourist: I was busy arranging placements for my students as well as lobbying to join the Australian Commonwealth observer mission for the forthcoming election in South Africa.

I did, however, indulge in some rare relaxation, including a trip to Bondi beach. A friend commented on the strapping lifeguards and their skimpy 'budgie smuggler' swimsuits: 'They pull their Speedos up their cracks to keep the left and right sides of their brains separate.'

I thanked Josie for her hospitality in a city I had grown to appreciate. Within a year or so I was back briefly for an interview for a university professorship. Fittingly, in a shortlist of two, I was pipped, fairly, by Sydney's leading feminist. She was the best man for the job, I had to admit.

My next outing from Deakin was to the vast empty Northern Territory. 'Crocodile Dundee put us on the map. Without that film I wouldn't have a job.' That at least was the verdict of Chris, a brawny Aussie game ranger who was leading me on a long bush walk in the Kakadu National Park. Many of Mick Dundee's film antics took place against the backcloth of this splendid location. Kakadu is just one of a number of parks – each the size of some European countries – that thrive in the Northern Territory. The locals call the area the 'Top End'. The Territory then had fewer than 200,000 inhabitants and roughly half lived in the scruffy capital, Darwin.

I had flown in to Darwin, a tough frontier town which was pummelled by the Japanese in the Second World War and then by Cyclone Tracey in 1974.

Despite its prefabricated look, it was a good place to buy Aboriginal art and craft, including bark paintings, carvings and, inevitably, didgeridoos. It also boasted a casino, strangely shaped like a sawn-off pyramid. It was said to be able to withstand winds of 200 km/h; the same speed as they take your money from you inside. I did a few touristy things like taking the 'Tour Tub', an open-air bus that shuttled around the main venues. I liked the names of the places we drove through: Humpty Doo, for example. I smiled at the signs – Hog's Breath pub and the Hard Croc café.

I dallied only briefly in Darwin because I was keen to get into the bush, lush when I visited in January because it was the rainy season which meant fewer package tourists – though it also meant abundant leeches. I wanted peace, quiet and rugged beauty and I got it. The park has rain forests and mangrove swamps, but my days of walking were mainly through pleasant open woodland. Some of the walks took in the fascinating rock paintings, some claimed to be 40,000 years old. The guides were well versed in local Koori culture (although all the rangers were whites). The rock paintings were explained in the context of the legends and customs of what may be the oldest living culture.

I also tried small boat cruises in some of the most important wetlands on the planet. It was a refuge for a galaxy of migratory birds. I admired most the sea eagles, but if you look up too often at them you'll miss the crocs stretched out on the banks. It was invigorating to see the most successful of earth's predators in one glance. Back on land I saw lots of 'frillies' – the pre-historic-looking frill-necked lizards. Fruit bats were everywhere and so were snakes. Nearly every Aussie snake is venomous, I was told. The vast majority cannot bite humans, however. Australia prided itself on the toxicity of its wildlife. Besides the snakes, the country boasted a cast of spiders and jellyfish that could kill you in eight seconds flat – it was always eight, never seven or nine. We were, however, encouraged to sample green ants, which were harmless, but tasteless.

After a few days of listening to Chris expound, interestingly, on bush life, I made the mistake of mentioning, briefly, that I had spent a little time in the African bush. This compounded an earlier error. I was talking to him while he put up a big wooden sign. I had picked up from my nextdoor Koori institute in Deakin some of their irritations about Aussie mistakes transliterating their languages. The whites always got some letter or other wrong, just as the English had done in Welsh place-names. To be correct, for example, 'Kakadu' should have been spelt 'Gagudu'. Chris was putting up more signs changing K to G.

'Being politically correct, are you?' said I cockily.

'Yeah, changing Kunwaddywaddy to Gunwaddywaddy. Do you know what it means?'

Thinking instinctively of the 1970s UK musical group, Showaddywaddy, I replied jokingly, 'It's a rock group.'

Chris missed the tongue in cheek. 'Hell, mate, that's spot on. It means "rock formation".'

Despite my protests, he started treating me like a world authority on ethno-linguistics and native cultures. More seriously, my hint about African bush experience prompted him to invite me to join the other rangers for a drink that night in their separate camp. Incautiously, I accepted.

I was sat down at a table and given a big pot of lager. 'This guy is going to tell us about the African bush,' Chris said with more emphasis than welcome. I didn't guess what was coming.

From behind me, one of the rangers dropped a large Olive Python on my lap. It immediately wrapped itself around my right arm. For some strange reason, I didn't jump up and scream – I find it hard to believe as I write this. Instead, I quickly reasoned that they were unlikely to kill a guest – it would look bad on their young CVs. Secondly, I knew enough to work out that it was a constrictor and therefore – in Africa – probably not venomous. So, in the only brave action in my life, I took a slug of the beer with my right drinking arm, snake and all.

I got a round of applause and the snake was removed. 'Free drinks all night for you, mate. And you gotta stay with us until you leave the area.'

I had to accept even though it was a sparse room, and my kit was in my luxury hunting lodge-type accommodation. Yet again, hoist by my own petard.

At least I had a keen audience for my tales of the African bush and nor was I patronized on the later walks. I had passed some sort of initiation test – probably rarely risked on tourists – probably because I had been such an obnoxious smartarse.

I understood, however, why the rangers played up their Crocodile Dundee image. They were right to act the tough bushman because I spotted a number of tourists doing stupid things like dangling a leg over a boat as live bait for the crocs. Tour operators sometimes dubbed the park 'Kakadon't', but I thought the restrictions sensible, not least to preserve the pristine and exquisite harshness of nature's bounty (especially against mining claims). I could understand why some visitors 'go troppo' and fall in love with the area.

I slumped back to Geelong with a lust to return to the wilds of Africa pounding in my heart. My trips out of Deakin had exacerbated not sated my wanderlust. I moved heaven and earth to get leave to fly to South Africa for the first democratic elections in early 1994. I had been selected as an official Aussie observer, but at the last minute my plan was wrecked: a UN regulation that required the observers to be a citizen of the country they represented. I had instead to go as a hack, and thus I had to run around to get commissions from Oz newspapers and radio stations.

Back to South Africa

It was April 1994 and the immigration official in the Johannesburg international airport hall was a fat, middle-aged Afrikaner. She was grumpy about my papers. Same old South Africa. Although a resident, I had to have a special journalist visa.

'Don't you tell lies about us,' she warned.

Once I explained that I was a returning resident, she spoke to me almost confidentially in Afrikaans. 'We're going to have a civil war here after the elections, you know.'

I drove straight to Melville, my favourite suburb. In a friend's kitchen, I asked why it was stacked with tins of baked beans and dog food.

'Strange mixture.'

'Ja, the dogs are gonna eat and the humans are gonna fart the siege away.'

The old defensiveness of white Johannesburgers. Living in Oz, I had almost forgotten about security. I had stopped locking my car. Now I was told not to stop at traffic lights at night. Car muggings had become endemic.

The international hacks expected the election to be a bloodbath.

I did the round of obligatory dinner parties, not because of my repartee, I suspected, rather for my expertise in getting into Oz. I had missed the lively soirees, full of survival politics. And in Oz you had to wash up yourself.

I had also missed the cynical black humour which infused white banter. 'There's good news and bad news about the new South Africa. The bad news is that the shit is going to hit the fan.'

'And the good news?'

'The fan ain't gonna be working.'

The whites I met were jittery in the immediate pre-election period. Hordes of international hacks streamed into the city expecting a bloodbath. I sensed a real fear in the white northern suburbs huddled around shopping malls shifting ever northwards, away from the now black town centre. The occasional bomb blasts didn't help, although most of the real violence was in Natal province and Joburg's black townships, not the white suburbs. My black friends predicted polling mayhem and extra violence too.

I was much more upbeat. When I had last lived in South Africa, six years before, Nelson Mandela and the African National Congress were absolutely taboo. The secular saint now beamed down at me from nearly every lamp-post. After being unpersons, the names of key black leaders were tossed around by even the most unwashed of whites.

One white business friend confided in me: 'The white man has had an easy ride up to now. They must expect that the black man will have his day too. And the whites are going to pay. They shouldn't be surprised.'

The awful local television service was better. Some of the brain-dead white presenters had been replaced by lively black faces. The end of sanctions had made a difference to the programmes: John Cleese's silly walk was far more entertaining than President P.W. Botha's silly finger-wagging. I watched a communist stalwart like Joe Slovo exchanging friendly televised banter with a white neo-Nazi. This was welcome in the inevitably short interregnum of press freedom between Afrikaner and ANC authoritarianism.

I visited Natal's capital of Pietermaritzburg, and was sitting in the office of the editor of the *Natal Witness* when it was announced, at the last minute, that the mercurial Zulu leader, Gatsha Buthelezi, was going to finally jump on the election train. Otherwise it could have been all-out civil war.

In the Cape Province, while staying on an elegant wine estate, the owner admitted, 'I benefited from apartheid. I felt guilty, but I made money. I'm glad it's all over.'

In nearby Stellenbosch, the Afrikaner Oxbridge where I had once taught, I enjoyed the boozy hospitality of an ex-colonel who knew his way around guns as well as the local hooch, *mampoer*. He was an admirer of General Constand Viljoen who had left the South African army and set up the right-wing Freedom Party. My host explained that the General's intercession had persuaded most white reservists to do their call-ups and police the elections.

'He will save the elections,' the Colonel said.

Church Square in Pretoria, the very heart of Afrikanerdom. The whole apartheid edifice was about to collapse.

That was my view too. Mandela's lavish praise of Viljoen also seemed to confirm this opinion.

Back in Johannesburg, the night before the elections, I visited Sue Ollemans, who owned an art gallery in the Rosebank Mall. She told me merchants were removing valuables from their display windows. Everybody was expecting looting – or 'affirmative shopping' as some cynics called it. Her black partner suggested they should put in the window some Africana, especially fetishes, to deter thieves. Must have been powerful *muti* (medicine/magic) for it worked on a grand scale. I heard of very little looting.

I had the right to vote. So on election day I planned to use it in my former suburb of Melville. The queues were too long, however. Yet the friendly multiracial atmosphere boded well. No voting rolls existed and so some chaos was to be expected. I had to vote on the second day in an area with smaller queues.

The arch maverick, Buthelezi, called the elections he almost derailed, a 'miracle'. Most of the 5,000 foreign hacks were clearly disappointed by Mandela's relatively peaceful triumph and so many trooped off to the genocide in Rwanda. Friends saw me off at the airport and we talked, as ever, of politics. I thought but didn't say that in a few years' time, as in Zimbabwe, local politics for whites would be like talking about the weather: interesting but nothing could be done about it.

The final comment came from a long-term South African colleague: 'South Africa was a first-world dictatorship, now it's a third-world democracy ... for a while.'

****

I got back to Deakin and noticed that, after some weeks away, the local newspapers contained almost exactly the same news as when I had left. Geelong, though, was safe, and friendly. Nearly every white I met in South Africa wanted to know how to get to Oz; conversely I was thinking of leaving the gilded country. Life was too easy there and I had a number of reasons to return to the UK, not least because my mother was dying of cancer, and I was her only child.

Meanwhile, I slipped back into the innocent abroad routine; by now my amiable buffoon turn had become almost a permanent habit rather than an occasional mask. It had been good for defusing angry African troops with shiny new guns, but it tended to backfire in Oz. For example, I was in the local supermarket dithering over different cuts of meat. A well-dressed woman in her fifties was standing next to me. I did my just-off-the-banana-boat routine and she responded with motherly advice. I thanked her for her comments on which cut of meat to buy.

As she walked off, she said, 'Please, if I can help you with anything else, then just ask me.'

If she had been a younger woman, I might have thrown her a more provocative line, but instead I said, 'Sure, you can adopt me.'

She dropped her bag and just stared at me.

'How did you know?' she asked earnestly.

A bit taken aback, I winged it by saying, 'I'm just rather psychic. I can't help myself sometimes.'

'*Really*, how did you know?' she asked again.

I just shrugged my shoulders. She would break first.

'It's amazing. I'm head of the state adoption services ….'

By this time a little crowd had formed and the woman was patently sincere so it was too late to say I had been joking. I didn't want to embarrass her. So I listened to a long charming tale of how she had been adopted herself and then ended up as the director of adoption services in Victoria. Then she invited me to dinner. I managed to avoid a specific date but, as she knew people in Deakin, word of my clairvoyant skills spread rapidly.

I continued to be restless in Deakin, not helped by messages from Slavka about the war in the Balkans. Her comments were affectionately cryptic along the lines of 'Has the tinman found a heart in Oz?' and 'I still want to iron your babies and have your shirts'. The kind messages degenerated into the less than tender 'I hope your dick falls off' after I had told her that I was not living a monastic life.

I never regarded myself as spiritual, but I was dragged into a number of esoteric pursuits. Previously Slavka had insisted on constructing a detailed star chart. Normally I would reply to any request asking about my sign by saying it was merely 'Keep off the grass'. Slavka also explained how to use runes. Then Jo, a witty young woman I'd met in Darwin, came to visit and insisted on our having a joint Tarot reading. The clairvoyant was explicit that Jo would betray me, which she did later. And so I was a little less sceptical about these dark arts. Though I learned in 2013 that eighteenth-century English laws condemning Tarot reading and witchcraft – which could earn a year in jail as well as a spell in the stocks – were still in existence in the Northern Territory (though they were set to be repealed).

My (slightly) expanded openmindedness still didn't explain why a chic Parisienne stopped me in the street in Geelong and asked for directions. I spent just a few minutes showing her the way and mentioned *en passant* that I taught at Deakin. The next day she managed to contact me to say that I was 'a very spiritual person', and would I come to dinner in Melbourne? I went because I had discovered that she was leading figure in Oz reiki and I wanted to find out more about the subject.

I behaved impeccably after her excellent cuisine at her house in St Kilda. She led me to a group of outbuildings containing a study and a bedroom. I said goodnight and went sober to bed. At three in the morning, I was woken by loud banging, then a rush of cold air entered through my open door. A hazy apparition stood next to my bed. It was the shape of a human, a little like a figure materializing when crew members are initially transported in *Star Trek*. I could see a human shape, but not a face. I sat up and stared at it. If a face had been discernible I think I would have addressed the thing. I was not afraid, just mesmerized. After perhaps thirty seconds, the figure dematerialized and a wave of cold air rushed through the door. I went back to sleep.

The next day at breakfast I asked Chantal, my French host, what had happened.

'Ah, you are 'onoured, he doesn't normally appear before strangers.' She explained that her father was so attached to her son who used to sleep in that room that the grandfather would visit even after his death. Mmm. I did ask Chantal's son a few weeks later and he reluctantly confirmed the story, in detail. Ten years later when the son, not the ghost, visited me in England, he told exactly the same story.

So I had seen a phantom in the newish colonies, when I had spent so much time in Ye Olde England and gory battlefields in the third world.

Chantal was very guru-like. She expended much time trying to help me with reiki healing – I was quite ill in my last few months in Oz. And she also did what she called 'distant healing' on my mother, even after I referred to it, mockingly, as 'spiritual Interflora'.

Some of my friends thought I was a spook taking long R and R in Oz. This was a comment by well-known cartoonist Nik Scott, who later married my friend Slavka.

Reiki didn't help me, nor did homeopathy, as recommended by some Deakin believers. I hadn't become a real SNAG – a sensitive new age guy – because of my feminist courses, but I had become more openminded – a little – about some New Age ideas.

On the other hand, perhaps I was going a bit (more) potty. Reporting in war zones may have helped to keep me sane. That was a reason for resigning, as well as telling the university that I had to go home to look after my mother. I recalled the so-called 'Deakin Prime Directive': the less you do, the less you get criticized for. After fifteen busy months in Geelong I had perhaps charmed as many people as I had antagonized. According to the farewell messages, many of the students liked me, but many of the staff – except my drinking companions – did not. Damien said simply: 'Thanks for being a mate.' I believe that was an Oz salute.

Nevertheless, most inmates at Deakin had been very kind and friendly to me in the end. I no longer was tempted to apologize for willingly being a foreigner. Most faults were mine and my permanent state of restlessness. I loved the wide open spaces and concluded that Oz was a great place to raise kids, but I wasn't sure about adults.

Back in the Europe, briefly

I came home to Britain to spend time with my mother before she died of cancer. My dog died shortly after her. I kept myself distracted by teaching journalism at Bournemouth University. I didn't start working in the seaside town, however, until I had kept my promise to Slavka.

In Europe you don't expect to find people foraging for grass to eat. That's what it looked like in Sarajevo, although I was told the locals were hunting for 'wild lettuce'. Passers-by in smart-looking clothes ignored the scavengers. I sat drinking a cappuccino in an open-air café while snipers were blazing away a few hundred yards from the relaxed coffee set. It was September 1994. I needed to remind myself why one of the most cosmopolitan cities in southern Europe was tearing itself apart.

I had flown to Vienna and then travelled by train to Zagreb. It was a very pretty journey, though I feared that my reception might be far from pretty. Slavka met me at the station. She was apparently alone. I checked carefully to see if any of her tough relatives were skulking around, perhaps carrying violin cases. Nope, she was flying solo. She was still sore with me, understandably so. The fact that I had come all this way to keep my promise did help ease the tensions.

Apart from the barely visible presence of tens of thousands of refugees, the Croatian capital appeared untouched by war. The cleaned-up Austro-Hungarian buildings and the green-domed churches were at their best in the late summer sunshine. The good company of a restored friendship added to the almost holiday mood. Slavka had spent most of her twenty-eight years in Australia, but spoke fluent Serbo-Croat. That was going to be a vital skill for what was coming.

As journalists, we both had UN accreditation and could have flown, with our flak-jackets and tin helmets, in a UN plane to Sarajevo … war permitting. Instead, we decided to go overland by bus. Before the war, the trip might have taken six or seven hours.

After twenty-seven hours of roadblocks in a bus crammed with Bosnian peasants, refugees, and food parcels, my holiday mood had dissipated. The shelled ruins of Mostar had depressed me. The sticky heat and pungent body odour were a minor problem compared with my concern at driving at night, without lights, in a large bus along hairpin bends on the tracks of Mount Igman, the only road access to the far outskirts of the Bosnian capital. The Serbs had largely stopped their shelling, but had tightened the siege by blocking all roads to the Bosnian government-held parts of the city.

Six miles short of Sarajevo, the bus was hit by cannon shells from a Serbian anti-aircraft position firing in a suppressed trajectory. The bus was overcrowded with mainly women and children. The first burst went through the windscreen. The bus stopped, a sitting target for the directional tracer bullets which kept up an intermittent fusillade for fifteen minutes in a flow of molten white hyphens against the night sky. In the confined space, the smell of shit, cordite, fear, and sweat was overwhelming. There was little screaming or panic.

I tried to impress upon Slavka, who had her leg jammed under a seat, the need to translate loudly: 'Get the bloody door open.'

I had been prepared enough to sit by the central door, with a quick 'grab bag' containing my basics — passport and bribes.

Eventually the door opened. I pulled Slavka out across the live, prone bodies jamming the aisle. After crawling on all fours through some undergrowth, we hid for a while as the anti-aircraft gun kept pounding away. Then came the crack of small arms and some shouting and what appeared to be torches. It looked as though Serb patrols were moving in for the kill.

I took off my light-coloured shirt; although bare-chested, I certainly didn't feel like Rambo. Bunny-hopping under fire, bizarrely leading Slavka, an old woman, and a young Bosnian female in a game of follow-my-leader, we found an old trench. The granny prayed, the Bosnian girl was in deep shock, and I was trying to remember the Serbo-Croat word for minefield. I told the young woman to take off her white top and dirty her white slacks with mud, because she was sticking out like a beacon.

It took an hour to sneak to the bottom of the mountain into a Muslim area. I traded some whisky for a Bosnian army unit's agreement to allow us to join their forceful attempt to get into the city. That failed, and we were left with the only other route, a tunnel under the main minefield (and air field). Only one Western journalist had managed to get through the tunnel and I was keen to try, even though it was just three feet high and airless.

It took twelve hours to queue and get permission; the locals were not keen on journalists using their precious tunnel. We were all crowded into a small courtyard. In it were some seriously deranged people, many straight out of central casting for Fagin's den in *Oliver Twist*; actually, some looked ready to star in the *Canterbury Tales*. An old crone asked for a sip from my water bottle: she drank some and then ran off with the rest, cackling loudly. Children were trampled and injured, but this went ignored.

A well-dressed woman said to me, 'We are behaving like animals. Look what the war has done to us.'

By this stage the Bosnian girl, Vedrana, was in extreme shock and turning blue. I gave her some chocolate and Slavka and I tried to comfort her. The tunnel would be almost impossible for Vedrana, even if Slavka and I tried to carry her.

It was time to use 'connections', the Bosnian way of doing business. A passing French armoured vehicle refused to take a local, no matter what state she was in, even though I climbed on top of it and implied that President Mitterrand was my close relative. I tried to get them to radio Brigadier Vere Hayes, the British commander in the area. He had been at Sandhurst with me. The French were at their obstinate best, however.

I finally persuaded a chivalrous British warrant officer to break all the rules (and risk his career) by taking the three of us on board his UN vehicle and negotiate the French roadblocks, arguably more touchy than their Serb counterparts.

*****

Slavka and I stayed at the ravaged Holiday Inn and joined the other hacks feeling their way around the pitch-black corridors. There was intermittent cold water and even occasional electricity. Vedrana's father, a local bigwig, insisted that we stay at his house on the snipers' front line. He wanted to thank us for getting his daughter into town. He insisted on giving me long candlelit lectures on the division of the Roman empire into east and west, accompanied by endless maps. We never got beyond twelfth-century Bosnian history. I found his broken German, and the distinctly twentieth-century rattle of constant small-arms fire in the street outside, rather distracting.

Many in the Balkans, especially Bosnia, seemed addicted to cartography. Journalist Ed Vulliamy, in his book *Seasons in Hell*, observed: 'The answer to a question to a Serb about a Serbian artillery attack yesterday will begin in the year 925 and is invariably illustrated with maps.'

Their memories were indeed long, like the Irish. I listened to a variety of Bosnian raves about a Serb crime in the dark medieval past. And I would have to say something along the lines of:

A tram still operating during the siege of Sarajevo.

Writing in the French base in Sarajevo. With so much lead flying around, it was a rare place to write in quiet.

'But that was in the fourteenth century.'

'Yes,' the Muslim soldier would say, 'but I heard about it only last week.'

I needed a bath and a drink. Water was scarce, but the Sarajevo brewery was intact. Vedrana was a Slovenian, her boyfriend, Tomo, a Serb, and their friends Muslims. After the rudeness of our initial welcome, I was treated to the most magnificent hospitality available in the old Muslim quarter of town. Because of the 10 pm curfew, the drinking started very early and very earnestly. I could see why the Balkan tragedy was dubbed the 'slivovitz war'.

Over a few drinks I asked Tomo what would happen if he — a Serb — was caught while fighting for the Sarajevo government.

'They would treat me as a traitor,' he replied. 'I would be tortured and then torn apart.'

Most of our conversations were punctuated by sniper fire, sometimes as close as from 300 yards away. Previous artillery shelling had deliberately targeted the city's famous historic buildings. Every Sarajevan I met wanted to know why the world had betrayed them.

And everyone I had ever encountered in the Balkans accused the other side's leaders of being bedwetting psychopaths. Long ago I had come to the conclusion that Serbs and Croats were right about their politicians. The Muslims, the cement of Bosnia, were caught in the middle, and the shortest-lived state in modern Europe had been almost destroyed. Maybe it was because the Balkan names were too difficult for Western foreign ministries. To adapt P.J. O'Rourke, the unspellables were shooting the unpronounceables and committing unspeakable atrocities. UNPROFOR, the UN Protection Force, 'monitored' some of the wholesale rapes and massacres, but their mandate allowed them precious little room to do anything about them.

'This hell of a crazy war,' said Tomo in broken English. 'I commute front line in a tram. I think I have a nervous fall-down.'

His Muslim friends were even crazier: they wanted to fight their only (unreliable) allies, the Croats, while the Serbs were strangling the city. This was Ruritania with lunacy and guns.

Like Romania, some of the besieged citizens asked me how to get out of their urban Hades, but most were surprisingly resigned to the day-to-day hazards.

'How do you cope with the drama?' I asked one resident.

'Drama gets lost when you live it.'

I talked to the assistant editor of the main newspaper, *Oslobodjenje,* who had somehow kept his paper alive throughout the two years of constant shelling. The children, he told me, had lost an average of over one-and-a-half stones in weight. Aid, a substitute for effective Western intervention, was now being flown regularly into the city. Water supplies and electricity started working a little better. Cynics said food aid just fattened them up to make easier targets for the snipers. It was a tough war for hacks, too. Nearly forty had been killed by the end of 1994.

Almost innocently, I said to Slavka: 'I don't know whether you've noticed, but it's bloody dangerous around here.'

She laughed. Slavka was more concerned with the lack of shower facilities than the presence of gunfire. It was time to leave, however. I had run out of whisky and cigarettes. Avid foreign members of the anti-tobacco lobby became 'Sarajevo smokers' because of the strain, and cigarettes were an almost compulsory icebreaker at roadblocks. It's hard for a man to kill you when you are doing your best to give him a Marlboro. I had eventually salvaged my luggage from the shot-up bus. It contained some food and especially two small bags of coffee, traditional presents to a good host. We gave them to Vedrana's family.

I did not intend to return by bus. Instead, Slavka and I flew out on an RAF Hercules, the UN route dubbed 'Maybe Airlines'. Maybe it flew, maybe it didn't. Forced to wear tin hats and flak-jackets, we had to run to the waiting plane with its engines revving. The plane, however, took us not to Split, where we had intended to go, but to Ancona in Italy. We were in no position to argue with a crew flying mercy missions.

After a pizza and wonderful wine we took a ferry across the Adriatic. The ferry broke down, which inspired an unplanned exploration of Dugi Otok island. It was charming, except that we had run out of Deutschmarks, and our credit cards were not accepted. We had to scrimp like ageing hippies for a few days until the next ferry came.

****

On the mainland, at Zadar, our credit cards were accepted: in a hotel full of refugees. Zadar, once the ancient capital of Dalmatia, boasted a long — and torrid — imperial history dating back to the time when the Romans enforced their strict town-planning rules: a rigid grid of streets around the forum. The city changed hands thirty times between the eighth and sixteenth centuries, and was bombed on seventy-two occasions during the Second World War.

We fled the refugees for the fleshpots of the Croatian capital. I tarried for a week or so in Zagreb, partly because of its architecture and partly because Slavka's fluency in the language helped me get to grips with the Croat mentality. I tried to find out why they were so constantly bloody-minded.

Slavka, herself a Croat, said, 'They will lie to your face, even when *they* know *you* know they are lying. They enjoy being perverse.'

Yet she is the most honest person I know, and a fine journalist.

I decamped to Vienna by train and then flew to London. The most difficult part of my journey back from Sarajevo was yet to come: my luggage was (temporarily) lost by British Airways, and strike-bound British Rail marooned me, at midnight, fifty miles from the stated destination. At least the BR official to whom I complained didn't bother lying to me.

Chapter 4

My Second Antipodean Base

New Zealand

I finished the unhappy nine-month stint at Bournemouth University. The ex-poly smelled like a school – over-disinfected corridors that failed to eradicate the gym sweat and faint aroma of urine mingled with stale food. I was glad to escape to the brisk freshness of Dartmoor where I tried to write in seclusion. Not in the prison, but in the wing of a friend's isolated mansion. Most hacks feel they are not proper writers until they have published at least one novel, even though there's usually no money in it. So soon I had to move to London and to the dark side, to do more lucrative PR work. Luckily, I ended up in a place of light, which is what Shere is supposed to mean in Anglo-Saxon. It was a romantic and historical village in the Surrey Hills, an area of outstanding natural beauty, south of London near Guildford. This was to be the location for a number of my novels. *Anchoress of Shere* became a minor hit in the USA. So far it's gone into twelve editions and languages, though inevitably I fretted whether I was a one-hit wonder. And a one minor-hit wonder to boot. Nevertheless, I decided that Shere was perhaps a place I could settle, find a little peace, and write, because of its lyrical setting. But, like the famous prayer of Saint Augustine, not quite yet … .

I accepted a job to set up a graduate journalism school in Hamilton, New Zealand, at the University of Waikato in the North Island. I had been happy to leave Oz, but, having done my family duty in the UK, I have no precise idea now why I dashed off to the Antipodes once more. Well, I do, but if you don't mind I would rather not share it with you.

It's easy to take cheap shots at New Zealand. Wags used to say they visited once, but it was closed. Or that it was a place for newly weds or nearly deads. I did find the ad-soaked TV unwatchable but, to be fair, the country offers many better things to do. It is an outdoor-pursuit paradise, though I didn't do that much yomping or white-water rafting. Much of New Zealand is an unspoiled arcadia with masses of space – bigger than the UK albeit with a population then of around four million. The sense of unfettered wildness prompted filmmakers to swoop. The terrain can be easily interpreted as Middle Earth and the Jurassic era, but also Sherwood Forest or the ancient Greece of *Hercules and Xena.* Despite feeling cut adrift by the Mother Country when Britain joined the EU, New Zealand produced

Waikato University in Hamilton, NZ – a very friendly place and like a reasonable provincial UK university in the 1950s. People went there to learn.

the world's greatest agricultural success story since 1945. The country also had an excellent public health service and a passable educational system.

That's where I came in: I was to teach undergraduate courses in international relations and the EU while setting up an MA in Journalism at Waikato University in Hamilton. It was the nation's fourth biggest town and about one-and-a-half hours' drive from the main metropole in Auckland. The customs people were friendly and warm at Auckland's international airport, always a good portent. I had been to Hamilton the year before for my interview and had been deliberately introduced to Sally, a petite blonde who was deputy curator of the museum. Perhaps the university thought that I could be added to the archives as an ancient Welsh artefact. So this time, late 1996, I would have a warm welcome for the coming Christmas. Sally had even modified her lovely alpine-style wooden house to add a study for me. The university had also kitted out my office with a phone and computer and even business cards. Waikato University had the ambience of a pleasant provincial rural college in the UK in the 1950s. It was relaxed, efficient and multiracial; about 35 per cent of the students were Maori, for example, as well as hosting a large number of students from Asia.

My friend in Shere, Tim Robinson, had sent me a jokey card saying, 'Enjoy your well-earned retirement in God's Waiting Room'. I was still only in my late 40s and had lots to do. One of them was to write a comprehensive history of war reporting, which was to be my first Kiwi project. Tim had also bought me a new tie, which I wore proudly in the upmarket Hamilton Club. One or two people greeted me extra warmly, but as I didn't wear the tie again until I returned to UK government service I didn't quite realize what I was sporting. The locals, I noticed, had no dress sense – they wore what I reckoned were mostly gardening clothes. To be fair, this was also true of me but not of Sally, who was usually elegantly dressed. She came from wealthy local farming stock, and so I soon learned to appreciate the finer points of animal husbandry. This also applied to many of my colleagues in the university. They had large blocks of land where they raised sheep. I soon gleaned an important fact: one sheep on its own will pine away. You require at least four sheep to make one contented joint sheep brain. I didn't know that before.

I soon slipped into a very comfortable lifestyle. Sally and I were not exactly a high-powered society couple, but we were invited to many events and enjoyed the impressive number of restaurants, pubs and cinemas in Hamilton. The

Sally was a gracious and cultured host to me.

centre's layout was strange; its main street seemed to turn its back on the main river-thoroughfare, unlike in most European cities. Maybe because the nineteenth-century settlers had tried to avoid the pestilential swamps on which the city once stood.

I found New Zealand more expensive than Oz, although being paid twice a month, as in Australia, still gave a false impression of being better off than in Britain. I couldn't understand how the often excellent local wines were so costly, especially compared relatively with their price on the other side of the world in the UK.

The locals were more than friendly, in a more genuine if eccentric way than the Aussies. First I fell in with Kiwi locals at a tennis club a stone's throw from Sally's hilltop home, not that anything was far – the university was a few minutes' drive away. Christine, a florist who said 'Good as Gold' at least ten times an evening (I counted as well as keeping the tennis score) paired me with her flamehaired sister, Carol. The two athletic siblings had obviously played a lot of tennis from an early age. My poor tennis was tolerated at the local club and so was my slightly better squash at the university where I played mainly with émigrés from southern Africa. I ended up as an unofficial counsellor for new refugees from South Africa. The Aussies used to call them 'boat people' – they bought boats as soon as they arrived. Many of the reluctant white refugees from Africa were poor and homesick, however, but they were grateful for the new safe life that NZ offered.

My past peripatetic lifestyle enabled easy access to other ex-pat circles. I fell in with the Israeli community, which was quite distinct from the local Jewish community. One flamboyant former Israeli army officer was always trying to get me to go shooting with bigger and better guns. My favourite Israeli-Kiwi was undoubtedly Gabriel, who looked and acted so much like the comedian Gene Wilder that he would have shot his own foot off given any kind of firearm. He was supposed to teach at the university, but he had ended up running a very successful polling company that proved remarkably accurate, not least for political results. Gabriel's English was vastly superior to my Hebrew, but both languages merged and cascaded over me regardless of my comprehension.

He was a master of malapropisms. Regarding his business plans, Gabriel said, 'I'm not keeping all my marbles in one basket.'

I quipped back, 'You've lost your eggs anyway.' At least Sally smiled.

He would talk about people behaving 'like an elephant in a Chinese store' and refusing to go home 'with my tail behind my knees'. He spoke very fast and would confuse not only phrases but also key words. In particular he had a disturbing habit of mixing up 'foreskin' and 'forehead'.

Gabriel was also very short-tempered. He was prone to fire staff at short notice. Nor did he spare his own family. He banned his teenage son from using his father's computer because he disliked the new shaven hairstyle – 'I am not having an

Auschwitz haircut in this house.' A few seconds later, Gabriel had to recant and offer his son thirty dollars to repair and use the same computer, despite the haircut. Gabriel fell out with nearly everyone, though I relished his irascible genius and inadvertent humour.

Naturally, I also dipped my toe in the political waters. For the white majority – the *Pakehas* – there was little to get upset about. For most indicators and for all races, NZ had the best standards of living in the world. Compared with Aussies, most Kiwis were very laid back, perhaps in the same way that Canadians are regarded as sedated Americans. The country was prosperous and peaceful and no enemy could be sighted for thousands of miles. Yet NZ had one of the highest suicide rates in the advanced world. It also had a problem with disaffected youngsters, especially in the Maori community but also among whites. They were called 'hoons'. Perhaps they were just bored. Except for sport – and it's a big exception – many young people, especially in the more rural areas, probably had little to do, except cause trouble, take drugs and drink.

The Kiwis had forged – early – a remarkable liberal democracy. It gave all women the vote as far back as 1893. Between 2005 and 2006 all the highest offices in the land (head of state – the Queen – governor-general, prime minister, speaker and chief justice) were all occupied simultaneously by women. When I was working there, much of the political debate was about which kind of proportional representation should be adopted.

At Waikato University I did not have to endure endless tirades from feminist harpies, maybe because they had quietly asserted all their rights long before. Perhaps also in a more conservative society women behaved, well, a little more conservatively. I came across few ladies of obviously questionable morals in Hamilton although one was described as possessing 'helium ankles'. I think it meant that she was prone to lifting them up easily and high, but as she was wearing trousers I couldn't decipher whether it was instead a comment on the shape of her ankles. Hamiltonians please e-mail me.

Nor did I feel aggrieved by poor race relations, as in Oz. Many of my students were Maori and they shared some of their issues with me. There were disputes about land, fishing rights and language discrimination, but many of the Maori were as concerned as the most rightwing *Pakeha* about Polynesian and Asian immigration. When I was there in 1996-97 probably the most popular politician was a lawyer, which was strange. Winston Peters was also of part-Maori descent. He was a constant thorn in the side of the ruling National Party which had, for a long time, to tolerate him because of his popular ratings.

Economics also intruded on my pub talk. Despite the apparent prosperity, food banks and soup kitchens began to appear for the first time since the Great Depression. Yet more political heat was generated by the anti-nuke stance of the government, which irked the Americans. But the most important talking point in

NZ was always the state religion – rugby. It was considered a divine right to watch the All Blacks play on free-to-air on TV.

I did occasionally wade into political debate with my colleagues in my department, the politics department, some of whom were considered national experts. More superficial and more fun was my dalliance with the McGillicuddy Serious Party. Although it had national aspirations, it boasted many specific Hamilton connections and origins. A number of my mature students – I use the word loosely – were active members. They tended to wear full tartan and kilts. The party's logo was the head of a medieval court jester, which clearly indicated its status as a joke party, akin to the Monster Raving Loony Part in the UK. The Kiwi equivalent was active from 1984 to 1999 when it was dissolved. The idea was to provide fun and colour so that Kiwis did not take their politics too seriously. Personally, judging by the political apathy on campus and the standards of local debate in the media, I could have argued that the country should have taken its politics more, not less, seriously.

Still, I quite enjoyed the silliness of the McGillicuddy Party. It had grown up in Hamilton in the early 1980s with 'Scottish' traditions and music. (In fact the clan was actually Irish.) Many Kiwis hailed from Scotland and hence the burr in the

The McGillicuddy Highland Army preparing for battle in Hamilton.

South Island and the ubiquitous use of 'wee' throughout the country. Some of the Scottish connections had faded, but enough survived to convince one of the leaders of the McGillicuddy clan, Bonnie Prince Geoffie the Reluctant, to claim sufficient Stuart pretender credentials to offer to replace Queen Elizabeth. The clan's armed wing, the McGillicuddy Highland Army, wanted to settle the matter by trial by combat: winner-takes-all pillow fight with the New Zealand Army. Surprisingly, the NZ Army declined the fight. Nevertheless, the party used pillow fights to select some of their parliamentary candidates. The losers in the fights were nominated. They also staged a large game of musical chairs in public squares to select candidates – as good a mechanism as American primaries, I guess.

Some of their policies were intriguing, not least an economic plan to return to a medieval lifestyle – 'the Great Leap Backwards'. Other policies included the abolition of cars and money. They also wanted to demolish The Beehive (the name for the parliamentary buildings) as well as other ugly modern edifices on the principle of last-up, first-down basis. Curbing unemployment by raising the school-leaving age to 65 was another bright idea. They also suggested that MPs be replaced by harmless jargon-generating machines.

*****

I slipped further into comfortable small-town life. I improved my tennis and the quality of my fillings at the very expensive Kiwi dental specialists. I covered my arse by travelling back to Melbourne to make sure that my time in NZ confirmed my permanent Australian residence. I didn't intend to live in Oz again, but after the massive bureaucratic hassle to apply for permanent residence I didn't want to lose it completely. It was good to see my old mates from Geelong, especially Slavka and Karen. I also made a very quick trip to London for an interview in the Ministry of Defence as a possible get out-of-jail-free card to exit NZ. I then planned to go to the South Island or at least some exotic islands such as French Caledonia but, in the end, I was persuaded to take a trip to Malaysia with Sally and then something more up my street: Vietnam and Cambodia.

Far East
I had already bumbled around parts of what the Brits used to call the 'Far East'. I had 'done' many of the cities on the tourist routes to break my long flights to Australia. Bangkok actually means 'village of the plum wine', but to me it meant traffic and ping-pong balls shot from unusual parts of the female anatomy (in my own defence, I explored most of its temples as well). Hong Kong always disappointed me because it had betrayed its history by not saving enough of its colonial architectural heritage. Singapore was far worse in this regard, although

it was also famously clean, efficient, and far too clinical. You could be fined for dropping chewing gum in a public place, a piece of sensible legislation that should be strictly enforced in London.

Like many journalists of my generation, I felt a trifle guilty about not covering the Vietnam War. It was a supposed rite of passage for all those hacks who could still actually remember the 1960s.That was in the past: Cambodia was not. If I were really looking for something difficult, interviewing Pol Pot was just the ticket.

In Cambodia Sally would be my cultural interpreter; she was an accomplished curator. She was also good looking, intellectually stimulating, and fit, all qualities I lacked. She didn't know that this holiday trip was intended as a recce; if all went well I would return with a cameraman. Like nearly all my female friends, over decades, she could not understand my visceral distaste for holidays, without a purpose or as cover.

The former French colony of Cambodia was totally destabilized by the Vietnam War and the US invasions and aerial bombardment. The country had all but been destroyed when Pol Pot's Khmer Rouge (KR) took over in 1975. Marriage, family, property, post, telephones, and medicine were abolished. Money and cities were also *verboten*. Peasant labour was worshipped, although many of the same peasants were worked to death. Perhaps as many as three million Cambodians were killed in the next few years; things were so bad that even the Vietnamese felt that they had to invade to sort out the mess. Since the Vietnamese were sworn enemies of the USA, Washington and London (and China) backed the resistance movement.

This was an unholy alliance which included the Khmer Rouge and the royalists they had replaced. To confuse matters, the UN stepped in to end the civil war. The 1991 Paris peace accords led to the elections of 1993, supervised by 20,000 international troops, police, and civil servants. Foreign investors began to move in, even though between 50 and 60 per cent of the government budget was funded by international aid. The monarchy of the shifty King Norodom Sihanouk was re-established. By June 1997, when I was there, the shaky two-party ruling coalition in the capital, Phnom Penh, had cost the international community as much as $3 billion. Tourism was beginning to develop. Pol Pot's men were still out there in the jungle, however.

The small airport at the capital was new, but it was seriously inefficient. Twelve officials, all in crisp new uniforms, were suffering from grand delusions of adequacy. Passports were thrown down a chain of these people and not a word was spoken. When we got out, the traffic was there, but it was mainly motorbikes and cycles. This was a welcome relief from the fume-choked arteries of most Asian cities. Traces of the imperial elegance of French architecture still lingered in bruised and battered form. In the hotel

I communicated with an aged receptionist, who spoke poor French. This in itself was a political act; during Pol Pot's rule, anyone who spoke French was considered an intellectual and murdered. Nobody had ever considered me an intellectual so I was treated just fine.

The enclosed city market was full of very cheap goods imported from China, as well as excellent fakes of famous brands. Sally lingered over the enticing array of jewellery. Beggars and war amputees were everywhere, though they were not aggressive. The Foreign Correspondents' Club, overlooking a tributary of the great Mekong river, was replete with swirling tropical fans, framed war photographs, and hackettes and groupies, all straight out of Graham Greene. I got up to speed on political gossip.

The ailing 70-year-old Pol Pot was said to have been taken captive by his own generals and put on trial. Would this lead to an international version? Judgement on Pol Pot would be the final catharsis for the emergence of democracy, although a public trial could have embarrassed many former Khmer Rouge politicians in both Phnom Penh and neighbouring states. The KR had excluded itself from the recent elections and government, but only 2,000 hardcore guerrillas were said to be holding out in their stronghold of northern Siem Reap province, with their HQ at Anlong Veng, about eighty miles from the world-famous temple complex at Angkor Wat. This was good news. I had always wanted to visit the place: I could mix reporting with tourism and keep Sally happy (and safe, I hoped).

So far, over decades, no foreign journalist had managed to interview or photograph the reclusive old monster. Most would-be visitors, whether lost tourists, aspiring hacks, or even former British soldiers working for de-mining charities, had ended up dead. More experienced journalists based in the region said that the whole story of Pol Pot's internal KR trial was a ruse to split the ruling coalition in the capital. Certainly, strains were evident in the coalition, which acted more like two separate one-party states. In early June minor skirmishing had erupted between the bodyguards of First Prime Minister Norodom Ranariddh (the King's son and leader of the royalist party) and Second Prime Minister Hun Sen, head of the former communist party. The two supremos were supposed to rule in tandem, but they hated each other's guts. (It reminded me of the simultaneous alleged partnership between the two chieftains of New Labour in Britain – Tony Blair and Gordon Brown.)

The prospect of Pol Pot being dragged in chains to the capital was an enticing media event, and I did not have a TV cameraman with me. Should I phone London and get one of my old mates over? On the other hand, although the royalists insisted that the mass exterminator would soon be in their hands, there were also reports of his death.

*****

Sally was still eager to see the temples, although I did try to spell out the dangers. We flew into Siem Reap airport in an old prop-driven aircraft. The town had an obviously decayed ambience, but enough of the 1920s French style survived to hold my attention. More importantly, a French expat ran a bar there. It was obvious from the jumpy soldiers and many roadblocks that trouble was brewing; best to see the temples while we could.

Between the ninth and thirteenth centuries a series of Khmer kings ruled from Angkor, using the wealth of the empire and a huge workforce to erect a sequence of massive edifices, many engraved with elaborate reliefs of Hindu gods. The grandest structure was Angkor Wat ('wat' means temple). Until the 1860s the temples were 'lost' to European scholarship. In 1908 French archaeologists started to clear away the jungle vegetation that had swallowed up the wondrous buildings, though the wars which began in the 1970s severely disrupted the restoration. By 1997 just a few French and Japanese experts were prepared to take the risk. Much damage had been done by both KR and Vietnamese troops, as well as robbers and smugglers who easily evaded the slack police presence. Land mines were also in abundance. Few visitors were around, which suited me fine; of my hotel's seventy-six rooms only twelve were occupied.

Angkor Wat.

The three most impressive temples were the Bayon, Ta Prohm, almost taken over by the jungle, and Angkor Wat itself. Angkor Wat, with its towers shooting into the sky and its amazing bas-reliefs, had to be one of the most spectacular monuments ever built. It was erected in the twelfth century by Suryavarman II to honour the god Vishnu. The building was intended as the funeral site for the king. The main temple had three storeys of squares and intricately linked galleries. Rising over 150 feet above the ground stood the central tower, which gave a magnificent sense of unity to the whole structure, especially when viewed across the moat in the late afternoon.

The Bayon site's most notable structure was the almost frightening third level, which had forty-nine towers carved with 172 giant faces. The Bayon also boasted almost a mile of bas-reliefs. The carvings on the outer wall of the first level depicted stirring scenes of life in twelfth-century Cambodia. The seventeenth-century Buddhist temple of Ta Prohm had been left largely as the French explorers discovered it. Elsewhere, international teams had tried to remove the arboreal tentacles, but Ta Prohm had been left to its fate. It was sad, and I am

normally a passionate conservationist, but here I empathized with Nature's triumph over man. It was reassuring, somehow cleansing, compared with the tremendous evils mankind had wrought so recently in Ta Prohm's vicinity.

My guide to the temples was Im Sophal, a gentle man who had worked at the site for nearly twenty years. Many statues, he said, had been despoiled or stolen during that time. After a few days, he started telling me about his past. All his family had been murdered by the KR during the years of the killing fields. Sophal was driven out of his home along with the rest of the inhabitants of Phnom Penh. He managed to bury just two books in his garden before his forced exodus in 1975. Proudly, he showed me the books, both in English – all that remained of his previous life.

I asked him why, if the Cambodians had such a reputation for gentleness, had they indulged in so much manic slaughter, especially of the professional classes.

A Cambodian child wanted to show me his collection.

'Pol Pot was crazy,' he said simply.

Sophal eventually escaped to a refugee camp in Thailand. He explained that he had adopted four orphans who had been living as street kids. Sophal had also taken in an old woman who was sleeping rough in the market.

'She replaced my mother, whom the Khmer Rouge killed.'

I asked him whether he had ever met anybody who had seen Brother Number One, as Pol Pot was called.

'No, he was always very secret,' he said.

Sophal took me to meet some of his new family and their friends. They were all very welcoming, especially after I paid for, and shared, rice wine.

I tried to find out more at the French bar. I mentioned to the French owner that I had found the locals to be extremely friendly; they fitted the old colonial stereotype of docile hospitality.

'Behind the smile,' he warned, 'they can be very dangerous.'

For some reason I thought of Glaswegian soldiers I had worked with.

'They all have guns,' he continued, 'although they won't show you … grenades cost two dollars, a pistol around five to ten dollars, and AKs about fifteen dollars.'

The owner had married a local woman, but was clearly unsettled.

Wasn't he encouraged that Pol Pot was possibly about to face trial?

'Pol Pot makes little difference now. There can be no solution until there is one prime minister, one government, one army. And they need another civil war to sort that out …. My suitcase is packed.'

So was Sally's. She had been holding up well, but was severely spooked by the flying crickets which were attracted to the lights in the bar at night. Children collected them in plastic bottles and later fried them.

Khmer Rouge troops, I was informed, were operating about fifteen miles from the town. But government (royalist) forces made it very difficult for foreigners to go far beyond Siem Reap and the temple complex. Anyway, this was just a recce, I told myself. So I indulged myself in attending a kick-boxing match, where I saw a young lady out-kick, if not out-punch, a male opponent. I thought this would go down a treat with all my feminist friends in Australia.

Sally refused to come to the boxing match, but she was happy to go to the floating villages on the massive Tonlé Sap lake, the largest inland water in the country. Houseboats, joined together way out into the lake, formed small villages. It was handy for fishing, but why live all the time at sea when there was so much land?

One elder told me: 'Our parents and grandparents lived in boats … we knew how to make money here. Not on land.'

They said that the Khmer Rouge let them keep their boats, but no fish could be sold as money was banned.

****

Back in the capital, we visited the Tuol Sleng museum. In 1975 this former high school was turned into the largest detention and torture centre in the country. Only seven survived out of about 12,000 inmates. I was told two of these were sculptors who made busts of Pol Pot, which was strange as he did not formally encourage a leadership cult. The museum housed many pictures of victims, including foreigners – an Australian journalist and an Indian diplomat. In some of the pictures taken of new inmates the victims appeared neutral, even defiant. Others were pictured after months of torture; their faces looked as if they had been robbed of almost all humanity.

There was a sign in the prison which said, in translation, 'Rules for prisoners: they are not to cry out while being tortured.'

Anyway, that's what my guide told me; I wasn't in a position to argue. Khmer is a complex language with the longest alphabet in the world – seventy-two letters, some of them apparently useless.

Military activity had suddenly increased in the capital. In the first week of July, Hun Sen, the ex-communist chief, drove the royalist forces out of Phnom Penh. He accused his co-prime minister of drug running and infiltrating the KR into the city to bolster the royalist components of the army. Royalist troops retreated into the countryside and in some cases lined up with surviving KR troops. The Prince's forces also pulled out of Siem Reap, slowing only to mine the roads, and maybe steal a few more statues, as they went.

While some of Hun Sen's men pillaged the capital, fifty-eight soldiers and civilians were killed in the few days of fighting. Tanks secured key points, while tourists were evacuated by Thai military aircraft from the ransacked international airport. Foreign businessmen quit in droves. Even the Cambodian brewery that made the famous Tiger beer was closed, a major blow to the small foreign media pack.

Despite the apparent dominance of Maoism and Marx, much of Cambodia's politics was personal, not ideological. The King had allied with nearly every internal faction and major foreign power in the region at one time or another. It seemed that the Cambodian hall of mirrors was best viewed by working out who attended what school with whom; naked ambition, however, led lifelong friends to torture ex-schoolmates to death, as the confessions found at the Tuol Sleng prison attested. At other times gross corruption was the key to conflict.

In 1997 the major powers were not likely to take sides in the renewed civil war. Cambodia was no longer a Cold War proxy. The Khmer Rouge government had abolished money, but Cambodia's neighbours were too busy making it. Guerrilla warfare is not good for business. That was the longterm lesson of the Vietnam war, at least for Hanoi. Their former proxy, Hun Sen, consolidated his hold on the capital; his forces perhaps controlled about three-quarters of the state. Pol Pot was off the hook, so long as he could survive his many reported ailments. Above all, Cambodia's 11 million people wanted peace. Hun Sen's strongman rule might do the trick; democracy would have to wait. So long as he brought stability, he was precisely the kind of authoritarian Asian leader with whom the economic tigers could do business. I wasn't about to do any business in Cambodia. And Pol Pot died from malaria. That, at least, was the official line.

Vietnam

Sally and I made it out of the strife-torn Cambodian capital in one of the last tourist planes to leave. We landed in Ho Chi Minh City, formerly Saigon. There was, of course, more traffic than on the rundown roads in Cambodia. I did the war-tourist number, first visiting the presidential palace, the gates of which Vietnamese tanks ploughed through in a final symbol of victory over US imperialism. Then I crawled through some of the infamous Cu Chi tunnels, once a palace of booby traps and an underground village for the revolutionaries. Next came the war crimes' museum, and markets with lots of fake Russian and US militaria. I did concede one thing to the Vietnam movies I had seen: the women were alarmingly beautiful, even though they screeched like ducks on speed.

The North Vietnamese tank which stormed the presidential palace in 1975.

The Mekong Delta was alluring, not least the markets and floating villages. Besides fighting, the Vietnamese are also good at cooking. In Saigon Sally and I ate in some convincing, if costly, restaurants. Later in the evenings I visited some of the former American wartime drinking holes. I recalled a passage from Michael Herr's brilliant book, *Dispatches*. While reporting for *Rolling Stone* and *Esquire*, he managed to catch perfectly the madness of it all. He wrote about officers debating the war in the roof garden of the Rex Hotel:

'This is where they asked you, "Are you a dove or a hawk?" and "Would you rather fight them here or in Pasadena?" *Maybe we could beat them in Pasadena,* I'd think.'

Exploring the Cu Chi tunnels.

I sat in the same roof garden, under cover, listening to the monsoon-type rains. So what was it all for? The Vietnam that I had encountered was very keen on modern capitalism, but was mired in old-style bureaucratic inertia; southern corruption had squeezed out northern puritanism. Still, if anybody could make an economic tiger out of these 72 million people, the USA could. That was the lesson: the almighty dollar would always outdo B-52 bombers.

****

Back in Hamilton, my short Asian trip had not sated my inevitable restlessness. Sally's charm and contacts meant that we were continually invited to events, connected to the museum or to the university. One evening at yet another Scottish event – it was Burns night – I was asked to join in some particularly energetic country dancing. My hostess worked herself into a frenzy like a whirling dervish which I was expected to match. I did. So did the hostess, until she dropped down stone-dead of a heart attack.

The party continued, but at a somewhat less frenzied pace.

Next day I felt obliged to write a special letter of condolence. The deceased's husband was very nice about my frantic dancing. He said that for his very Scottish and homesick wife, who was not in the bloom of youth, it was the perfect way to go – dancing the Highland Fling. I thought that very understanding of my embarrassing part in her demise, though some of my superstitious female friends refrained from ever dancing with me again.

My penchant for singing in public was still encouraged, however. Perhaps friends thought it irksome, but not fatal. The most memorable was a demand to sing nearly the entire Connie Francis songbook in a Japanese restaurant with an ardent Japanese Connie fan. Trying to match her register, it was my turn to sound like a screeching duck.

If my evenings were often bizarre, my post-midnight phone calls were even stranger. I was being extensively vetted for a new MoD post and this involved a charming and patient lady called Mrs Roberts ringing from Bath in UK office hours, in the middle of the night in NZ. As I had lived around the world, often under very strange regimes, the calls were frequent; eventually I ran out of steam with the very nice Mrs Roberts. She finally had tracked my whole life, except for one year. The missing period had been innocently spent teaching at Cardiff University, but I couldn't help myself. It was three in the morning, I'd had a few drinks and I was grumpy at being woken yet again. I told Mrs Roberts, 'Ah, you've finally rumbled me, that missing year I was training with the KGB in Moscow.' The late-night vetting calls suddenly stopped. I thought: if they can't take a joke then I won't take the job.

So I gave up on thoughts of a return to the Ministry and concentrated on learning about sheep. The terrible TV was still obsessed with animal programmes. I watched a repeat of a TV docie on merino wool for the third or fourth time. I was learning something each time, but why was I watching another rerun? Why was I wearing (not indoors) a matching Driza-Bone hat and full-length, waterproof coat designed for horse riding? I imagined perhaps that I looked a bit like the chiselled star of the Oz western, *The Man from Snowy River*, but I think the hat may have actually made me resemble Benny Hill on a bad day. I found myself genuinely excited by tractor racing at country shows and even slightly aroused by advanced farming machinery. I was going native.

Luckily, the MoD phoned and said I should start in October, four months from the call. At the same time I had been informed that the funding for my MA programme had been canned. I was offered either promotion to professor of war studies in another department or all my expenses paid to return home plus a small amount of compensation for the broken contract. The latter suited me just fine. Sally was sad, but she understood that Hamilton could not be my whole life. Gamely she threw a big farewell party for me, and read a kind poem she wrote specially that had a slight sting in the tail as to my next travels: 'Heaven won't have him and hell thinks he'll take over.' I knew that my forthcoming job would involve some travel, probably in danger zones, but I decided I would keep in one place an English base – I might as well call it a 'home'.

I was misty-eyed to say goodbye to Sally; I had not always been as good to her as she had been to me. I would miss the friends I had made. I would not miss Aotearoa, as the Maori called this 'land of the long white cloud'. I felt so cut off from the rest of the world. Yet I could appreciate that Waikato University was well run and people mostly went there to learn. They were unlike some contemporary Western university students, who, to quote novelist and university professor J.M. Coetzee, were 'post-Christian, post-historical, post-literate; they might as well have been hatched from eggs yesterday'. New Zealand was inevitably a little old-fashioned. It was certainly friendly. And it was undoubtedly beautiful. The country was one big picture postcard. There was not a lot for me to write on the back of it.

Chapter 5

Whitehall Warrior

In October 1997 I returned to live in Shere. I had opted for the MoD post partly because I could live and write in the Surrey Hills, while also working as a member of the directing staff at the brand new military staff college in Bracknell. It merged for the first time officers' training from all three services as well as foreign officers. I was reasonably content, living in a favourite place and teaching some of the smartest and keenest students in the world – military officers.

I soon resolved the mystery of the tie that Tim had given me. In the first week in the officers' mess a British brigadier came up and chatted in a more than tribal way. Rightly assuming it was the tie I was wearing, I mumbled something about not being 'in the Cambridge sheep-shaggers' association'. Tim was a Cambridge man and so I made that sort of guess. The brigadier thought I was insane and shuffled off. That night I found out that Tim had given me an old Etonian tie, which I had innocently worn in New Zealand and now at the Joint Services Command and Staff College. I gave Tim his present back straightaway. Tim continued to interrupt my serious work at the Staff College with endless practical jokes, including forging numerous 'lonely hearts' ads, seeking a variety of unsuitable encounters such as six-foot-six female partners in their early 20s with various curious hobbies. And so once more my beauty sleep was interrupted by strange calls, most of which I tried to pass on to Tim, who had the time, money and, above all, height to satisfy the callers' demands.

For three years I taught mainly on a MA course in War Studies, granted by King's College London. I also did a special media ops (media operations) course, both the theory and practice. I used my position to make sure I worked in the field as well. I managed to chopper into the centre of British operations in Bosnia, but more challenging was being in the vanguard of the British Army's move into Kosovo in 1999. It was here that a British general refused a direct order from his US commander to attack a Russian armoured push into the airport at Pristina, the Kosovan capital. The precise words were, 'I am not starting World War Three for you.' Happily, London got Washington to back down, and the offending US general, Wesley Clarke, was shifted sideways. Mike Jackson, the Brit general, was exonerated at the time and by history.

With Major (later Lieutenant Colonel) Robert Partridge in Kosovo, media ops team. He was not the first officer to ask me whether I was dressed for fishing rather than fighting.

I liked Kosovo. I wore standard army camo and was given privileges as an army colonel, including a driver. I adjusted my uniform so much and also wore a fishing jacket to cater for media purposes such as lenses and tape recorders, one proper colonel asked me, not without humour, 'Are you dressed for fishing or fighting?'

My abiding memory of Kosovo was the strange popularity – idol worship is not too strong a term – of the British prime minister, Tony Blair, for pushing the Americans into the humanitarian invasion. It was a strange region, however. The pin-up in next-door Albania was British comedian Norman Wisdom. So perhaps the Blair-worship should be set in context.

Besides bashing around the Balkans, I did a little of what was called 'defence diplomacy', visiting unlikely places in Africa. I was in the MoD, but some of this work was directed by the Foreign Office. I mentioned earlier that I was asked to visit my old warlord friend, Afonso Dhlakama, because he was considered a possible contender as future president of Mozambique. As I write this, Afonso has left his post as opposition leader and returned to the bush, perhaps to resume the civil war. It was almost as nutty as the then UK Labour leader Ed Miliband donning Rambo gear and heading off to rampage in the Cotswolds.

I was also tasked to visit Zambia, to give a lecture at the Zambian army's staff college. I was warned sternly, a number of times, in London and in the Lusaka

High Commission, that I 'should not mention the war': the war next door in Angola, and above all never, ever mention Dr Jonas Savimbi and never, never, never mention that I was acquainted with the bearded warlord. I did what I was told, but twenty years on, I can get some little relief by letting it all out now. And who cares?

I started visiting interesting military and intelligence places in the US, usually on low-level liaison visits, sometimes with US officers at the staff college. I later went on book tours in America. Apart from constant hassles at airport immigration, especially once when I was on a scheduled visit to the CIA HQ, I must register that I had a 100 per cent good experience of the US. The same goes for working with US military personnel around the world.

My quasi-diplomatic if low-level trips came to a temporary halt in Kiev in the Ukraine. For some reason, no doubt related to excessive vodka toasts earlier in the day, I ended up singing, in the correct Norfolk dialect, 'Have you got a light, boy?', the 1960s hit by the briefly acclaimed Singing Postman. My excuse was that it was a requested duet with a member of the Royal Family who was wearing full-dress uniform. It was at a small formal dinner hosted by the British ambassador, who never spoke to me again.

I did three years at Staff College, but was not keen to move to the new Defence Academy near Swindon. I didn't want to leave Shere or move to Swindon (although my colleagues found pleasant rural retreats in the Cotswolds). So I was the only civilian instructor who stayed in the MoD. I suggested a posting to somewhere useful in the field, such as Afghanistan (this was 2000) and requested that I go practically anywhere but defence procurement, because I am severely number blind. Of course I was posted directly to the defence procurement HQ in Abbey Wood, outside Bristol. I was in good company perhaps because the billions wasted there suggested that it was a citadel of dyscalculia.

After four unhappy months, I was posted to Main Building, the Defence HQ in Whitehall. I was reasonably happy there, as I could commute from Shere. My job, which was related to internal communications, meant that I could roam around Whitehall and parliament. I could sit in outer offices of the ministers and listen to senior mandarins display the precise disdain for politicians satirized in *Yes, Minister*. For a defence journalist it was heaven. I was also a relatively junior member of the civil service, so I remained faithful to the code and kept Her Majesty's secrets. Not once did I leak to a fellow hack. I was by and large trusted, even when I went on one or two sensitive trips with ministers, although I doubt whether the mandarins would really trust 'their' ministers with anything really sensitive.

Though I could not write about defence matters, I kept myself active by scribbling my historical fiction, which could not offend the Official Secrets Acts.

To be honest, I hardly came across that many secrets, though there were also titbits which could embarrass politicians. I kept schtum about those too. Sometimes the MoD was a bit sniffy about my old hack connections, and certainly later some hacks thought, incorrectly, that I was a spook. My sometimes wild and eccentric behaviour was considered a kind of double bluff. I was in a kind of limbo, yet it was a fascinating limbo to be in, at the centre of power, not least when the tectonic plates of world politics shifted on 9/11.

I was due to leave the MoD in September 2001 to take up a commercial job as editor of a small group of security magazines, with its offices in Southwark, south London. It was run by a former cavalry officer. I was due to leave Main Building in a few days, then the war on terror was declared by George Bush Junior after al-Qaeda's attack on the Twin Towers. A MoD mandarin rang the ex-army officer to explain that I could not leave the Ministry, because of my alleged expertise on Afghanistan. This showed how desperate they were. My magazine job would have to be held open. That made me feel wanted and no doubt helped my street cred with my new employers. I did stay on to set up some infrastructure to do with the forthcoming attack on Afghanistan. To be discreet, and polite, all I will say is that Whitehall was even more surprised by, and ill-prepared for, 9/ll and its aftermath, than Washington was. I don't think the Brits were aware of the dots, let alone the need to join them up ….

I contributed my widow's mite and then moved to the commercial world where ads were much more important than good copy. My colleagues were all in their late twenties or early thirties and there was some initial concern that my new editorship would mean that an old fart was taking over. They soon changed their minds and wondered whether perhaps I was too juvenile for the job. Fortunately, the man I worked most closely with, Gwyn Winfield, was also a wild Welshman.

I continued to work closely with the MoD, going on what was called 'press facilities', the first to Afghanistan as British troops moved into Kabul in early 2002. If they had to send in bloody press people, then I was at least trusted more than most. I tried not to take advantage of this leverage, but sometimes it was difficult. When I arrived in Kabul some of the senior officers, some former students or colleagues, insisted on accommodating me in the officers' mess and not in the large tents for hacks. I was also given a special pass to use in the HQ, which I suppose definitely compromised my role as a hack. Nonetheless, the foreign correspondents duly elected me, as their elder statesman, to be the spokesperson to air grievances or offer thanks where appropriate. And I made sure I went out on as many foot patrols as possible and did not just sit drinking coffee in the mess. I must admit that I did appreciate having my own relatively comfortable room to sleep in. I'd had a bellyful of communal living and roughing it in combat zones.

Above: With British army on outskirts of Kabul, 2002.

Left: I took this picture while on patrol in Kabul in 2002.

I had vowed I would never return to Afghanistan. I had spent three months around Kabul in 1984, when the West was helping the anti-Russian insurgents, who included Osama bin Laden. I had been unnerved, to put it politely, by being in daily contact with the Russian bombers and Hind helicopters, as well as ground attacks by pro-Russian Afghans. I had been with four experienced ex-soldiers from southern Africa, who no doubt saw me as 'a bit of a granny' (I was then 34). I was technically the leader. That was tough when I was Danny DeVito in charge of a bunch of Rambos. We were making a film on the fifth anniversary of the Russian occupation of 1979. The cameraman kept telling me 'If it was easy, everybody would be doing it' or 'If you can't take a joke you shouldn't be in Afghanistan.' We made the film and everybody survived three fairly deep penetrations of Russian lines, not that proper front lines existed. I lost about three stone in weight, partly through endless marches with large Bergens and amoebic dysentery. It almost finished my war reporting career. Peter Jouvenal, the old Afghan hand and star BBC cameraman, used to say, 'There are two kinds of people – those that visit Afghanistan once and those who come back.' I was definitely in the former camp. I eventually partly recovered from the dysentery, but not my fear of Hind gunship attacks.

Years later I would occasionally lecture about my time in Afghanistan and say it was a 'weightwatchers' paradise'. Inevitably someone would look at my middle-aged gut and shout out, 'It's about time you went back then.'

Author with Coke (centre) with Mujahedin after crossing from Afghanistan into tribal area of Pakistan, 1984.

So I did, but with the British and NATO armies around me. The initial entry into Afghanistan using special forces, local militias and heavy bombers worked well. But right from the start, I was vey sceptical about occupation. From the months I had lived alongside the insurgents in the 1980s I realized that Afghans would resist the Anglo-Americans as heartily as they did the Russians. That disaster lay in the future.

In 1984 I got in and out of Afghanistan by illegally using an ambulance travelling through the deadly tribal areas, and then walking in camel trains or sometimes mounted on horseback. It was hard and dangerous and I was essentially on my own. There would be no casualty evacuation if we hit a landmine. This time, 2002, I rode in armoured vehicles and came home in a giant C-17 aircraft, courtesy of the RAF. This was more comfortable war reporting.

The siege of Jenin in May 2002 was a return to the old style. I ended up in the middle of the besieged West Bank town in the excellent company of Marie Colvin,

I took this pic of Tim Lambon (Channel 4), Marie Colvin (Sunday Times) and Lindsey Hilsum (Channel 4) during the siege of Jenin in 2002. Marie was later killed in Syria.

Lindsey Hilsum and my old wartime buddy Tim Lambon. We were arrested twice by the Israelis for illegally entering Jenin. I suffered the indignity of having to strip to the waist, but I thought it a fair cop as my gut could easily be confused with a hidden suicide vest. I had a soft spot for Marie, which was not entirely reciprocated. I enjoyed this hard graft of front-line reporting a big story with world-class reporters. We also explained that it was not an Israeli massacre, a story which Al-Jazeera supported, an unusual example of the new channel countering Palestinian propaganda.

The old Arab-Israeli story continued to rumble, but the main event was the looming war with Iraq. I interviewed George Galloway, the maverick Labour MP, in his House of Commons office. I always found George entertaining company, despite the fact that he was considered a stooge for Saddam Hussein. I thought he had a point, not least about what sanctions were doing to Iraqi kids. In a throwaway line to George, on the eve of the war against Iraq, I said, 'If you go back to Baghdad, can I come with you?'

He took me at my word and I flew out to Jordan with a few hacks and then went by road to Baghdad. I argued with George for a week that Saddam had some bio or chem weapons – I didn't buy the official Anglo-American propaganda about nuclear weapons ready to strike Cyprus *et al.* I didn't get to meet Saddam, which was the purpose of my trip, but we met a lot of the other main Iraqi players. I said to George that if, after the war, no WMD were found then I would eat my hat.

I had something of an old-fashioned scoop in the lead-up to the war. Rowan Williams had just been appointed the new Archbishop of Canterbury, but was avoiding all interviews until he was formally invested, because of endless media brouhaha about gay priests and female bishops. He also didn't want to comment on the politics of the war. I asked the Archbishop-designate's press secretary whether I could secure an interview to discuss some arcane theological points about just war doctrine. The press secretary, who had been instructed to enforce a three months' moratorium on all interviews, said in an offhand way that Dr Williams was doing

The massive armoured Israeli bulldozers had sliced this lady's house in Jenin in half. She was sitting there with stoic dignity and I asked her politely whether I could record her plight for posterity.

interviews only in his native tongue. The guy hadn't spotted my long-lost Welsh accent. I jumped at the chance and so had to resuscitate my equally long-lost (and piss-poor) Welsh. Dr Williams had to honour the offer and I spent weeks swotting up on obscure Welsh terminology for WMD, deterrence and dual containment etc.

I met the wild-haired Welshman in a Jesuit college, of all places, in Oxford. He took pity on my stumbling Welsh and gave me an immaculate interview on what the war in Iraq would bring, along with warnings about the fate of Christians in Iraq and later in the whole Middle East. Williams was proved correct. I had a powerful, prophetic interview which was syndicated worldwide as well as in the magazine I was editing.

As Britain and America went to war against Saddam, the debt collectors waged a blitzkrieg against the publishing company I worked for. It folded. Gwyn, who was an expert on WMD, was busy doing lots of freelance work in the run-up to war. I was the only civilian included in a small band of retired military officers

I visited Saddam's famous Mother of all Battles Mosque in Baghdad on the eve of the 2003 war. The 'sermon' sounded very fiery so I went in and listened to what was a long homily on the joys of faithful marriage.

who were given detailed private briefings by the MoD. The intelligence briefers believed that the Iraqi army would topple Saddam and hold the country together when the 'Coalition' forces invaded. The Ministry and probably MI6 got it wrong. And it was not just an academic point for me. I was recalled to duty at the start of the war, which suited me fine. I needed a job *and* good access to Iraq.

I went back to my old desk in Whitehall, and soon started flying it in the direction of Basra. I wasn't exactly in the front line, but managed my usual number of idiocies, not least allowing my head-torch battery to run out, and so confuse my toothpaste tube with Preparation H pile-cream (very useful in desert conditions). It tasted awful, and the colonel I was with said, 'Your teeth may not stop itching, but your arse will be gleaming white.' I was off on an early morning patrol with the troops from the Duke of Wellington's Regiment and my episode was the funniest part of the day for my team. I was technically doing media ops and reporting on Iraq for internal communications at home. It was soon obvious that our official political fiction that we weren't going to war, and if we did we would go through Turkey, not via Kuwait, caused all sorts of problems, not least the fact that the Brits lacked lots of basic kit and not just the occasional armoured vest mentioned in the media. We had very little of nearly everything and we deserved the nickname the Yanks gave us – the Borrowers. My Bergen was two-thirds full of chem-bio protection kit. I had been on the pre-deployment training and, like everyone else, believed that Saddam would use some local WMD if we crossed this or that red line en route to Baghdad.

I didn't spend long in the operational area. I was soon back in Whitehall dealing with all sorts of media problems, not least the disastrous occupation. The Brits had the right idea: they wanted to keep the Iraqi army intact. So did the US State Department. But the Pentagon, via the adamantine personality of Donald Rumsfeld, was determined to de-Nazify Iraq as in 1945 Germany, to get rid of the army and the ruling Ba'ath party apparatus. Remove that and you'd create a vacuum for civil war. I could see that plainly. The Pentagon couldn't or wouldn't.

I took this pic while on patrol with the Royal Military Police in Basra, just after the city was 'conquered'. Note the berets, not hard hats. Soon six of the military policemen were killed and then the British army itself was under siege by Shia militiamen.

I had rejoined the Ministry on a temporary basis and, although it was potentially dangerous in Iraq, my new terms did not count towards my tiny existing pension. A bit unfair, but I was keen to get out to the war. Later, the MoD offered to effectively double my salary and return me to full civil service status, pension and all. I said yes, so long as they posted me to be PR officer to Wales, where I had the contacts, and – at a push – the language. It was all agreed and they eventually drew up a new contract, but for a posting in *Edinburgh*. Maybe in Whitehall all the Celtic natives looked the same. More importantly, like many in the MoD, I was disturbed by the Dr David Kelly affair. He was supposed to have tipped off the media about the sexing up of the government's 'dodgy dossiers', part of the pretext for going to war. Very unusually, the Ministry summoned a general meeting of all media-related staff to discuss the general grumbling about Kelly's treatment and alleged suicide.

I had a tangential role in the press handling of his suicide. On my last evening in the Ministry, I spent hours arguing about what I felt was a rather unfair press release about Kelly's service in the MoD. I'd had enough of New Labour's politicization of the intelligence machine and defence media spin. I finished my press assignment and walked out of Whitehall. It was a sunny August evening and I had no job – I felt good.

I was still loyal to the MoD, and did some occasional freelance Whitehall work later, sometimes unpaid. Despite being a crap businessman, I raised some money to resuscitate a few of the magazines which had been lost in the bankrupt company six months previously. Gwyn and I set up a new office in Esher, Surrey, and renamed the magazines. I was also keen to set up a new homeland security magazine, which I called *Resilience*. It wasn't very resilient, however, and lasted just two issues. Another magazine, on chemical, biological and nuclear weapons, was to flourish. Gwyn was keen to sail off on his own, which he did with great success. I had already left to set up a small think tank, the Centre for Foreign Policy Analysis, to deal with conflict resolution. My idea was to apply the media ops principles I had taught and used in government service to the commercial world. I was never much good at moneymaking, but I was good at travelling around war zones and getting in, and usually out of, difficult places.

George Galloway was another man for getting into tight spots. After the Iraq Survey Group reported the total absence of WMD in Iraq, I rang up George to offer him lunch. I had promised to eat my hat if no WMD materialized, so I said, 'Can I have cream or custard to go with my hat?' He had the grace to laugh and say, 'You know, you are the only person who has apologized to my face for being wrong about Saddam's WMD.'

Yes, I had been very wrong about Iraq and started defining myself as 'a recovering interventionist'. British intervention in Afghanistan, Iraq and later Libya were to create disastrously unintended effects. That didn't stop me busybodying in all sorts of bizarre places ….

Chapter 6

Asian Sideshows

The superpowers naturally devoured much of my intellectual attention. As the director of my small think tank, I spent a lot of time in the United States, especially Washington, and was soon frequenting Beijing as a counterbalance. In the Chinese capital, I organized, for example, a conference on Darfur. I had visited the Sudanese region over eight times and had reached the conclusion that the only people who could bash heads together and bring peace to the area were the Chinese.

I have written about my Chinese and US travels elsewhere as well as my clumsy derring-do in major war zones in Afghanistan, Iraq and other hotspots. Here I would like to talk about the perhaps more intriguing sideshows largely unexplored by the media.

The mountain kingdom
It wasn't just ageing hippies from the 1960s who should have felt concerned that the former Shangri-la of Nepal was descending into chaos. The Himalayan state which borders two giant neighbours, India and China, was the sole Hindu monarchy. Yet the monarchy which had ruled for centuries was on its last legs when I started visiting the country in 2005.

It was an intriguing country with eighty ethnic groups and 123 languages. Nepal was the only state without a rectangular flag – rather, it consisted of two triangular banners. It had never been effectively invaded, partly because of British influence. Nepalese Gurkhas had been part of the British army since 1816, and still are today.

For decades, Nepal seemed to have been inoculated from the revolutions that shaped Asia, despite the feudal conditions of its 26 million inhabitants. 'Only 1,000 people matter here,' a member of one of the three dominant families proudly told me. Nepal had appeared immune to the Maoist upheavals in China and the emergence of the world's largest democracy in India. Then Nepal awoke from its long political slumber. In 1991 a semi-democratic system was introduced after popular protest. The major parties in the new parliament were fractious, ineffective and often corrupt, however. Prime ministers went in and out like a cuckoo from a clock. The monarchy was little better – it even made the British royal family look entirely sane.

In 1996 a Maoist rebellion broke out in the countryside; thereafter it claimed perhaps 13,000 lives and displaced more than 100,000 peasants. Yet life in and around the capital, Kathmandu, was largely peaceful; the charming rituals of the distinctive Buddhist and Hindu cultures continued to seduce the tourists, which the disciplined insurgents avoided harming.

The Maoists demanded a republic, but the majority of the traditionalist population, while sometimes attracted by the rebels' egalitarian message, voiced active or passive support for the monarch, whom many regarded as a living incarnation of a Hindu deity. Others in the countryside, however, were coerced by Maoist violence into toeing the communist party line.

In June 2001 King Gyanendra ascended the throne in distinctly inauspicious circumstances. The drink-and-drug-addled Crown Prince Dipendra massacred most of the royal family before killing himself. The new king vowed to end the Maoist rebellion. Gyanendra assumed executive powers in 2002, and then in February 2005 took complete control, though he promised a general election in the future. The ambassadors of Nepal's chief allies, Britain, the US and India, had personally been assured by the king that he would not assume autocratic powers. He did anyway, and the Western allies cut many of their ties. Now all that stood between the King and the Maoist rebels was the 80,000-strong Royal Nepalese Army (RNA).

When I first investigated the war in Nepal, I asked an obvious question, 'Why is the army, which has a similar make-up to the famed Gurkhas in the British

Irwin Armstrong and I made our film on the war in 2005.

and Indian armies, losing the war?' I knew from working with Gurkhas since my days as a Sandhurst instructor that they were the finest warriors. They were also a disciplined ingredient in UN peacekeeping missions around the world.

And the reply from Nepal experts? 'Gurkhas are on the other side too.'

Previously, India, Britain and the US had supplied weapons and training to the RNA which doubled in size and became more professional. The UK Ministry of Defence, for example, assisted in human rights training and monitoring. But weapons supplies and offensive military support from the West and India officially ended in February 2005.

The Maoists stepped up their campaign against an army that had lost its main allies. The rebel force numbered up to 15,000 troops with, perhaps, 50,000 part-time militia. They controlled up to 70 to 80 per cent of the countryside, but could not conquer the area around the capital, which was defended by 40,000 royal troops. The war, in Asia's poorest country, made no economic sense; nor was there much political logic. The seven major political parties continued to squabble amongst themselves, whether in or out of the king's prisons. Even the Chinese Communist party in Beijing was embarrassed by the 'retro' ideology of the Nepali rebels; and the king's solution – divine autocracy – was equally outmoded.

*****

Britain had officially stopped supplies to the Royal Nepalese Army when the king assumed total control. I had a strong sympathy with one of Britain's oldest allies, and I believed, *inter alia*, that a Maoist victory could have denuded an overstretched British army of its excellent Gurkha troops. Moreover, a victory for communists, fifteen years after the collapse of the Berlin Wall, would be a psychological and propaganda blow for Washington, already reeling from setbacks in its war on terror. Bereft of allies, there was a gap in the market, so maybe I could do some good. I went on my first visit to Kathmandu in May 2005, via an ordinary tourist visa. I had, however, spoken to experts on the country and made contact with the Nepalese embassy in London.

As I hadn't had any formal leave or any holiday in about five years, I decided I would try to behave like any normal tourist. I couldn't help making mental notes about the heavy security at the airport. The driving was chaotic, but the ramshackle charm of the city was instantly alluring.

The tourist Himalaya Hotel was relatively empty, though friendly and efficient. I looked at the pool and pleasant garden and promised myself some relaxation. The phone soon started ringing, however, even though I checked in early on a Sunday morning. My groundwork in London had obviously been too thorough. Siddhartha Thapa (Sid to his friends), to whom the London ambassador had introduced me, was all geared up to show me the political entrails of the capital; despite being just 19, he came from one of the elite families. Also, a Dr Manju Mishra rang to ask me to lecture at her journalism college that day; I deferred until the Monday.

As I waited for Sid to pick me up, I marvelled at the colourful saris of the women attending a function at the hotel. The strong colours, of the people and places, were my first and lasting impression. Sid arrived spot on time – what a pleasant change from Africa and the Middle East. I asked him whether the gossip that I had already picked up was true. Yes, he said, his grandfather was likely to become the new prime minister. I asked to meet him. He did even better. I soon spoke to the leaders of *all* the seven main parliamentary parties. Their highly nuanced political disputes reminded me of one of the wars in *Gulliver's Travels*, fought over which end of a boiled egg should be opened. The debate then current was how to go back to the political dispensation before the king took over in February 2005. The politicians all spoke good or even excellent English; some had been educated in the US and Oxbridge.

Sid also took me to meet his mother, Sangeeta, who looked about 28, and was elegantly beautiful. My mind turned to the famous Frank Capra film, *Lost Horizon*, starring Ronald Colman, about a Himalayan valley where the population ages very slowly. I soon discovered that Sangeeta had almost a Princess Diana status in Nepal. She ran an art gallery, but was a patron of all the arts. Sangeeta became my gracious host and guide, and we discussed in particular her views on reincarnation. Sid, with his younger friends, continued my cultural education in debates about arranged marriages, love, and cross-caste relationships.

To reinforce my education, Sid took me on a brief temple tour. Kathmandu was an anthropologist's and architectural historian's dream, with shrines on nearly every corner. He wanted to show me the Kathmandu valley from a good vantage point: Swayambhunath, one of the world's most glorious Buddhist Chaityas. This stupa is said to be 2,000 years old. Teeming with monkeys, painted on the four sides of the spire's base were the all-seeing eyes of the Lord Buddha. I made some quick notes, as I intended this trip to be a recce for the film I planned to make later with Irwin Armstrong, my ever-patient cameraman-colleague. A little tourism would be an inevitable part of that later expedition, or so I told myself to excuse my eighteen-hour working days.

*****

I gave my lecture the next day at the so-called college of journalism. It meant well, as did its director, Dr Mishra. Over seventy students crowded into a small room and seemed so pleased to hear anybody from Europe that they laughed at all my jokes. They must have been desperate for entertainment. I asked if they had freedom of speech.

The student leader replied, 'Only in this room.'

I was then dragged on to the local celebrity circuit. I did an interview for Nepal TV, and a glossy magazine. The British embassy requested I give a lecture for ex-pats, which went down very well, I was told. Nobody commented on the intellectual content – the title of my talk was 'The War on Terror: The Blackadder Approach' – but numerous drunks suggested I should do regular stand-up comedy. Everyone was well-oiled because of the late start. And the Ambassador introduced me as a Del Shannon fan, and sang a few bars of *Runaway*, in which I joined in. That set the tone for the evening. The Ambassador also challenged me to a one-hit-wonder singing competition in the bar afterwards. I liked him a lot, and he was most helpful when we had a serious lunch later.

*****

As ever, my main interests were security and so I sought access to the military. The British military attaché, whom I also liked but who seemed wary of me, arranged for me to visit the main Gurkha recruitment centre. I was escorted around by a female Gurkha, which was new to me. She had the long and famous *kukri* on her back belt.

'How do you sit down?' I asked, perhaps too obviously.

'With some difficulty, sir.'

I was more interested in the Nepalese army. A meeting with the senior generals was arranged. Clearly there had been a misunderstanding. I thought they were going to brief me, but I had to give an impromptu talk on the security situation in various countries where the RNA served in peacekeeping roles.

I asked, 'Why send crack troops to monitor elections in places such as Sudan when you say you don't have enough troops to monitor elections here in Nepal?'

I was met with evasion, but I knew the answer: the military experience and above all bigger salaries and perks were strong inducements to wear blue helmets.

The generals were fiercely loyal to the King. Yet even the devout monarchist, Lieutenant General Rukmangat Katwal, the chief of the general staff, admitted to me that 'there can be no military solution … we can only hold the ring for an election … and follow the constitution.'

I asked the generals whether I could return to film the war. The BBC had tried it a few years before, but had little success in gaining real access. I had to do better. As down payment I was asked to visit the RNA staff college to give a formal lecture on the war on the terror. I even got a fancy embossed mug for my troubles.

*****

Sid took me around the famous Durbar square. The old royal palace (Hanuman Dhoka) takes up more space than all the other famous monuments. Dating from the sixteenth century, the royal family last inhabited this palace in 1886. Small intriguing parts were open to the public. Kumari Chowk, the home of the 'living goddess', overlooked the square from the south. The temples were not mere museums: this gilded cage of the goddess was an active contemporary example of the fusion of Buddhist, Hindu and indigenous religions. A prepubescent girl had to be chosen from the Buddhist Shakya clan, in a similar way to the Tibetan Buddhist method of divining reincarnated lamas. She was worshipped as the living incarnation of Durga, the demon-slaying Hindu goddess. Apart from religious ceremonies, in which her feet must never touch the ground, she lived a cloistered life until she menstruated, or bled heavily from other causes, thereupon she retired with a small pension, and had to live life as an ordinary mortal. Apparently, these goddesses had trouble finding husbands, not because of any illusions of grandeur, but because their husbands were reputed to die young.

I soaked up Sid's extensive local knowledge, but was unnerved by his driving. The Nepalese seemed such gentle and polite people yet they became reincarnated demons behind a driving wheel. Cows, sacred animals, roamed all over the place. Hitting and killing one brought an automatic one-year jail sentence. Car horns created a constant raucous cacophony in the polluted city atmosphere. I asked Sid, if he were forced to choose, whether he would give up his car horn or his mobile.

'Definitely my mobile would go first,' he said laughing.

*****

Nepal was full of architectural splendours: the pagoda in the main square of Baktapur, a medieval city. Luckily we filmed before the later (2015) earthquake did so much damage to Nepal's heritage.

I'd done the diplomatic and cultural rounds and scoured the bookshops and tourist markets. One thing was missing: I wanted to fix up a later film interview with the reclusive monarch. That would be a tough call. I went to see the man who could fix it, the 80-year-old Dr Giri, who ran the King's Council. He was not too optimistic about the revival of democracy. 'Even Jesus Christ couldn't resurrect this dead parliament.' I thought the reference unusual in a Hindu/Buddhist country. Later I discovered that he was one of a handful of Jehovah's Witnesses in the country. It was a pity I didn't know at the time, as my detailed knowledge and personal experience of that religion might have secured a better regal result. I failed to secure an audience with the King.

In less than a week I had prepared the groundwork for the film. I had not been much in the countryside, and since I was courting the royal army did not talk to the Maoists. The flight back was one of the worst I had endured. Cattle class was full of Nepalese labourers working in Doha. Next to me sat a young man with St Vitus's dance and the eating habits of crazed monkey. I couldn't get an upgrade in Doha without paying thousands of dollars, and so got stuck this time with a well-mannered evangelical who insisted on reading scripture to me, nearly all the way to London. Whether it was a bus, boat or plane, the nutter would always sit next to me. Perhaps other passengers thought that of me.

After my first visit, I concluded that Nepal was an intensely beautiful country with an intrinsically peaceful culture. The passive allure of Karma (and dope) attracted hippies, as well as the Beatles' guru, Maharishi Mahesh Yogi, to save the world through transcendental meditation. The Yogi failed, but well-meaning intervention by foreign powers could work. And Nepal had many friends, and not just those who aspired to climb Everest.

Seeing the war

I returned, with Irwin on camera, in November 2005. This time we would have a tight timetable, according to the itinerary organized by the Royal Nepalese Army. At the airport we were met by a charming colonel, Surya Khanal, who smoothed our entry and took us to the more upmarket Yak and Yeti hotel. Sangeeta hosted us for dinner on our first night at the exquisite Dwarika's Hotel. Many of the dinner guests stood up as we came in, in deference to the ever-modest and ever-elegant Sangeeta. I was none too deferential as I drank far too much of the ever-excellent Everest beer.

I was groggy as I started the next day's series of military briefings. I perked up in the psy-ops session, which was impressive and sometimes amusing. I could not afford any levity, however, with the Chief of the General Staff, Lieutenant General

A Nepalese soldier on roadblock duty near the capital.

Rukmangat Katwal. I took a few hours to persuade him to give his first-ever TV interview to a foreign journalist. After the formal session, the general was prepared to give us an off-the-record briefing. Sam Dealey, my friend from Washington, had joined us.

Marcia Chadwick, the down-to-earth, Bolton-born PA to the British Ambassador, had done much to finesse arrangements, not least with the prickly Americans, on my first trip. She now fixed our TV interview with a somewhat reticent Brit Ambassador: no singing, all cautious realpolitik this time, and even that was off-camera. Surprisingly, the French Ambassador was prepared to talk to our camera.

Sam, my American companion, went down with a bug and so missed a diplomatic dinner in the Yak and Yeti, to which Luna, the pert young marketing director of the hotel, invited us. (Beautiful and pushy, she later invited herself to stay with me in England, for some weeks more than was polite.)

*****

Our trip to the war zone was due to start at 6.30 am next day. Sam still had a raging temperature, which did not help the rather heated debate about how we were going to all fit into a brand-new, though small, French chopper. They didn't have time to make more room by stripping out the under-seat armour that morning (though why they didn't do it beforehand was unanswered). The army wanted one of us to drop out. Sam had come all the way from Washington, Irwin had to shoot the film so I was the most expendable, but Irwin knew that I could be useful in our two-man team. I appealed to our escorting colonel to pull rank at HQ. Eventually the pilot was ordered to stand down – the second pilot, that is. Flying in the difficult thermals and mists of the Himalayas, as well as possible rebel groundfire, it was standard, and sensible, operational procedure to deploy two pilots. We signed numerous documents exonerating the military from any responsibility for anything that might possibly happen to us. Fair enough.

Enjoying splendid vistas of the cloud- and-snow-tipped Himalayas, we flew south-west to an RNA base at Kasara. It was very British army in style, but of the 1960s. An obviously bored and geeky base commander spent more than an hour briefing us with PowerPoint. The commander had used every extra colour and moving part in the menu, fashioning his presentation into an art form: pretty, but didn't say much. Sam was obviously bored, so was I. And I had spent three years being PowerPointed to death daily at the Joint Staff College in England. Sam, explaining he was ill, jumped back into the chopper returning to Kathmandu. The escort colonel, Surya, who had spent months preparing our media facility, was very upset, but was too well-mannered to show it. He did question implicitly my leadership skills. I explained that journalists do not operate in a command hierarchy. That was the umpteenth time I had been compelled to explain that to the military all over the world.

Sam had missed out on a wonderful photo opportunity. Kasara was bang smack in the Chitwan National Park, abutting the Indian border. Over 500 Asian one-horned rhinos and a hundred Royal Bengal tigers were said to live in the dense forests of the park. We soon joined an army elephant patrol, a first in my war-reporting experience. Three elephants, each with a mahout, plus two to three soldiers, glided into the long grass. Sitting targets, true, but silent, and the elephant smell overcame that of the humans so all the other game in the park ignored the patrol. It was a useful means of surprising insurgents. With the help of a mounting tower, Irwin climbed on one of the elephants and obviously enjoyed the unusual vantage point for his camera.

Patrolling on elephants – a unique military experience for me.

Afterwards we patrolled in jeeps and on foot in nearby villages. I witnessed charming, almost medieval, scenes, of little thatched huts, bullocks drawing ploughs and villagers threshing corn by hand. It was like revisiting the Hobbit shires in the *Lord of the Rings*; though Tolkien did not include a bus that had recently hit a land mine planted by the Maoists. We talked to nearby villagers, including those who had survived the blast, and asked them about their response to the incident. The close presence of the patrol and my army interpreter did not encourage independent replies.

Irwin and I tarried too long in this Q and A, and we had lost the light. It was moonlight when the Land Rover forded the wide Rapti river. It looked impossible to cross, but we had managed it earlier, albeit in daylight. At night, however, one of the rear wheels smashed into a large submerged rock, and the vehicle had to stop on a small mid-river pebble island, in order to change the wheel. I took the opportunity to walk away to some reeds to relieve myself.

I spotted a sudden commotion to my right. I thought it was a very large bullock coming towards me, though its speed surprised me. I had never seen a bullock move that fast. I looked and looked again and realized it was a rhino charging straight at me.

From my African days I knew that rhinos have poor eyesight, but so do I. They have, however, a keen sense of smell, and will charge anything that they perceive as a threat. I remembered (later) that if a rhino is about to charge it will lower its head and take a step back. If it did that the best way to survive, if you couldn't instantly climb a dirty great big tree, was to zig-zag and throw off a piece of clothing, hoping the animal would stop to smell it. I am afraid that my instant reaction to this rhino, already in a headlong charge, was to run directly for the armoured Land Rover, knocking aside two armed soldiers who were also trying to get in, though slightly more slowly than me. Some of the other nearby soldiers distracted the rhino which charged past us.

Later that night at the charming Tiger Tops lodge, I endured much teasing about my moonlit member sexually arousing a female rhino. Much more likely, she was defending her calf, hidden in the reeds. We had seen rhinos early in the day and had been told about a rogue who had a habit of charging at, and severely damaging, vehicles. I will stick, however, to my protective rhino theory, as next day, from the safety of a mount on an elephant, I saw perhaps the same rhino with her calf alongside her.

I was out in the early morning mists on a dawn elephant ride. Even deer, normally skittish, seemed unable to pick up our human scent as the elephants strolled past, with a strange lolloping gait; it was more like riding a camel than a horse. I had no illusions about their ability to move much faster. In northern Botswana, I had been

filming mock elephant charges and noisy flapping of the ears and much bellowing. I had previously insisted that we had an open jeep, with the engine running, right behind us, as we were filming. It was my job to decide when a mock charge became real. Heaven knows where our expert guide was. It was a decision way above my pay grade, as they say in the MoD. I called it right, more by luck than judgement: we threw ourselves into the back of the jeep and accelerated off at full speed, and even then that big bull elephant almost caught us.

*****

Filming from an elephant's rear tested some of Irwin's video skills.

We now made a series of visits to far-flung RNA bases. The most interesting was Khara, a eyrie high up in the mountains to the north. We choppered in because the roads were far too dangerous. On 7 April 2005 thousands of Maoist insurgents vowed to take the symbolic base at all costs. It was the rough equivalent of the Khe Sanh siege in the Vietnam war, though shorter and with far smaller casualties. Just over 150 defenders killed 300 guerrillas in the close-quarter eighteen-hour battle. The base commander, a major who had trained at Sandhurst, clearly was a born leader, and an inspired engineer. He had constructed one of the most intricate defensive fortifications I had ever seen for such a small rocky outcrop.

We toured other front-line bases and went on occasional foot patrols. Afterwards we were treated to the usual propaganda tour of captured weapons. I was supposed to be impressed, that was the purpose of the facility. For a developing country, Nepal's army looked professional enough. The police were not. The problem the army faced was its poor record of human rights. I was no tree-hugging, sandal-wearing liberal: in war lots of people get killed. For moral and practical reasons, however, prisoners and innocent bystanders should be considered even in the most savage firefight.

I persuaded the army to let me visit a rehabilitation camp for former Maoist prisoners of war. (They had refused me access to the jails and camps where recent Maoist captures were held.) The inmates spoke of boredom, but not of ill-treatment. And I managed to get a few interviews out of earshot of the military minders. It didn't seem like a Potemkin village. The Brits had briefed me on human rights abuses, and the British Army had spent a lot of time helping to train apparently enlightened middle-ranking officers to incorporate human rights issues in the training of the rank and file.

I had asked Sam not to chase up Maoist contacts, because we were on an RNA facility. In our absence he had done what a good journalist should. He had made some Maoist contacts in the capital, and we went to interview them. Some made serious accusations about the army and the police, and we filmed one of the victims of maltreatment.

*****

Irwin needed some 'colour' for the film, and Sam wanted to take stills of the cultural sites. We explored the *ghats* of the Bagmati river. Elaborate temples and statues were jumbled along the stonepaved embankments. Irwin shot a funeral pyre and then the dumping of the ashes into the river. I noticed that

We were choppered into a high-altitude eyrie.

an office had been set up to collect corneas before immolation. We filmed and shopped again while riding the rickshaws around the magnificent Durbar Square.

East of the capital, we travelled to Bhaktapur, a well-preserved jewel of a medieval city. Founded in the ninth century, it ruled the valley until 1482. Tourists had to pay a smallish entrance fee in dollars. It helped to reduce perhaps the volume of less dedicated temple fans. Presumably the money fuelled the rampant corruption in the country, but some must have been put to good use. Restoration work was evident everywhere, and not just from German government generosity.

Bhaktapur's Durbar square was not as grand as its namesake in the capital nor entirely genuine. It was spruced up for Bernardo Bertolucci's 1993 film, *Little Buddha.* Most of the buildings and narrow alleyways were the real thing, especially Taumadhi Tol. There we sat on the balcony of a restaurant and filmed the wonderful old buildings. Most graceful was the five-tiered Nyatapola pagoda, Nepal's tallest. Nearby was Dattatraya Square, the place to explore ornate woodwork, once a much more common craft in the country. In the Dwarika's Hotel in Kathmandu part of its grandeur comprised the various carved doors and windows saved and restored from demolished homes throughout Nepal.

*****

Sangeeta Thapa was a most gracious host. To her right was the American member of our team, Sam Dealey. The author to her left.

Sangeeta once more was the generous host and organized an elegant farewell dinner party at her home. There I met a very sophisticated Indian businesswoman who ran the upmarket Hyatt Regency Hotel in Kathmandu. She invited me to coffee the next day. On arrival, I noticed an expansively long red carpet, with schoolchildren waving little flags. I thought for a moment that this was a rather over-elaborate welcome for a coffee appointment. Before I started to wave back at the kids, I stopped and turned around at the head of the red carpet and realized that the infamous Reverend Sun Myung Moon was my Tail-end Charlie. If ever there was a bad moon rising, it was him. The head of the Unification Church was also the publisher of the right-wing *Washington Times*, for which I occasionally wrote, so I shouldn't call him a nutter. But I will.

Colonel Surya was late picking us up that afternoon, and the traffic was clogging the road to the airport. The colonel delegated a tough-looking regimental sergeant major to escort us quickly through customs. Even with the RSM's help, it was a nightmare and we were also hit for a few hundred dollars excess baggage on our film kit. Nobody was likely to demand a security inspection of our film, however.

Irwin had used a new high-definition Sony camera; the quality of our film was tip-top. We had not been actually attacked so we didn't have bang-bang, but the elephant sequences and the wonderful aerial shots, as well as unique access to foot patrols and bus searches and the like, had produced almost unrivalled footage on the army. What we didn't have was anything on the Maoists. We did not pretend we were shooting both sides; it was just an investigation into the RNA. Moreover, the sexy shots of female Maoists waving their AKs had been done a number of times. In short, visually, it was the best film Irwin and I had made, but we couldn't sell it. The only time I had failed to broadcast a film. The RNA was not on the side of the politically correct angels as far as my usual film contacts were concerned. Being an 'Indie', an independent freelance producer in war zones, was a dying profession in all senses of the word. I thought seriously about giving up.

*****

The king, however, was soon forced to give up. In late November 2005 the seven constitutional parties did a deal with the Maoists. The rebels said they would accept a democratic route and they also cosied up to India, which had a Maoist rebellion of its own – in thirteen of its states. The seven-party alliance demanded elections for an assembly to change the constitution, and to end or alter the monarchy's role. The palace refused. The parties started mobilizing street protests, most dramatically in the capital; the tumult grew in size and anger, as Maoists, many from the countryside, infiltrated the disorder. The Nepali *intifada* took on a life of its own as a worried Indian government said that Nepal was 'spinning out of control'. The role of the army was central. A coup was always unlikely, but some of the middle-ranking officers, reluctant to fire on their own people, increasingly sided with pro-democratic forces. Diplomats feared a replay of Saigon in 1975 or the fall of the Shah in Iran: King Gyanendra might have had to be spirited away in an American helicopter from his palace if anarchy totally enveloped Kathmandu.

With Indian, US and British help, and later UN involvement, the parliamentary parties and the Maoists signed a peace accord in November 2006 to end the ten-year civil war. The army was officially confined to barracks and the Maoist fighters were supposed to be corralled in cantonments, not unlike the assembly points in 1979-80 in Rhodesia. Elections were finally held in April 2008 and the Maoists unexpectedly emerged as the largest single party, although without an overall majority. The monarchy was abolished a month later. A Maoist-dominated government took office in August 2008. But the army, although demoralized by the effective communist victory, still was a powerful force, privately encouraged by the Indians who did not want an unbridled communist government in Kathmandu. In May 2009 the once secretive and mysterious Maoist leader, Prachanda, resigned, over his inability to sack the army chief. Yes, my old friend Katwal was still there, and refusing to integrate what he called 'indoctrinated' guerrillas into his professional force. Still, the 19,000 frustrated Maoists languishing in their camps did need jobs, in civvie street, if not the army.

Poverty and unemployment were still endemic, but the war was over, probably never to return. A perhaps more stable political system would allow the restocking of the game reserves, better restoration of the many historical buildings, more (upmarket) tourists and more jobs. The kingdom in the sky had been brought down to earth: the monarch had been sacked, though Nepal now had at least a chance to rebuild (especially after the major earthquake of April 2015).

In Britain, the fate of the Gurkhas who fought in the British army and wanted to settle in the UK was widely publicized by the actress Joanna Lumley. Ms Lumley outfoxed and outcharmed a number of British ministers and politicians, but she has not personally addressed the social issues of a large influx of poor Nepalese families into one small area of England, namely Aldershot. The fate of the Gurkhas is one of the final fiscal legacies for the post-imperial return of the legions.

****

Trouble in Paradise: The Maldives

The Maldives could be the first liberal democracy in the Islamic world: such was the claim of reformists in the chain of over 1,200 islands in the Indian Ocean. When I first visited, with Irwin, in November 2006, pro-democracy groups demonstrated to create the conditions for an 'orange revolution'. Prompt police action preserved the dictatorship, however. The peaceful demonstrations were declared illegal.

About 200 islands were inhabited, a paradise for the hundreds of thousands of upmarket tourists who visited every year, many for honeymoons. They went to the beautiful archipelago to explore the seas and each other, not the country's social conditions. Underneath the holiday-brochure image, trouble was brewing in this Sunni Muslim state. The islands converted to Islam in 1153. But, unusually for a 100 per cent Islamic society, the Maldives had the world's highest divorce rate.

The crime rate was low. No beggars populated the streets of the capital, Malé. And there was little rubbish; the public buildings were immaculate. It was also one of the lowest countries in the world: none of the islands measured more than 1.8 metres (six feet) above sea level. The archipelago was immediately threatened by any rise in the oceans caused by global warming. The December 2004 tsunami killed eighty-two people. The Maldives was like the proverbial canary in a mine: it was the first warning of catastrophe. 'Our entire nation could be wiped out,' said one government minister.

The country's president, Maumoon Abdul Gayoom, was Asia's longest-serving leader. He had been in power since 1978, two years more than even Robert Mugabe. This was a 'beach dictatorship', to use the phrase of novelist Hari Kunzru. Gayoom's relatively benign rule had brought a tenfold increase in the economy for the 340,000 inhabitants, partly because of the tourist boom. Tourists outnumbered the local population, so there was a major incentive to avoid friction with Europe, from whence came most of the visitors.

Much of the tourism money went into Gayoom's elaborate patronage system. The president had always emphasized the role of the family, but it turned out that he was talking about his own family. Powerful and squabbling factions among his many relatives behaved as if they had a dynastic claim on power.

Some of the boozy holiday islands boasted $1,000-a-night rooms while, in the slums of the main island of Malé, Maldivians were living eight to ten people to a cramped room. Unemployment was 40 per cent, especially among the three-quarters of the population that was under 35. Maldivians were not permitted to work in the bars of the islands reserved for foreign tourists. Alcohol was strictly prohibited to Muslims, though hard drugs were common. There was little else to do, youngsters complained, in a society which strongly discouraged dancing and pre-marital liaisons.

The Maldives, like China, faced a paradox: increasing economic prosperity was not matched by political reform. 'We don't have oil, so the world doesn't care,' said Mohamed Nasheed, the chairperson of the Maldivian Democratic Party (MDP), the main opposition group. He argued that a pro-Western liberal democracy in the Maldives could be a beacon for reform, not least in the Middle East.

The European Union, however, did threaten sanctions after the 2004 upheavals, which the opposition saw as their version of Beijing's Tian'anmen Square. The reformers did not want to kill the golden goose by encouraging sanctions on tourism, though they did advocate travel bans on the ruling elite. 'This won't affect ordinary people, but it will be some sort of restraint on the lavish lifestyle of the leadership,' said Mohamed Nasheed.

The archipelago was roughly 200 miles north of the crucial US base on the British Indian Ocean Territory of Diego Garcia, and approximately the same distance south from the tip of India. Through its three main channels over $300 billion-worth of oil was shipped annually. The islands had been a British protectorate, not least because of the strategic position; it was used as a major imperial military base, until full independence in 1965.

The Chinese were negotiating for a base there, claimed the MDP (although Beijing vehemently denied this). India donated military equipment and training, and also helped to suppress the 1988 coup attempt led by Sri Lankan mercenaries. Britain and America also provided some military training, but this was usually low-key – provision of places in military colleges, for example, for selected officers. A few of the more remote islands had become radicalized by al-Qaeda, and some of the young people in the capital, where the veil had returned in force, were becoming attracted to jihadism.

President Gayoom told the outside world that his regime was a bulwark against Islamic extremism. At home, the former Egyptian-trained Islamic cleric played the religious card for all its worth, though he was not a religious fundamentalist himself. He warned locals that Christian missionaries would take over if the (entirely Muslim) opposition came to power. The two Islamist parties on the island had little influence in the *Majlis*, or parliament, while the opposition party, the MDP, held a small number of seats in a system dominated by the governing party controlled by Gayoom.

*****

My first impression of the Maldives was the view from the plane: set in an azure sea, little circles of green made up a series of atolls. It certainly looked like the archetype of paradise. At the airport, the luggage conveyor moved at a snail's pace. 'Indicates the pace of life here,' Irwin noted.

We travelled from the airport island in a small launch for the ten-minute journey to the main island, Malé, where we settled into an average hotel near the water front. Irwin and I had recently been in Darfur, staying in a slum room in the governor's so-called palace. 'Sure beats staying in Darfur,' I said. 'And we can at least get a beer here.' In that I was wrong. Casual visitors could not get booze in the capital, although it was available in the nearby islands. I could see that Irwin and I would spend a lot of time at sea.

I went straight to the offices of the opposition '*Minivan*' ('*Independent*') newspaper group. I was lucky to meet Aminath Najeeb, the editor. Everyone called

Ferry terminal in the capital, Malé.

her Anthu. We immediately got on very well. She was small, lively and brave –
though she was at first reluctant to tell me about her ordeals in Gayoom's prisons.
She was more keen on talking about Nepal when we shared a dinner together. We
were introduced to Seena, the only supermodel the country had produced. Again,
I was to be lucky with an 'escort officer'. She took us immediately to the chief
press officer to sort out our accreditation which was done with alacrity because
the government official was obviously smitten with Seena, though he was also
attentive to Irwin and me. And our beautiful guide helped to arrange a meeting
with the foreign minister the next day. It was a small place and, with the right
connections, things could be fixed quickly.

   That night Irwin and I met up with Hari Kunzru, the novelist and travel writer;
he had a dry wit and easy manner. We three took the ferry out to the airport island
so we could chat over a beer and discuss the fate of his photographer who had just
been turned around at the airport. It could be a strict place. After the locals got to
trust me, the young women I met confessed that they drank alcohol and had sex.
'Just don't get caught,' one told me. 'You could get forty lashes for drinking.'

*****

The people on the island were very small, even by my Welsh standards. The foreign minister, Dr Ahmed Shaheed, was less than five feet tall. Sitting on his chair like a forlorn Ronnie Corbett, his feet didn't touch the ground. Tactfully, I had to suggest he sat in a lower chair for our TV interview. He had studied at Aberystwyth University and the Welsh connection quickly cemented our rapport. He was clearly a nice guy, despite being a front for a dictatorship.

Amnesty International had regularly condemned suppression of political opposition and the media, as well as the use of torture, especially after the anti-government riots in 2003, and the state of emergency proclaimed in 2004. Some improvements had been made after international concern about the complaints of police and prison brutality. The catch-all accusations of 'terrorism', particularly for journalists, became less frequent. Allegations of arson and drug abuse were deployed instead. Abdullah Saeed, an independently minded journalist, had recently been jailed for twenty-five years. Summoned by the legal authorities, the prosecution alleged that he took the highly unusual precaution of stuffing his pockets with heroin before attending the police station.

The new younger breed of ministers in Gayoom's government claimed that there was a proverbial 'road map' to a multi-party democracy. Many of them were anglophiles, educated in the UK, like Dr Shaheed. The highly articulate foreign minister told me that 'things are changing fast. The Amnesty reports refer to conditions of two years ago. There have been monumental changes. Then there were no opposition parties, now there are three or four.' He pleaded for his 'young country' to be given time.

The opposition groups considered twenty-eight years to be quite long enough. That's why they had called for a series of protests which were to culminate in a mass rally on 10 November 2006. They promised the downfall of the authoritarian system.

Irwin and I had to get in the middle of the protests. This is where Irwin's experience in Northern Ireland really came in handy. He had to walk or run backwards to film the advancing riot police. Quite a skill. And it was my job to run behind him, with my hand on his back, and my wider vision to avoid collisions or deflect any flying objects.

Everything went well for a while: we got some great shots. The demonstrators were restrained, and the heavily protected police anti-riot squad, looking just like Star Wars stormtroopers, were disciplined and apparently well-trained. Occasionally a snatch squad would grab a protestor. We filmed one arrest sequence outside the college for training tourist personnel. Our pictures, juxtaposing the big tourist college sign with protestors being dragged off by police, would not help the tourist industry.

We had already grabbed a short interview with the leader of the MDP opposition, Mohamed Nasheed. So we tried to keep up with him as various groups

Arrest by police looking like Star Wars stormtroopers, November 2006.

'Anni', leader of the opposition, in the middle of the protests.

of protestors were rallying around him as he popped up in different parts of the tiny capital. We lost contact during his various disappearing acts. I stopped to ask a pretty young bystander whom I noticed had a picture of 'Anni' – as Nasheed was universally dubbed – as a screensaver on her mobile phone; presumably she was a supporter. I urgently needed to locate the deliberately elusive opposition leader. It meant that I had left Irwin's back unguarded for a minute or so.

The streets were very narrow, and private cars were few. The pride and joy of particularly the young people were the highly polished scooters and small motorbikes. They were lined carefully, and closely, alongside the street. These were the equivalent of the sacred cows in Nepal; I noticed that both sides in the demonstrations were careful to avoid knocking over any bikes. But that's what Irwin did. He backed into one shiny red bike and the rest started to topple over in painfully slow motion, like falling dominoes. The police, protestors and bystanders let out a collective howl of anguish. Everyone stopped what they were doing and rushed to catch the bikes. Only three or four fell because of this prompt action. And Irwin was rightly miffed.

All he had seen was my talking to an attractive young woman.

'Can't you concentrate on the job instead of chatting up the women?'

He was not entirely convinced by my very genuine reason for taking my eye off the ball. But I did secure the location of Anni and we sped off in our hired car to find him.

The protestors were not as many as expected because the government deployed its tiny navy to prevent supporters assembling in the capital, including threatening to sink one vessel. We were in the middle of the final protests, and observed police restraint, by and large, though we apparently missed the use of gas sprays and heavy-duty baton charges. I stood alongside Anni as the police charged. He informed me that it was the presence of our two-man film crew that discouraged police violence, not least against him personally. There were also rather eccentric so-called peace monitors from the US and Europe.

Next day the would-be peaceful revolutionaries called off their protests because they feared bloodshed, they said. In truth, geography, successful police tactics and perhaps the fear of jail combined to produce a damp squib.

Inevitably, having been filmed by police cameras in the middle of the mêlée, we were stopped by a police colonel and his team. A few Western journalists had already been arrested and deported the next day, although they were treated well. Now it looked like it was our turn. As the colonel was about to take us away, I handed him the card of the foreign minister.

'Why don't you ring him? I had a meeting with him this morning.'

Luckily Dr Shaheed answered his phone. The colonel's attitude to us changed immediately, especially when the Minister wanted to speak to me directly. He suggested that we get out of trouble by visiting one of the offshore islands. Good idea, I thought. We needed some colour material to supplement our good action shots.

The foreign minister allocated us one his people and we set off next morning for one of the islands, about an hour away by boat. We were offered a longer trip in a seaplane, but we needed to get back to the airport for our departure the next day. Irwin and I were each given a palatial wooden house on stilts above the sea. Each had a small pool, and steps down into the ocean. They were well-stocked with the finest soaps and other toiletries and, more important, the best wines and champagnes. It was the most romantic place I had ever visited – pity Irwin wasn't in the mood.

We had only a short time to film in the fading light of the evening, and in the very early, rainy, morning. The French manager entertained us royally for dinner. We had secured our soft colour sequences, and Channel Four News loved the action scenes. It went on air less than twenty-four hours after our return to London.

Helped by our film, according to opposition leaders, the week's protests focused some international attention on the Maldives, and the Gayoom government pledged to accelerate multi-party democracy. Maybe the friendly and well-educated people of these beautiful atolls could do what all the military might of the US could not do in the Middle East. Rapid reform, allied to the generally laidback nature of Maldivian Islamic culture, could create a Western-style liberal democracy. One former longterm detainee had told me, 'It might have been paradise for tourists but it was hell for us.' The gentle, diminutive islanders deserved a change for the better.

So I kept trying to help the islands. I went back again, on a quiet visit with no cameras, to talk to the security people, so see whether they would accept regime change. I also met Mohamed Nasheed in London to talk about his plans for peaceful reform.

******

In late October 2008 an American-accented voice rang me to ask 'Would you like to attend the president's inauguration?' I thought Obama, but why the hell me?

My mind cleared and I realized that the caller was speaking from Malé. The official was talking about Anni's inauguration. Veteran foreign correspondents are accustomed to guerrilla leaders and exiled politicians promising that when they win power they would give the favoured hack the first interview in the presidential palace. Mohamed Nasheed kept his promise to me. After thirty years of dictatorship, he won the first free and fair presidential elections in the Maldives. The 41-year-old former political prisoner had been likened to Mahatma Gandhi, but he would have trouble keeping his head above water. In the short term he faced a looted treasury and in the long term his country could be sinking beneath the waves.

Anni deserved his success. He had served a tough apprenticeship on the long walk to freedom: he was jailed twenty-three times, and was sometimes tortured on various prison islands. The young politician, who had been schooled in England, always had impressed me with his straightforward decency. He was almost too honest to be a successful politician.

I recalled the old adage that people who start revolutions rarely finish them. I was almost wrong in this case. Like Robert Mugabe, also in a 2008 election, the former Maldivian dictator wrongly assumed he would win more than 50 per cent in the first round of presidential elections. He didn't. Nasheed instead won the second round of the elections in October and he was made president elect. And so I received the promised invitation to attend his inauguration on 11 November 2008, two years after I filmed him standing alone on the streets of the Maldivian capital, Malé, after the failure of his attempt to foment a peaceful revolution.

Irwin and I attended the formal pre-inauguration ceremony. Naturally, Anni was thronged by local supporters and foreign dignitaries. I waited for an hour or so to catch his eye as he glad-handed the hundreds of guests. Frustrated, I came up behind him and tapped him on the shoulder. Two heavies moved aggressively towards me, but Anni quickly spun around and hugged me.

'Are you going to keep your promise for the first interview?' I got straight to the point.

He said yes, and delegated a new minister to make the arrangements. I then bumped into Dr Shaheed, whose liberal instincts and defection from Gayoom's government, had persuaded the new president to keep him in his old portfolio.

He smiled at me and said, 'You've put on weight.'

That might have been a compliment in his culture, but probably not. I almost replied, 'And you've lost some height.'

*****

Next day, on his busy first day in office, Anni, now 'Mr President', found time to give me an hour interview – before the waiting and impatient Chinese, Indian and British diplomats who were clicking their heels in the corridor outside the presidential office.

'Not many Islamic countries have had free and fair elections to form a multi-party democracy,' he said. Despite his brutal treatment, Anni preached forgiveness to the old regime, because it was an Islamic principle and practical politics. He said Mandela and the South African Truth and Reconciliation process were his model.

President Nasheed had also been compared with Barack Obama. Did he face the same crisis of expectations as the US President-Elect? 'No,' he said, 'I have already delivered on my main promise: democracy.'

Interview with President Mohamed Nasheed on his first day in office, 2008. (Irwin Armstrong)

The previous regime had emptied the treasury. 'Our finances are in bad shape. We can't consolidate democracy if we can't pay wages. The economic fundamentals are good, the problem is the next few months.' He said he was appealing to Britain, as well as China and India. I suggested that Britain was not in great shape to hand out any money, although Anni was asking for just $200 million in emergency loans.

I also asked him whether I could visit the prison where he was shackled to a generator that had temporarily deafened him, and fed glass in his food. 'Before you sack your police chief, order him to take me tomorrow to that island.'

The next day the senior police officer picked me up in a launch. I had persuaded my friend Anthu to come as well, because she could form the central link in the film sequence I had planned, and also, as a former inmate, she could tell me if the authorities were trying to pull the wool over my eyes. She wanted to exorcise some ghosts, so she accompanied me to Dhoonidhoo prison island.

Her gentle face contorted in anguish as we were led by her former jailors to the prison cell where she had been held, now inhabited by a Chinese prostitute. Anthu recounted the depravities of her treatment: shackling, blindfolding, threats of rape and being thrown into the sea. The accompanying senior police officer claimed that he had never heard of such maltreatment to anyone. Well, he would say that, wouldn't he?

As someone who was likely to play a leading role in human rights work in the new government, Anthu went around the cells, listening carefully to the complaints of the inmates. No political prisoners remained on this island, though Anthu explained that others were held elsewhere on fabricated charges of drug-dealing.

After bravely confronting her former jailors, some of whom she thanked for the little kindnesses, such as giving her cigarettes, she talked at length about her experiences. Was it all worth it?

'I am proud to have helped bring down the dictator. He is gone, but his set-up still is here. We need to clean up the Maldives.'

Did she support the forgiveness policy of the new president?

'I believe in forgiveness,' she said, 'but I also believe in justice.'

President Nasheed faced a huge task of rebuilding his country's economy, besides issues of jihadist infiltration and long-term challenges of global warming. In his interview with me he talked of eventually – in fifty years or more – planning to relocate his people to Sri Lanka, India or even Australia: 'I don't want my grandchildren living in a tent in a refugee camp.'

The young president insisted that his revolution was a beacon to the Islamic world, and beyond. Maybe London's cash-crunched government, or Washington, could help this kind of Islamic transformation – it would be a tiny, and very cost-effective, sum compared with the billions spent in Iraq and Afghanistan. It was the first time there had been a transition in a free and fair election to a multi-party democracy in the Islamic world, and without a drop of blood spilled and without the presence of a single Western soldier.

The outgoing dictator had called on his security forces to declare a state of emergency and abort the election victory, but they had simply refused. Anthu's emotional testimony had added a human interest angle to this uplifting story, though it only just made Channel Four's second-tier More Four news a week or so later. After all, it was a rare good-news story.

****

I had worked so hard on the Maldives film, but secured just a few minutes of air time. So it was rather ironic that I got extensive exposure for a very trivial story, and in my own Surrey village. The *Mail* and the *Daily Telegraph* had run articles on the fuss about the new vicar of St James's in Shere. It really was a storm in a parochial tea-cup. He hadn't been caught with his hand in the till or up a parishioner's skirt; rather, he had been accused of being 'too High Church'. Also, he had refused, with accurate, though strict, interpretation of Church law, to allow people to marry who were not sufficiently connected with the parish. His congregation had dwindled and some had complained to the press and bishop. Personally, I liked the vicar, though I saw little of him, especially in St James's. I mean *he* was always there; I wasn't.

Above left: St James's church in Shere, a beautiful village in the Surrey Hills.

*Above righ*t: Jenny Muddiman and I attending a wedding at Shere church, 2015. I am the one without a hat.

Picturesque Shere had been featured in a number of Hollywood movies, most recently *The Holiday*, starring Kate Winslet, Cameron Diaz *et al*. Coincidentally, Parliament was revising a series of laws relating to wedding rules in the Church of England. As I had been quoted in the *Telegraph*, because of my book on Shere, the Beeb asked me to do an interview. I was reluctant to talk on Church matters, but I was prepared to talk from a *community* perspective, especially as the Bishop of Guildford had also suggested my name to the BBC.

I did a piece of impromptu Nimbyism, and happened to invent the term 'wedding tourism'. Must have been a slow news day as this soundbite was on the main BBC news all day, and bits of the interview were on Radio Four's Today and PM programmes, and that led to a whole series of radio interviews, including a

The launch of my novel, *Anchoress of Shere*, in a village pub, 2000. Although Shere was chock full of eccentrics, wearing medieval dress was not the norm.

30-minute live debate with two bishops. And I knew bugger-all about ecclesiastical law.

I had my first reaction phone call at 8.00 am from Alan, an old college friend in Cardiff.

'Saw you on the news this morning. Quite spoiled my breakfast. Anyway, I thought you were a Muslim.'

Another called to say that he was surprised to see that the caption on the news read 'Professor Paul Moorcraft, church member'.

That surprised me too.

My friend suggested, 'Pub member would have been more apt.'

I had to agree.

A journalist colleague called to say, 'You didn't quite get into your stride. You didn't mention female priests and gay bishops, nor the return of flogging and the white five-pound note.'

I had to take the phone off the hook. I was stopped in every shop in the village and on the main street for days afterwards. I had spent over thirty years of serious endeavour writing numerous books, endless articles, and doing much broadcast punditry on vital issues such as Iraq, Afghanistan, Palestine and Darfur. I had lectured on the importance of journalism around the world, and for years at Cardiff University, where I had recently been made a visiting professor. It was, however, my very short impromptu comment on wedding tourism that had inspired much more media attention. My fifteen minutes of (minor) fame had come from a throwaway line.

I was bound to wonder why I had spent most of my life reporting in so many hellholes.

****

The Maldives wasn't a hellhole, at least for me, and I was keen to go back. I was asked to set up courses in journalism in the islands' embryonic university, and I recruited some lecturers. Funnily enough, I thought I would have no problems finding experienced hacks to teach in paradise for a year on a reasonable tax-free salary. I was wrong. I also offered to train the police and military in media ops in particular, while throwing in some good governance/human rights advice. I shared my concerns about the police and army with the charming new Maldivian High Commissioner in London, Farah. I had worked hard to help democracy in the islands, and apart from the friendship of the new president and small amount of payment for the films shown on British TV, I had worked *pro bono*. (My accountant said that, since I worked non-stop for so little, then I should seek charity status for my small think tank.) I still nagged about the need to train the small army and police and perhaps to shut me up I was asked to attend the islands' inclusion in the Hay Literary Festival outreach. That sounded like a nice bonus. Authors are much more prone to accept such jollies than hacks, it seemed.

In February 2012 my friend the president was ousted in a police/military coup loyal to the old regime. Well, that's what he said, although the Commonwealth somehow regarded it as a voluntary resignation. Many Commonwealth leaders, however, wouldn't recognize a forced resignation even if a shotgun were shoved up their own backsides. I did a little quiet lobbying for the deposed president – now plain Anni again. He contested the presidency again, only to be pipped at the post by the return of the Gayoom family dictatorship.

Anni was eventually jailed for thirteen years on trumped-up charges of 'terrorism'. I did some more lobbying although Anni had a powerful advocate in the shapely form of Amal Clooney, George's famous lawyer wife. Amal worked *pro bono* facing Mrs Cherie Booth (the wife of Tony Blair) who was representing the dictatorship for a large fee (albeit briefly). Anni stayed in prison despite a little pressure from the Commonwealth and a lot from Number Ten Downing Street.

I had to do my bit and persuaded Irwin to come with me again. We flew to Sri Lanka to see Anni's ministers in exile or conveniently on holiday. Then we made the short flight to the islands as tourists with rather a suspicious amount of camera gear. Anni's beautiful young wife, Laila, gave us a powerful interview and my old friend Anthu managed to get us to the new prison island where Anni was held. But we couldn't see him.

We made a number of digital copies of our film just in case we were arrested. We weren't and we got the film safely back to London. Unfortunately, all the convulsions in the Islamic world made our story rather insignificant, especially for Channel Four News which had run two of my previous films on the Maldives. I needed a short interview with Amal to add celebrity power. Instead, short parts of our film were used by the American NBC station. It included both Hillary Clinton and Amal Clooney. That film, perhaps, and the personal intervention from Prime Minister David Cameron persuaded the Maldivian government to allow Anni thirty days out of prison to secure urgent medical treatment in London. There I spoke briefly to him and Laila and it was obvious that he wasn't going back. Anni's two children were also in England. The Islamic world had lost a good leader, although some of his followers had told me he was suffering from acute Post Traumatic Stress Disorder after so many tough times in prison. A few of his ex-ministers said some of his actions in government had been erratic or eccentric. I thought one of his first gestures as president – holding a cabinet underwater – was genius PR, to accentuate the dangers of global warning. He was an idealist perhaps and not cynical or focused enough to rule. Now the black flags of the Islamic State are appearing on the streets of the Maldivian capital. That's not genius PR for the vital tourist industry.

*****

A rare victory in Sri Lanka?

Before 2008 I had stopped over at Sri Lanka's Colombo airport a number of times, but had never ventured into the luxuriant tropical island outside the air-conditioned modern terminal. I had also followed the long war there quite closely and even opined publicly on its unusual conclusion, despite the fact that I was not, for once, an eye-witness. Shortly after the twenty-six-year civil war ended in May 2009, I was asked to visit Sir Lanka. Would I be interested in writing a history of the war? I was a little worried about official invitations, but I would be happy to talk to the political, intelligence and military leaders for a book to be produced independently in the UK by Pen and Sword, probably the best-known UK military publisher.

I did my initial homework on the former British colony of Ceylon. I found out about Kandy, a small inland kingdom which hid itself away, far from the first European colonizers. A shipwrecked British sailor called Robert Knox was held in Kandy for 19 years in the mid-seventeenth century. His largely favourable impressions – except for the occasional executions by spurring elephants to gore or trample condemned prisoners – were recorded in a journal, which was later filched by Daniel Defoe as a source for his *Robinson Crusoe.* In 1796 the British wrested the island from the Dutch and by 1815 the independent kingdom of Kandy, once protected by forests and warrior spirit, was crushed, though minor guerrilla wars spluttered on. The last rumblings of resistance were inspired by a (false) rumour in 1848 that women were to be taxed according to the size of their breasts – which perhaps indicated the less lofty preoccupations of the British colonizers. Generally, however, the Brits did their usual civilizing thing, not least building roads, railways, and lots of tea plantations. It is of course against union rules to describe the benefits of colonial rule in any detail; Ceylon did prosper, however. The Brits largely kept the peace, but were accused of over-promoting the minority Tamils in the civil service and the economy because of their perceived higher levels of education, entrepreneurial skills and, colonists argued, work ethic. The rivalries between the Hindu Tamils, Muslims and other minorities (some Christian) as well as the overwhelmingly Buddhist Sinhalese majority were sometimes tempered by anti-colonial alliances. In other respects, parallels existed with the Palestinian versus Israeli cycle of violence: two peoples fired up by different languages, religions and ancient histories contending for the same small piece of sanctified land. In the same year, 1948, Britain extricated itself from the Rubik's cubes in Ceylon and Palestine. Independence was achieved peacefully in Ceylon, unlike the

The island of Sri Lanka (formerly Ceylon).

savagery of partition in the next-door Raj. The war of secession was delayed for a few decades.

Soon I was visiting the island regularly for interviews, research trips and battlefield tours. Everybody kept talking about itchy this and itchy that. I was perhaps missing the effects of some peculiarly debilitating insect bites. Eventually, after tuning into the local variant of English, I twigged they were saying not 'itchy' but 'HE' – His Excellency – the popular abbreviation for the island's president, Mahinda Rajapaksa. I knew the first thing I had to do was to get HE onside. I was quickly granted a two-hour breakfast meeting with him at his personal residence, where I sat next to His Excellency and engaged him closely.

After the early breakfast (my second of the morning), he invited me to join him alone, in his prayer room/personal temple. I understood this to be a token of favour, and I had the good sense to take off my shoes before entering. Outside his personal retreat were family photographs, especially of his sons playing sport – with emphasis on rugby rather than the more expected cricket. The inner sanctum hosted numerous statues of the Buddha, many in precious metals or adorned with jewellery. About a quarter of the room was also populated by a pantheon of Hindu deities. Presumably, the president was covering his spiritual bases for religious or PR reasons. From our brief discussion on reincarnation – I explained I'd written a book about past-life experiences – I felt Rajapaksa was genuinely religious. I might just have been naïve. I liked him not least because he was very courteous to me, an unimportant military historian.

A rather unflattering portrait I took of President Rajapaksa.

I guessed from my experience of autocracies that if you win over the support of the big man, the rest will follow much more easily. And so it was. I was given incredible access, usually going where I wanted, often at short notice, to avoid Potemkin set-ups. I was given individual use of VIP helicopters and an impressive personal protection unit, plus an armoured personnel carrier when travelling in the north (though why I should have needed all this security when the war was supposed to be over, I didn't discover). Naturally, the leadership, especially in the military and intelligence, was keen for me not to get blown up or shot, but rather to buy into its perspective, as it was understood that HE had given me *carte blanche* to write a history of the war, the first 'authorized' one by a Western historian. I would speak to anyone I wanted – from any side – to get at the information I required for my book.

I asked first for access to the 'seat' of the war, the Jaffna peninsula. I flew up in a small Russian Antonov passenger plane. The Sri Lankans, I soon realized, had a hotchpotch of equipment, bought in whatever market they could find, especially when the West cut back on supplies. The army, however, was very British in its origins, dress and style. A very articulate major general, another Mahinda, gave me a comprehensive briefing on the war around the northern capital, Jaffna, which fell to both sides on a number of occasions. I was taken on a tour of the massive old Dutch fort, typically laid out in a star formation. The Dutch and the Portuguese had preceded the British as the island's fortifying colonizers.

Because of my love of trains, I wanted to see what remained of the railway system that once passed through some of the most beautiful routes in the world. Trains, which first appeared in the Ceylon colony in 1864, were initially called by the locals (in translation) 'coal-eating, water-drinking, sprinting metal yaks'. A few years after independence from Britain, steam gave way to diesel locomotives. The Yal Devi, or northern line, used to run from the modern capital, Colombo, to Jaffna and beyond. The railway would pass Anuradhapura, the island's ancient capital, once teeming with monasteries, royal palaces, pleasure gardens and artificial lakes. Then the train would travel on to Kilinochchi (later the Tamil Tiger capital) and Elephant Pass, the scene of much fighting after 1983, before traversing the narrow Isthmus into the Jaffna peninsula.

I insisted on visiting the Jaffna station – it had been torn apart by war. Just one man was camped in the shell of the building. Amid the encroaching undergrowth, I could see that all the rail lines had gone, used as reinforcement for the bunkers that the rebel Tigers had built throughout their former domain in the north and east of the island. They claimed this area as Tamil Eelam, their own independent state. The most attractive surviving building in Jaffna was the ornate library which had been

The rebuilt library in Jaffna, a centre of Tamil Hindu culture.

destroyed and rebuilt twice. Considered the central repository of Tamil Hindu culture, its white exterior gleamed in the unforgiving sunshine. Inside, despite the scattering of ancient computers, it seemed largely defunct.

I also insisted on leaving my military minders to talk to people in the shops and banks. One trader told me, 'When the Tigers were in control they took protection money from us. We have to do the same now, but the government calls it tax.'

I was given the standard tour of what Western armies call 'CIMIC' projects – military aid to the civilian population, in this case nice new brick bungalows for Tamil resettlement. Again, I managed to chat to some of the local Tamil leaders, out of army earshot. It was clear that, while the fighting war was over, many residents sullenly resented what they saw as an army of occupation. This impression was partly confirmed by my visit to a fancy army holiday resort near Jaffna called Thal Sewana. It was to become an international hotel, one day, when overseas tourists could risk coming north. The same major general was an attentive host and very urbane, except for his eccentric affection for Engelbert Humperdinck. It was a boozy occasion and I tucked into an elaborate buffet as well, until I realized that it was just a starter. I was often caught out by the procession of meals, never sure how to measure the beginning, middle and end. Another culinary factor also surprised me. At every military meeting (between meal times) I was always served with Jacobs cream crackers and Dairylea cheese triangles, with no butter. It was a very British affectation.

During the course of the evening I fell in with a colourful colonel who was either under instruction to talk to me or was too fond of booze; the former I suspect. He had attended and removed the body of the rebel leader, Velupillai Prabhakaran, from the battlefield when he was shot in May 2009 in the Tigers' last stand. He gave me a detailed, almost forensic, description of the warlord's wounds, which did not match the official version published at the time. He described three rifle-shot entry wounds on the side of the chest – the official version and pictures emphasized one forehead wound. I sensed that my questioning would soon reveal many more apparent discrepancies.

The next day I travelled with my escorting officer, a war-wounded major with a prosthetic leg. That was fortunate as it meant he was less keen on walking long distances than even I was. We moved around in Vietnam-era Hueys, which always felt safe and reassuring – veteran but reliable choppers. I wanted to visit de-mining sites, because I had been told that the remaining resettlement of Tamils had been delayed in some areas because of former intensive mining by the LTTE (Liberation Tigers of Tamil Eelam) – as the Tigers were called officially. At the de-mining site at Kumarapuram, a smartly dressed sapper colonel briefed me on the variety of foreign and locally improvised mines used. Generally about the size of a large can of baked beans, they came from Singapore, China and Pakistan or were made by the Tigers themselves. I examined the defused mines – I was told they were inert – laid out on trestle tables. (I had once foolishly picked up a Russian 'butterfly bomb' in a similar display in Afghanistan to discover it had *not* been made safe.) I asked an array of what I thought were intelligent technical questions as a prelude to my request to move beyond the standard display for occasional VIPs. Could we actually go into what was perhaps the most intensely sown minefield in Asia? I was genuinely interested in de-mining; I also wanted to see first-hand whether I was being given bullshit excuses about the delay in Tamil resettlement.

The colonel spoke to the brigadier present who made a quick call to their HQ. I was expecting the usual official 'no' couched in 'Elf and Safety' jargon. In this case it would have been reasonable, but I had to ask. Surprisingly (and unnervingly), I was given the go-ahead and a Lady-Di-style helmet and body armour along with an important lower padded flap to protect what I jokingly called my 'Welsh member'. It was a well-dressed way to go boom.

The brigadier took over from the colonel and warned me, 'You must be very careful – lots of active mines remain. You need to step in my footsteps, if you can.'

I couldn't because I could see so little. And the dappled sunlight under the forest cover made my very limited vision even worse. Trying to keep up with the fit senior officer in the midday heat, I started to sweat profusely under the protective and bulky clothing. Once again, I asked myself, 'What the hell am I doing here?' The incursion into the minefield took far longer than I expected. I had asked for it so I had to shut up and concentrate on following the brigadier in front of me and keeping an eye out for the small pegs and white tape all along the poorly defined path.

Another hot sticky mile passed before we came upon a small clearing where sappers were scraping away, very carefully, with metal prods. Used to the perhaps more advanced techniques I'd seen in Iraq and Afghanistan, I asked a daft question, 'How dangerous is this method?'

'In the last few months twelve of my men have lost a hand or two,' the brigadier said in a somewhat blasé tone.

Doing my Lady Di impression – wearing some of my mine-protection gear.

A sapper working next to me in one of the most dangerous minefields in the world.

Just then a sapper shouted that he had found one. He gently raised it out of the ground and looked at it carefully. It was another baked-bean-can-size mine. Presumably satisfied with his examination, he started unscrewing the top. I knew that perhaps 10 per cent of these mines were booby-trapped precisely to stop sappers unscrewing the top to defuse the mechanism. I couldn't be seen to cower, my natural instinct, though I shifted myself slightly behind a small tree and behind the brigadier.

Since everybody seemed to be disobeying standard procedures, I lit a cigarette in a stubborn display of macho nonchalance. This was a bit bolder than might appear, because a friend who hated my smoking had doctored some of my cigarette tips with heads from the highly volatile local matches. Too thrifty to throw away my contaminated packet I took a chance in the minefield. I thought, *if I gotta go, I may as well do it in style*. Nobody cared much in that steamy ex-battlefield, anyway.

Neither mine nor fag exploded.

The sapper finished unscrewing the device; it was not booby-trapped. A very brave man doing this all day for a pittance. For some reason I thought of fat-cat bankers in London being compelled to do internships in mine-clearance to justify a little of their massive salaries. And with luck a few of them might blow themselves up instead of a poor corporal trying to feed his family.

I took some pictures of the sapper, and then carefully retraced my steps, closely shadowing the brigadier. Still sweating intensely, I was glad to remove my protective gear. I had taken just an hour's risk and had lived to scribble my tale, with my Welsh member still attached. I celebrated with fresh coconut juice.

*****

The Tigers had spent most of their long war turning their-ever morphing statelet into one massive armed garrison: not just mines everywhere, but bunkers everywhere too; and cleverly camouflaged command HQs underground. I was flown to see the Tiger generalissimo's main bunker in Puthukudierupu. It was brilliantly concealed by tree cover bent over a small hut. Beneath the simple hut was a three-tier concrete structure. It was very austere, even Prabhakaran's small personal room.

The territory initially held by the Tigers was reduced to a rump by early 2009.

The Tiger boss was always on the move and would stay for only a few days in a command bunker. Due to air supremacy and constant drone reconnaissance, the Tiger leaders were frequently targets for government air strikes.

The bunker was encircled by eighteen timber-and-earth strongpoints for Prabhakaran's personal protection team. The Sri Lankan air force devised a partly successful strategy of decapitating the Tiger leadership by air power, sometimes accompanied by raids by teams of special forces. That was enough to make any military leader paranoid; the Tiger chieftain was also nervous about internal challenges to his dictatorship. Like Stalin, his leadership cult brooked no dissent. Nevertheless, he also had a cutthroat charisma that forged one of the most successful insurgencies in modern history. The LTTE developed a guerrilla and semi-conventional army, very successful navy and also a tiny air force, the only guerrilla force to possess its own combat fixed-wing and rotary aircraft. The five light Czech-made planes were occasionally effective in raids, but more psychologically disruptive when used in kamikaze urban attacks. Most international security experts believed that the Tigers could not be defeated by military means – almost till the end of the war, when they were defeated.

My army escorts took me to see the site of the final *Götterdämmerung*. The Tigers had forced hundreds of thousands of Tamil civilians to become human shields, although some no doubt also supported the separatist cause. By May 2009 the government forces had squeezed the Tiger fighters into a tiny enclave, a small spit of land alongside the sea and a lagoon at Nandikadal. The whole area was like a scene from a post-apocalypse movie. A large Jordanian ship had been hijacked and driven onto the beach and used as the final redoubt of the gutsy Tiger navy. Wrecked cars and buses were strewn everywhere. Bombed buildings and shell holes were evidence of intensive artillery strikes – the government forces were accused of war crimes in shelling civilians, but the Tigers also set up artillery next to hospitals and a UN hub. This was the first war in a long time that I'd covered post-hoc, yet the sense of death and destruction still hung like a miasma over the place. Strangely, the only orderly spectacle was a field full of neatly stacked bicycles, rusted now and waiting patiently for their dead or interned owners.

I was taken to the small outcrop of mango foliage on the lagoon's outskirts where Prabhakaran had hidden with his thirty final guards. They were killed, according to my army sources, by a fusillade of automatic fire. Prabhakaran did not have time to take his suicide pill hanging around his neck, an adornment carried by all Tigers, men, women and child soldiers alike. The Tigers had fostered a cult of martyrdom.

Inevitably, I was also taken to the nearby victory monument – part of the triumphalism that had swept the largely Buddhist Sinhalese, who constituted roughly 80 per cent of the islands' 20-odd million population. I was more interested, however, in seeing the army's museum of captured Tiger weaponry. In a near-miracle of self-help, the Tigers managed to build a navy of small attack craft, out of fibreglass and plastic. They also built six (unused) submarines, as well as their own armoured vehicles. What they couldn't build they usually bought from the North Koreans in a brilliant logistic effort to thwart the government's naval blockade. The Tigers were utterly ruthless to their own side and to the government forces, but they fought with great bravery and determination, and often operational

The last bit of coast held by the Tiger navy was based on this captured ship deliberately run aground.

skill. The Tiger leader, Prabhakaran, did not know when to quit, however. Before 2005, as a three-year ceasefire crumbled, he should have declared victory and negotiated. He had humbled the government forces, which were quipped by the major regional powers, especially India, China and Pakistan, as well as Israel and, intermittently, the USA. Prabhakaran had carved out roughly the territory he claimed for his Tamil supporters. A federal solution, negotiated by the Norwegians, was on the cards. But his years of martial success against a stronger foe made him believe in outright military victory. He believed his own propaganda that he was an Asian Napoleon. And his dictatorship prevented any of his advisers gainsaying his beliefs. By playing for everything Prabhakaran lost everything and the Tamils suffered a comprehensive military defeat. The war did not determine who was right, but who was left.

President Rajapaksa and his family-dominated government had secured a tremendous and rare military victory, but until he won the peace he was condemned to face mounting UN and Commonwealth criticism for his alleged war crimes, especially in the final stages of the conflict. Critics claimed that as many as 40,000 civilians were killed either in crossfire or outright atrocities. My later research indicated a much lower body count and much of that was caused by Tigers executing Tamil civilians who were trying to escape from their enforced role as human shields or slave labour building defensive earthworks.

Sri Lankan special forces in the last stages of the war. (Sri Lankan Ministry of Defence)

I needed to talk to the Tamil survivors. Around 300,000 had been interned yet almost amazingly – especially compared with the large permanent internally displaced refugee camps I had visited elsewhere, for example in Darfur – most of the Tamils had been rapidly resettled. Some remained because their villages had not been de-mined. I went to a number of camps for displaced people, including Manik farm. It seemed rather well organized and presumably on the regular VIP tour, though some of the inmates complained to me of minor issues, so perhaps it was not one of the concentration camps depicted by Tamil supporters abroad. I also visited rehabilitation centres where hardcore Tiger female cadres were being retrained to work in the Sri Lankan garment industry. Their feisty replies to my questions, despite the army interpreters, suggested they were not at all cowed by defeat. Their comments appeared more like disgruntled union workers in the north of England rather than Asian slave labour. Nevertheless, I was with army minders and so the picture might have been blurred. I would find out more, for myself, on later visits.

I returned to the island regularly, mostly to military sites and for interviews with top brass, though I also managed a little tourism. Throughout the war in the north and east of the island, tourism had continued, sometimes stutteringly because of occasional air raids and much urban bombing by the Tigers. I enjoyed the lush countryside even in tropical rainstorms (unusually, the island has two monsoon seasons) which reminded me of the single rainy season in Zimbabwe. A number of the shops in downtown Colombo were reminiscent of colonial Bulawayo too. Cargills department store, near the Hilton, was an architectural gem. Many of the old imperial street names had survived as well. It demonstrated a post-colonial confidence, unlike the heady passion for renaming nearly everything in Africa, when they swapped one set of foreign predators for another – Karl Marx Street or Kim Jung-Il Avenue and the like.

Tourists who visited the south – for years the guide books left out references to the north and east because of the fighting – would find excellent beaches, fine temples (for example, the Buddhist Temple of the Tooth near Kandy), good food and hotels often at reasonable prices. And foreign cricket fans could share the Sri Lankans' often semi-religious fervour for the sport. First-time visitors would inevitably be shaken by the apparently homicidal driving, especially the trishaws in the towns. From their drivers' windscreens dangled a variety of charms – dedicated to Jesus, Buddha, Ganesh and the odd guru. The trishaw drivers needed all the divine insurance they could get. Many Sri Lankans, especially the older generation, were deeply superstitious and took astrology very seriously. In terms of rural driving, tourists would be warned by notices: 'in areas of human-elephant conflict do not venture out after dark.' The elephant reserves were a popular tourist draw – in daylight.

As with most of my travels, I was usually too busy with politics and war to indulge in much casual tourism. In Colombo I visited a few excellent restaurants and even a night club where a Sri Lankan companion cautioned: 'Never ask the local girls to dance if you don't know them or the group they are with – their men will kill you.' Sri Lankans of all political and religious persuasions seemed friendly and anglophile to me – at social gatherings I was instantly called 'Uncle' by the younger generation and made very welcome – but my study of the island's history, recent war and many interviews suggested the polite passivity could sometimes mask savage souls.

My first visits had been to the north and north-east, where most of the fighting took place. I'd spent time mainly with the army, including a long and detailed briefing by their impressive commander of special forces. He mentioned that even when he was a defence attaché in London, he was not invited to Hereford. Arguably, the Sri Lankan special forces were world leaders in jungle warfare; even the famed British SAS could have learned a thing or two from its Commonwealth ally.

The air force was also very cordial – I attended special forces training with the Hueys, and after talking a little about my phobia-fixation with Mi-24 gunships, spent time with the squadron which flew them. In exchange for telling my stories (or maybe *curtailing* them) about tactics I had experienced in Afghanistan in the 1980s, I was entertained in the mess, and was allowed to see some of the flying logs of the conflict. That was useful information when I later interviewed the (Christian) head of the air force, when he assured me that at no stage in the conflict was the chopper fleet grounded for lack of parts. The logs had clearly shown sometimes desperate cannibalism of parts and cancellation of some or part of operations because of worn-out kit, especially the rotor blades. Call me a dupe, but the more I questioned, the more I was told. Sometimes the information was contradictory. Except perhaps for the official version on the Tiger casualties of the last stage of the war, I didn't feel I was getting a party line. I wasn't enclosed in a tight PR loop.

I visited a whole squadron and base which serviced the sole surviving tiny Searcher drone, purchased from Israel. I had not outgrown my passion for steam trains, obviously, but I had largely transcended my professional interest in pilotless planes. Still, the squadron was a hobbyist's dream. The airmen had been paid to build their own small multi-coloured balsa-wood planes to practise their manual launch and landing skills – once out of sight the Searcher was flown by (fairly) modern electronic controls. The small fleet of Sri Lankan unmanned aerial vehicles, to use the proper term, was very effective in providing real-time surveillance. On occasion, the president even brought in foreign diplomats, especially at the end of the war, to watch what his forces were doing and not, he would argue, committing any war crimes against the besieged Tigers.

I needed to get to grips with the navy as well, and so visited Trincomalee, one of the best natural harbours in the world. That's why Admiral Lord Mountbatten used

My fascination with steam trains was temporarily replaced by an interest in UAVs, pilotless planes. This was the sole survivor at the end of the war of a squadron of Israeli UAVs.

it as his base in the Second World War. During the Tiger war, the former British base had been attacked from, and under, the sea and from the heavily wooded hinterland. Any British visitor would immediately be struck by the colonial heritage: the streets and junctions were named after Oxford Street and Piccadilly Circus. Monkeys clambered over verandas of places called Seymour Cottage in Drummond Hill Road. It was all very orderly, very Royal Navy, including smart waiters in the mess/wardroom serving up a perfectly chilled gin and tonic in the oppressive heat.

   In the morning, after too many gins, I was given a tour of the harbour in one of the fast attack craft. And it did move fast, almost leaving my heaving gin-soaked stomach at the dock. Its captain told me that during the war no one bothered with flak-jackets as the close encounter battles – some lasting a whole day – meant that the large-calibre Tiger naval guns could cut a man or his ship in half. The Sea Tigers gave no quarter – this was not a naval war involving prisoners. The insurgents specialized in swarm tactics using attack craft and suicide boats fighting in large wolfpacks. The Sri Lankan navy had to learn to out-guerrilla the guerrillas by developing their own swarm tactics and even larger numbers of boats. The key element of their victory had depended on sinking the so-called 'Pigeon' ships, the large armed warehouse vessels the Tigers deployed. One of the actions took place as far as the edge of Australian territorial waters, assisted by Indian and occasionally American naval intelligence. The main naval weakness of the government was its regular supply convoy from Trinco, as it was always called, up the north-eastern coast to reach the often besieged Jaffna outpost. As many as 1,000 troops were conveyed in one large former cruise ship, the *Jetliner*, heavily escorted by the navy and air force. The Tigers tried everything to sink this ship. Its loss might have been a turning point in the war.

Back in Colombo, I focused on senior intelligence people. Initially, I rendezvoused with colonel-level operators. They would tell me they would meet me in the comfortable and possibly discreet foyer of the Hilton hotel. Inevitably, a bit of cloak and daggery was involved about names and contacts. The first time, no problem. The second meeting with a different officer did not go to plan. A middle-aged man in a well-cut suit approached me and asked about German *Oompah* music. I had to think quickly – had I forgotten or misunderstood a coded meeting technique? I bluffed for a while by slipping into my bad German. The man looked as confused as I felt. Eventually, it emerged that he was a hotel manager. The Hilton was holding an Oktoberfest with an *Oompah* band. And the manager had assumed that my European appearance and beer belly – and perhaps my hairstyle redolent of a failed violinist (which I was) – indicated that I was a member of the visiting band. He made some polite enquiries about what sort of tunes I would be playing and when.

I made my excuses as I'd noticed a man of obvious military bearing and approached him, without mentioning any German music. It was the right colonel, and we soon began a useful working relationship. He was the handler of the country's most important political prisoner – K.P. (Kumaran Pathmanathan). Everybody in the country and LTTE called him simply K.P., however. A close friend of Prabhakaran, he had even been the equivalent of best man at his wedding. For a while, he was technically the leader of the Tigers after the warlord's death. K.P. interested me because he controlled the international LTTE network. He was a financial and logistical genius who managed the billions of dollars that supplied the movement in arms. He also controlled the fortune made in drugs and people smuggling as well as the money raised by Tamil charities throughout the world. Only a small percentage of it had been spent on the administration of Tamil Eelam in the island. K.P. had operated a shipping fleet of twenty large ships and numerous smaller fishing boats that brought in the foreign weapons, as well as running front offices to launder money in Asia, the Middle East and Africa. He concentrated on the ungoverned spaces, especially the sea.

After the war, he had been seized in Malaysia by Sri Lankan intelligence and brought to Colombo. K.P. had been kept under house arrest for over two years, although he was allowed to visit resettlement farms that he had founded as part of a reconciliation exercise, and for this reason rivals in the extant foreign network had claimed he was a collaborator. Except for one FBI visit, no Westerner had spoken to him, or so I was told by my new colonel friend, K.P.'s handler. The colonel was a fount of all knowledge on the LTTE; he had devoted all his waking hours to analyzing the Tigers. No man alive knew more than he did. Very earnest, he seemed to enjoy our long discussions on counter-insurgency. I explained that I was good at getting information from people and, jokingly, I asked if I could spend some hours with K.P. not least to find out where the tens of millions were stashed. K.P. had resisted all blandishments from the colonel. I said I would do my best, provided that I could keep 10 per cent of any money I managed to find.

Next day I sat down with K.P. in the Intelligence HQ. We chatted for about two hours, with two secret servicemen at the other end of the long room. I don't know if our conversation was bugged, but K.P. seemed completely at ease. We talked about the war, about Prabhakaran and about K.P.'s attempts to save his boss at the end, when the Tiger leadership was trapped in the final 'Cage' by the army's advance. I didn't ask where the money was; I was too involved in his personal story, not least about the boss's personal habits: he loved cooking and shooting, but hated smoking and homosexuals. And he enforced rules more fit for a monastery than a guerrilla movement. I could see why so many *bien-pensants* in Europe thought he was a cool dude. K.P. later e-mailed me in England, so he had some freedom to communicate, if not to leave Sri Lanka. I liked the guy because his answers were straightforward. He was still a believer in the cause, yet appeared to accept the war was lost and now political reconciliation was the only solution. Under the circumstances, he would say that, wouldn't he?

I spoke to other Tamil supporters, NGO people and independent journalists, mainly about the mass killings in the controversial final weeks of the war, as well as disappearances of Tamils and independently minded Sinhalese journalists after the fighting was over. Some of this could be done outside Sri Lanka. I was gaining the trust of the local intelligence community and so concentrated on that. I spent hours with the head of National Intelligence, Major General Kapila Hendawitharana, and found him fascinating and informative company. We sat in his office which provided no hint of his personality – not a plaque, picture or book. I thought this might be his 'interview' office, but later found out it was his actual workplace. I have met a number of intelligence heads – director generals as they're often called – and mostly they seem to be apparently very ordinary men, albeit nearly all good listeners and curious, by definition. Except for a few colourful African variants, they all appeared to be the neutral types you could chat to in a golf or bowls club. This is where John le Carré's vision of an understated George Smiley was so accurate, and a reflection of that author's own real experience of the spying game. Fleming's Bond was the comic-book exception, not the norm.

The owlish Sri Lankan intelligence supremo, who had insisted on creating a unified service, the equivalent of merging MI5 and MI6, had a good story to tell and he had been given clearance by the president to talk to me. He was happy to do so. It could not be one-way traffic. I had learned that senior intelligence people like to swap gossip. There was an unofficial rule: in this game, you could of course omit stuff, but passing on actual disinformation was not considered the done thing, old boy. I had no formal intelligence to trade, I was a mere historian, although I did voice general opinions on Iraq and Afghanistan, based on direct experience, not editorials in the *Guardian*.

I asked him to rate the Tigers compared with other guerrilla movements:

> Definitely one of the deadliest. They had the ground fighting troops. They had a very strong Sea Tiger wing. Their air wing spread a lot of fear and then there was a culture of suicide among the suicide cadres. No other terrorist group had all three arms.

I asked about his successes. The general beamed when he talked of sinking the Pigeon ships, the floating arsenals, and explained that his organization had persuaded one of Prabhakaran's top commanders to defect to the government side, with thousands of his fighters.

What was his greatest cock-up? He told me that he had assembled a crack team of special forces to assassinate Prabhakaran on the eve of the ceasefire in 2001. At the last minute, it was called off, and his team was stood down in a safe house near Colombo where a group of over-zealous police officers arrested them for planning a coup and the assassination of the then prime minister. General Kapila had a lot of explaining to do. And some of the plot was leaked to the media.

We were in our stride now, so I said, 'The war has ended, surely some old secrets can be told?'

He smiled mischievously, 'We suffer in silence.'

The spy chief was a man quietly suffused with a righteous anger, as well as charm. Many of the other top brass may well have paid formal obeisance to Rajapaksa Incorporated; while probably believing in the official mantra, they also had to say it publicly, and often. With the director of national intelligence, however, the fire of commitment burned deep in his psyche. He had seen so much intelligence gold turned into base metal by the fatal vacillation of previous political administrations.

I was given almost free rein to investigate in intelligence and defence HQ, particularly film footage of the war, both real and faked. I spent two whole days examining – with forensic experts and IT geeks – footage offered by LTTE sympathizers after the war and used by western TV stations, especially Channel Four News, which triggered a moral panic in some quarters, including Number 10 Downing Street. From years of film editing and despite no-doubt-biased expert analysis in Colombo, I was able to draw my own conclusions on what was faked – much of it – and what wasn't. I studied details of earlier pogroms against Tamils in the early 1980s especially, a main cause of the conflict. Atrocities had been committed by both sides in the prolonged and savage war, but I just didn't buy the claims of deliberate genocide voiced by the human rights industry. The Colombo government clearly understated the fatalities in what they called a humanitarian intervention and a massive hostage-release operation in the last months of the war. I felt, however, that Channel Four News – a programme I had produced films for and which I respected – had gone along with the exaggerated figures sold by the still highly effective LTTE propaganda lobbies in the West. In my writing I didn't and couldn't attempt a definitive number of deaths – I could try only to create a balance between extremes. Maybe neither side could really claim the moral high ground, nor would I take shelter in American or EU official labels of terrorism for the Tigers, although their urban attacks on civilians could not escape that epithet.

I was soon spending long days talking to senior intelligence people and

Everywhere I went in the former operational area I had a serious close protection unit, including this armoured vehicle. Maybe it wasn't as safe as the army had indicated.

to the man who had actually run the war effort, Gotabaya Rajapaksa, the president's brother. Gotabaya did not want to trade information. He wanted to talk, at length. I taped hours and strained my wrist with my own version of shorthand. Gotabaya had been a highly decorated fighting colonel when the war had been run by politicians who had no will to win. Disillusioned, he had quit his service and country and gone into IT in the US. When his brother, Mahinda, narrowly won the 2005 election, Gotabaya was drafted in as permanent secretary of the ministry of defence. The beefy Mahinda managed the politics, and the wiry and wily Gotabaya ran the war, while another brother, Basil, partly ran the economy. (Other relatives were also busy in the state structure and private economy.) Despite the smell of nepotism, this tight fraternity brought a fresh cohesion to the anti-Tiger conflict. Gotabaya completely revamped the armed forces, and finessed the Indians, the regional superpower. The Chinese – with their blocking vote in the UN Security Council – also provided top cover for Colombo. The Rajapaksas thus created the focus for a determination to win outright victory and the capability to ignore Western pressure, especially from Britain, France and Norway, to negotiate a compromise peace. President Rajapaksa passionately wanted to end the war that had ravaged his country for twenty-six years. Peace deals had been tried and failed, he told me. No one would derail him, he said, not even the great powers. Only India – with its 60 million Tamil voters in Tamil Nadu – could stop Colombo. The main mechanism of the government's victory was how Gotabaya worked day and night on his mobile phone to talk to India's key intelligence and security players to keep New Delhi on side, despite the bloody finale in the so-called Cage. He gave me chapter and verse of this backstairs diplomacy, all of which added extra authority to my book.

I also spoke to the police counter-intelligence people in Colombo and asked, late one evening, whether I could visit, next morning if possible, the hardcore Tigers still in captivity. I was collected at 06.00 to drive south to Galle, well known for its cricket ground. Less well known is a large nearby prison called Boosa. I wanted to go there at short notice, if possible, to avoid any set-up. The prison staff gave me relatively free access. I managed to identify the senior Tiger officer; the prison authorities denied that the prisoners operated under an internal hierarchy. The Tiger colonel spoke good English – he worked in the tiny library. Low-ranking prison officers hovered for a while, but I secured a number of conversations with the Tiger colonel and some of the inmates, chosen by me; the translations were done by the Tiger officer. Conditions seemed relatively humane although Boosa's rule of no booze, smoking or TV would cause riots nationwide in UK prisons. The main complaint was the slow pace of justice. Many of the hardcore Tigers were eventually freed and the remainder tried on specific criminal charges, though the process was cumbersome. I also investigated the handful of government servicemen who had been tried for crimes in the war.

I had covered a lot of ground in my research. I wanted, however, to speak to the president again and also get access to the Svengali of the war effort, Lalith Weeratunga, the head of the civil service and a man who seemed always at the president's side. President Rajapaksa gave me a more formal interview this time, as he was suffering from a heavy cold. His amanuensis, Lalith, amused me by finishing off some of the sentences of the ailing leader, especially when the president occasionally searched for a word in English. Most of the Sinhalese leadership spoke English well, but very fast and with a heavy accent. The president came from the rural south and was not part of the traditional Colombo political elite in which a small coterie of family dynasties indulged in ping-pong control of the presidency. Rajapaksa's trademark was always a tawny scarf to represent his rural peasant upbringing, on top of his white flowing gown symbolizing Buddhist purity. Rajapaksa was not as poised as his often Oxbridge predecessors, yet he was no fool – he had once been a campaigning human rights lawyer, an irony as half the Commonwealth was on his back in 2013 for alleged human rights abuses. The prime ministers of India and Canada refused to attend the contentious Commonwealth heads of government meeting in Colombo in November of that year.

I needed one more interview to complete my book. Lalith Weeratunga was not only the head of the civil service, but also the president's personal secretary and effectively the keeper of all the secrets. We arranged to meet in his office on his day off and he was dressed very casually. I knew he was a yoga fanatic so that perhaps added to the impression I had of a Gandhi-like figure almost levitating on his sofa. He explained that he was the only one who had kept the record of the inner war council, in spidery writing in small notebooks He showed me one, but didn't let me read much of it. That added to my impression of his pre-modern technology style. We chatted for more than the thirty minutes I had thought I had secured. I was using a trusty old-fashioned reel-to-reel tape-recorder. It had never let me down, over decades. This time it did. On the second tape change, the reel started spitting out yards of tape. An interview disaster. I pretended it was business as usual, as I stopped my notetaking to wind up the lost tape with my pen. I carried on talking, though he asked if I was getting it down. I lied and said yes. I somehow repaired my machine and also carried on with my clumsy shorthand.

I learned much about the inner workings of the National Security Council, especially the personality clashes of the heads of the army and navy. The president was always calm and collected, Lalith said, though he did once or twice get rattled enough to tell his service chiefs that they were behaving like naughty children.

The president had previously admitted to me that he had lost his temper on a few occasions in the war council meetings, especially with the quarrelsome army and navy chiefs. 'I used to laugh at them,' HE told me, 'because they reminded me of my own children when they started squabbling.'

The president was no patsy. When the then British Foreign Secretary, David Miliband and his French counterpart visited Sri Lanka to try to enforce a ceasefire in the last stages of the war, Miliband was so arrogant that HE told him in effect to fuck off, adding, 'We are no longer a British colony.'

The successful operation of the National Security Council was the key element to winning the war (and explaining my story). This is where the two brothers finessed their strategy of victory based upon: determined and unified political direction; no negotiations; ignoring Western diplomacy but keeping India in the loop; and controlling the media on the island, especially the few foreign hacks who were allowed near the fighting on the government side. (My brave colleague Marie Colvin had tried the Tiger side and lost an eye to government mortar fire.)

The military were largely given operational freedom. Like all military top brass, they quarrelled, however, not only in the war council, but also in the field. In the council, President Rajapaksa kept a tight grip, though the air force commander took it upon himself to sit between the army and navy chiefs, to block the bickering, much of which came from schoolboy animosities. Sinhalese politics was based on old-school loyalties as much as formal obeisance to Buddhist or party creeds. My fascination with how the war was conducted in the NSC, as well as the formal intelligence briefings that preceded it the day before, taught me a lot about how the war was won. It also partly explained postwar politics – why the army boss, General Sarath Fonseca, was sidelined. Seen as a popular hero, he made the mistake of standing against the Rajapaksa clan in the 2010 elections, and ended up in prison, not least because of the *lese-majesty* of an ex-army boss challenging a civilian political leader.

My detailed conversation with Lalith helped to add the final bits of the command-and-control jigsaw. We also talked in depth about how the Indians almost pulled the plug in the last days of the war, and how Gotabaya Rajapaksa schmoozed them. After two hours of talking, the Gandhi-like figure pulled out a shiny new iPad from under a pillow on the sofa.

'You should try one of these – you can record up to ten hours, or use a smartphone which can do about six hours,' he said reassuringly.

 Presumably he had been recording our meeting, much more efficiently than I had. Here was I, a professor of journalism, posing as a Western sophisticate, and I was getting – clearly much-needed – advice on interview technology. I learned much about the war, but also much about my own technical failings. I bought a smart new digital recorder as soon as I got to back to England.

When my book was published it was somewhat controversial. I explained it was not a moral tract, rather a purely military analysis of how the war was won. I made a comparison with the British Army being allowed to wipe out hundreds of IRA gunmen at the beginning of 'the Troubles'; and *perhaps* ending the war the Sri Lankan way instead of suffering the longest insurgency in Europe. I also pointed out that some Western experts, including impeccably liberal NATO top brass, had noted the possible correlation between outright victory and keeping the hacks out of the way. As a journalist I could not agree with that conclusion, but I took flak for writing such a neo-Machiavellian text. War can never be divorced from morality, and the Rajapaksa regime could not have secured real peace without real reconciliation with the Tamils. Triumphalism had to give way to healing, perhaps along the lines of the flawed but sometimes inspiring South African truth and reconciliation model. Optimists about Sri Lanka might recall the Buddhist saying: 'What the caterpillar calls the end of the world, the master calls a butterfly.'

****

In all my travels in the region, I had ignored a mate's request to visit the Doon school in the foothills of the Indian Himalayas. Peter McLaughin, an old friend from Rhodesian and Romanian adventures, was the headmaster. Doon was the equivalent of Eton, I was told. And very impressive it was too. Peter and his wife Elizabeth were wonderful hosts when I visited between Sri Lanka trips in early 2014. It was in Dehradun, an old hill station, now overpopulated and clogged with traffic. The school, however, was an immaculate island of tranquillity and discipline amid the chaos, a little bit of Victorian England in India. I did the usual temple visits including to the Rishikesh yoga centre where the Beatles had presumably stood on their heads and had their pockets emptied by the Maharishi. I was amazed to see so many old hippies from the 1960s as well as their current variants. Personally, if I wanted peace, it was the last place I would visit.

I was not over-impressed by the area, not least because of the projectile vomiting – mainly my own. It was lucky that I was in a comfortable house, with a big en-suite bathroom, and a school doctor on immediate call. I recovered by sitting in the well-tended garden of the headmaster's house. The head gardener was called Gunga Din. No, really. I spent hours trying to work out a possible conversation with Mr Din, which would end with 'You're a better man than I am, Gunga Din.' Not easy when the head gardener spoke not a word of English and I knew nothing of Hindi.

I spent a few days in Delhi, partly to visit the grand buildings designed by Sir Edwin Lutyens. My home village of Shere owed much to the master imperial architect. He had spent four years in the village because of an unrequited love affair with the daughter of the local lord of the manor. Perhaps to pass the time and vent some of his frustration he did much to improve Shere's style. Delhi's Viceroy's Palace was his masterpiece. Designed in the early 1920s though not completed until 1929, it was hubris in marble. Created to represent the permanence and power of the Raj, it was clear even then that the days of empire were numbered. I enjoyed visiting the Red Fort too. The museum inside the grounds displayed details of the 'Indian Mutiny' – or first war of independence. Schooled as I was in the history of imperial India – I had read my M.M. Kaye and Flashman of course – it was refreshing, and disturbing, to see Indian re-assertion from the other side. My time working in Pakistan had always suggested to me that partition was a crime and a disaster; getting the Indian perspective was moving and instructive.

In the Red Fort, I was accosted by an American army officer who had served in Iraq. He heard my English accent and came up and asked whether I had an intrinsic affinity with the country because of the past legacy. I explained that as a historian I had grown up with tales of the Raj, so yes. It was true, I seemed to know a lot about the history and the names all brought back memories of my more youthful reading (and stamp collecting). Yet of course I knew little about modern India. And it was unlikely that I would find out the truth. My airline ticket had been purchased before I tried to secure my visa. What an elaborate, time-consuming and expensive exercise that was. If I hadn't already paid for a ticket I would have given up. I knew that the Indians were making it tough for Brits, in retaliation for visa restrictions on Indians, but it was a bureaucratic nightmare, made worse by the fact that the application had a special section on applicants with military or defence backgrounds. A famous friend had recently been invited to an all-expenses-paid trip to an Indian literary festival and simply turned it down when she started trying to get a visa. Brits travelling to India independently – be warned.

The Red Fort in Delhi.

Chapter 7

Africa's Longest War

Sudan: a tale of two countries

The civil war started in Sudan in 1955 even before the British had upped sticks. I began covering the conflict there from 1996. It was not a popular war for journalists, not just because of the inaccessibility of the fighting. Khartoum in the Muslim north was very dry, in all senses. In the largely Christian and animist south, booze was technically available, but rare. And it sometimes involved long hikes to find it. I achieved something of a record for arrests when I first visited. In the first hour in the country in August 1996 I was arrested with cameraman Irwin Armstrong, despite being in possession of a hard-earned press pass, for filming a male tailor working in a Khartoum bazaar. I had asked the tailor very politely. His old-fashioned treadle-powered machine would add a touch of colour.

Someone had been watching us. We were soon shoved into a Mercedes by some heavies. I asked the driver under whose authority he was arresting us.

'Mine,' he said with a pukka English accent.

I almost asked him which Oxbridge college he had attended. Instead, I said, 'And who might you be?'

'The Minister of Justice.'

A fair cop, I thought. He raved about our filming people and saying they were slaves. I refused to give him the tape and we were politely released from the central police station after a few hours. I met the minister a few times over the years and it became something of a joke in government circles. Because of the condemnation of human rights abuses, Sudan had gained a reputation for being not a country but a near-death experience. I had much rougher times in the south and in Darfur in the following years; by and large, however, the Sudanese reputation for hospitality was justified during my following, often extended, visits.

Sudan became a country the US loved to hate and imposed heavy sanctions on Khartoum. Sudan had made a basic error in hosting Osama bin Laden from 1991 to 1996. I had long been interested in Osama, ever since I worked in Afghanistan in the 1980s and my temporary base was next to an Arab jihadist camp which was said to host the Saudi warlord. Whenever we got too close the 'Arabs' would fire on my Afghan companions. I had tried to interview Mr bin Laden in Khartoum, but, rather ungraciously I thought, he quit the country, under American pressure,

Sudan and the Darfur region.

a few days before I could try to speak to him. Osama called Khartoum 'a mix of religion and organized crime'; the Sudanese had booted him out, leaving over $50 million of his assets behind. Thereafter it was rumoured for years that he had taken refuge back there again. One Canadian diplomat teased me with, 'There have been many sightings of Osama – about the equal number of times as alleged sightings of Elvis.'

I served my time in Sudan, going to the eastern war, along the border with Eritrea, and to the south, including visiting the besieged town of Juba, and numerous visits to that massively misreported war in Darfur. I accompanied government forces in Darfur as well as the Sudan Liberation Army rebels, festooned with their amulets, which they (wrongly) believed turned enemy bullets into water. Eventually, I got my feet under the table a little: I interviewed President Omar al-Bashir at his home, as well as the main spiritual mentor of the 1989 revolution, Dr Hassan al-Turabi. Parodied in Khartoum as the 'Islamic Pope', I ended up as his house guest on a number of occasions. He was equally at home in tie or turban, and could run circles

The SLA (Sudan Liberation Army) rebels in Darfur. I took this picture in 2008.

around his political rivals in French, English and Arabic. He had all the charm of a snake-oil salesman, but he was very intelligent, an enlightened theologian though a poor political tactician. In trying to set up an international jihad, based in Khartoum, which became 'a jihadist Davos in the desert', he fell out with the more pragmatic General Omar al-Bashir who eventually kicked him out of power. I also became friendly with a wide range of opposition politicians, north and south.

The key to influence in dictatorships is always first getting to know the president and then the intelligence and military chiefs. It took me some years, though I managed it. I was the first Westerner to interview the 6-foot 4 defence minister, General Bakri. He was a thickset towering figure who was said to terrify even his superiors. He certainly terrified me. The intelligence chiefs in the secret police (the *Mukhabarat*) I found more amenable and urbane. After 9/11 they went out of their way to court the West, especially the CIA and MI6. The enhanced demonstration effect of the US-led invasion of Afghanistan and Iraq transformed the *Mukhabarat* into one of the CIA's closest 'friends'. So much so that its chief, Saleh Gosh, spent a week at Langley, the HQ of the CIA, as an honoured guest. He was feted in a fashion usually reserved for senior spooks from major NATO states.

In October 2005 I attended an elaborate garden party in the grounds of the new National Security HQ in Khartoum. Saleh Gosh was the host; he was in good spirits, backslapping his peers and even dancing on stage while the band played. Many of the top spooks in Africa – it was a summit for director generals of intelligence agencies – had assembled in the Sudanese capital. It was officially called the 'Fourth Conference of the Committee for Intelligence and Security Systems in Africa', which operated under the AU umbrella. No one could complain about the quality of the food, and big water fans kept the guests cool. Spooks rarely let their guards down, but this was a unique occasion to relax among very discreet peers. MI6 and the CIA had sent senior people. They were incognito of course, so they did not expect Major General Gosh to call the senior CIA officer forward, by name, to step up to the well-lit platform and give him a handshake and a hug, a mark of a close male relationship in northern Sudan. The CIA man smiled awkwardly when he was given a spangly carrier bag full of small gifts. Then the MI6 spook was called up and given the same treatment. It was a touching display of rapport in the intelligence world, but a tiny bit awkward as a sprinkling of senior press people had been invited (to advertise that Khartoum was respectable again). I sat next to a distinguished journalist who wrote for the UK *Guardian*, a newspaper not always favoured by the intelligence community.

My good contacts in the country, with various shades of opinion, led to requests for my Centre to run an observer mission for the 2010 election. The British, Americans and Norwegians had helped to end the longest war in Africa's biggest country in 2005, when Khartoum signed the Comprehensive Peace Agreement (CPA) with the southern rebels, the Sudan People's Liberation Army, led by John Garang. (The usual abbreviation was SPLA for the army and the SPLM for the political movement.) Despite Garang's suspicious death soon after, a government of national unity was set up in Khartoum. The southern ministers now had smart cars and offices. What really mattered, though, were oil money and security.

The new autonomous government of South Sudan (GoSS) in Juba, led by President Salva Kiir, appeared to have earnestly adopted all the bad habits they learned from Khartoum (as well as Kampala and Nairobi). The wealth was centralized in Juba among fat-cat commanders-turned-politicians and most of the oil money was spent on weapons. The SPLM officials were quite open about this; they said it was a prudent policy of insurance against the north should the CPA fall apart. As in Pakistan, the SPLA was an army that happened also to run a country. By 2009 GoSS had received about $6 billion in oil money, though perhaps as much as 90 per cent was ostensibly spent on re-equipping the army. Amid a sea of corruption and cronyism, very little was left over for funding education, health and agriculture as well as infrastructure, which was largely provided by foreign donors.

South Sudanese cohesion was required not least to begin the shift from army politics to the development of the country. One visiting Western economist told me he thought Juba was 'a scrap heap built on a rubbish dump'. To be fair, it had been under siege for over twenty years. The standard yardstick usually quoted was that only thirty miles of tarred road had been built by GoSS, and these roads were in the capital, around the new high-walled villas owned by senior politicians. Smart new government buildings had been erected, with carefully marked-out white lines in the car parks for the fleets of government Land Cruisers.

Outside Juba, the country was starving and wrecked. In early 2010 I stopped off at a small village halfway between Juba and Torit. I was invited to take tea with the headman, who introduced me to the sole teacher in the village school. The teacher pointed at the dirt track – supposedly a main highway – and complained of no road-building.

'Nor have we been given any schoolbooks,' he said. 'We have none at all.' He listed other things that he'd asked Juba for, but not received. 'There is not a single tractor for miles,' he added.

What have five years of your own government brought you then?

'Nothing – but we'll all vote for the SPLA, for freedom next year.' And he smiled.

Entrepreneurs had moved in from Uganda, Ethiopia and Kenya and developed small businesses in and around Juba, including the occasional hotel. For thirsty travellers from the *sharia* north, a new South African brewery had been built as well. The local Equatorians, however, felt doubly squeezed – by the Dinka tribal dominance in the new government and job competition from foreign workers. Overall, South Sudan had developed very little in five years, despite the often tireless efforts of foreign NGOs and lots of American money. In the words of one British

Some of the observer team in South Sudan, 2010.

financial journalist, 'Southern Sudan was beginning to resemble a new African phenomenon, a pre-failed state – prostrate and enfeebled before it was born.'

Khartoum in the north had enjoyed boom times, however. The oil bonanza, championed by Chinese, Malaysian and Indian companies, had created lots of new infrastructure, from the massive Merowe dam scheme to roads and power stations as well as the sparkling new international airport. Despite the UN arms embargo on Darfur, China and Russia continued to supply the bulk of imported Sudanese weapons; both nations insisted nothing was going to Darfur, although it was the main centre of fighting once the CPA was agreed with the south.

Armed by China, Russia, Ukraine and Belarus, and boosted by new investments from, especially, Qatar and Turkey on top of Beijing's financial largesse, Khartoum had less need to bend to American diktats. Paradoxically, massive amounts of food aid from the West, especially America, were going not only to the south and Darfur, but also to the north, not least for the large refugee camps around Khartoum. An American UN worker told me that he had questioned a Dinka tribesman from the south who was wearing a cross but standing at a Red Crescent feeding centre in the capital. The American asked the Dinka about the cross. The man laughed. 'I might be a Muslim in the morning, a Christian in the afternoon, but at night I pray to my own [Dinka] god.' No synagogue had survived in the capital, but I used to make a point of visiting church services in Khartoum and saw no problems, just as I have visited mosques freely throughout the world.

*****

Even before the intervention by the International Criminal Court, which branded Sudan's president a war criminal because of his actions in Darfur, Omar al-Bashir had despaired of working with the West – he constantly felt betrayed by their broken promises, not least on sanctions and removal from the terror list. US sanctions did make life difficult. One senior finance minister told me that removal of Washington's restrictions would improve the economy by perhaps 40 to 50 per cent. Because nearly all Western credit cards worked through a central system in New York, it forced northern Sudan to be a totally cash (or barter) economy. Paying for everything in wads of US dollars created numerous problems, not least for visiting foreign businessmen and diplomats, and it encouraged corruption inside

Omar al-Bashir, photographed at his farm where I interviewed him in 2014 (Tony Denton).

the country. It also led to actual shortages of dollars, not always provided by the Chinese who often preferred barter deals – oil for projects. The cauterization of the Sudanese economy did, however, prove a boon when the Western economic depression hit in 2008; by accident, Khartoum was largely immune.

By 2010 Darfur had been largely contained as a military problem. There was no peace, but the conflict was low intensity, and the food programmes were working. Health, education and nutritional standards had surpassed pre-war levels and were often higher than the east and south of the country. Yes, the scorched-earth tactics of both sides had driven hundreds of thousands into camps, now increasingly looking like the permanent semi-towns inhabited by the Palestinian diaspora. Few could expect to return to their villages, destroyed or re-settled by nomadic tribes. The refugee camps would store up anger for the desert *intifada*s of the future.

The Elections

The presidential elections in 1996 and 2000 were highly controlled affairs with limited electorates, although the government made much of Bashir's popular mandate. The last reasonably democratic elections had been held as far back as 1986. Now, under the aegis of the Western-backed CPA, a free and fair election had to be held in the whole country, despite Bashir's dominance in the north and the equally dominant SPLM in the south, as well as trying to run elections in the devastation that was Darfur. It was a tough call and worrying for Khartoum because lots of foreign busybodies had to be allowed in as election observers.

I included myself as a 'busybody'. I was head of mission for fifty independent British observers, organized by the Centre for Foreign Policy Analysis, the small London think tank of which I was director. The team comprised experienced British civil servants, mainly from the Ministry of Defence, former British officers, lawyers, academics, and local government officials with election expertise, as well as observers from previous EU and UN missions. Some were long-term observers, serving in the country for two to three months, but most were short-term, placed throughout the south and partially in the north. We were excluded from Darfur. On the eve of the arrival of the main body of my foreign observers, plus the larger influx from the EU and American Carter Center, President Bashir made an ill-tempered and ill-judged intervention. He warned any foreigners who tried to delay or interrupt the elections that 'we will cut off their fingers and put them under our shoes'. I had some trouble explaining to my teams about to leave from the UK that this was mere hyperbolic Arab rhetoric and could be dismissed. They would be met by hospitality, I said, and they were. What could not be so easily dismissed were the many obstacles that could prevent a free and fair election: inaccurate census numbers, gerrymandering (especially in Darfur), censorship and limiting air time and rallies for opposition politicians in the north. In the south, the SPLM were intimidating their much smaller rivals.

My teams traversed the country and were generally met with friendliness and co-operation, not least from the UN. One female member of a team in Wau, Maggie, was assaulted by an SPLA policeman, but she bravely stayed at her post. She had endured worse during protests in Belfast, she told me. We came across many irregularities; for example, party members – innocently or maliciously – often tried to 'help' people to cast their ballot, especially among the vast majority of the illiterate voters in the south. The voting method – for national president, regional president, governors, state and national assembles – was very complex, based on a mixture of US, French and British models. Twenty-five per cent of seats in the assemblies were reserved for females, and women, especially in the south, were vocally enthusiastic voters.

Bashir did a lot a better than his own party expected: he won 68 per cent of the vote for national president, although most of the northern challengers were straw men and women, and some dropped out because of the government's restrictions on campaigning, especially free and equal access to radio and TV. Salva Kiir took 93 per cent for the southern presidency, although the old warhorse Lam Akol complained to me personally, regularly and bitterly, by phone and e-mail, about how he and his candidates were bullied by the SPLM. In the end, in north and south, the elections confirmed the existing domination of the two leaders. The results were predictable, but were they fair?

The larger EU and Carter Center observer teams basically said 'good try, but you didn't meet international standards'. Nevertheless, the earnest and affable former president, Jimmy Carter, said the elections were 'relatively peaceful, calm and orderly'. Of course, the AU and Arab League, many of whose representatives would not recognize a free election if it bit them on the backside, raved about the election process. The verdict produced by the Centre for Foreign Policy Analysis came somewhere in between the two extremes. Its final report said:

> After continuous disaffection or war since 1955, the fact that a national election was held in Africa's largest country, with few traditions of democratic contests, widespread illiteracy and poor infrastructure, especially in the south, is to be commended. We consider the election to be a credible and important step on the road to political pluralism.

The Centre's teams did offer a number of recommendations to improve the process for next time, especially the forthcoming referendum in the south. To temper what some might judge to be the patronizing tone of the Centre's final verdict, it was also noted that these elections would have confused even a sophisticated Western electorate. In the concurrent UK national election, foreign electoral observers in Britain noted failures, not least in postal voting, lack of IDs, shortage of ballot papers and closure of some polling stations while angry queues remained outside.

Some of the observers grounded, literally, in the grounds of the Hilton, Khartoum.

In South Sudan, the fact that the presidential candidate, Salva Kiir, had to go to three polling stations to find his name could be forgiven, perhaps, in the first and most inclusive and free elections ever held in the south. The Brits, on the other hand, should have known, and done, better.

Then I faced one of the most difficult problems of my career. The all-volunteer team I led worked hard to help the electoral process in Sudan. They were just about to fly home from Khartoum airport, when suddenly all flights to and from much of the northern hemisphere were stopped because of the ash cloud erupting from an Icelandic volcano. I faced my toughest challenge: keeping fifty irritable and homesick Brits happy, occupied, housed and fed in an expensive city where they could not use credit cards or alcohol. I asked Marty, a tough and affable former Royal Marine, to act as 'entertainments officer' to keep the troops occupied. Equally important, I appointed an 'escape officer' to work fulltime on trying to tunnel out. Most eventually got home to Britain ten days later.

Herding so many eccentric Brits had been demanding. A few, I came to realize, might deserve to be sectioned in the UK – although I suppose it took a mad kind of courage to volunteer for the trip in the first place. None were paid, although expenses were covered. Some of the conditions were tough, even dangerous. Four of the team, including two women, were surrounded in a small hotel-cum-brothel in Bentiu by drunken and aggressive SPLA soldiers. It was later alleged that I tried to call in a UN air strike to rescue them. That was an exaggeration, but it was my job to move heaven and earth with endless calls to UN HQ that did almost set off a column of armoured cars to rescue them – at night. I persuaded an influential oil man to fly them out in the end – the UN was often over-extended. At one stage one of the most experienced observers, a former RAF officer, sent me a formal signal warning me that I should abort the southern part of the mission because of the dangers. I didn't, but spent the night working out a plan to keep the less militarily-experienced and older people (and lawyers) in the safer north. Even they managed to get into scrapes. I was obsessed by security and safety – all the team members had received detailed verbal and written warnings about obvious things such as not taking photographs of bridges. It was no use arguing in London that you could see all the bridges on Google Earth. That cut no ice with an illiterate drunken jobsworth with a new gun. I had to deal with one major and one minor incident to do with people taking photographs of damn bridges. The daily sitreps [situation reports] from the UN began to include embarrassing references to my teams' cock-ups. And I had to take all the responsibility, of course.

Luckily, many of the observers' tales were good-humoured. Marty had been on tough tours with the marines in Afghanistan, but he was almost brained by a large falling mango in Juba. 'Death by Mango,' he quipped, 'after all I've been through.' A female observer was very bossy and very efficient, but she enjoyed

The rarely visited pyramids to the north of Khartoum. We organised a few excursions, not least to the wonderfully unspoiled pyramids, to keep the troops entertained.

her (well-earned) nickname of 'Sergeant Major'. Most of the team did their jobs quietly and efficiently and caused me no hassle, although one lady, let us call her Dolores, caused 75 per cent of the problems. Extreme conditions – though Sudan did not compare with Iraq or Afghanistan – often produce surprising results. As I had seen before, some of the macho males were tearfully overcome, especially when the flights were delayed for two weeks by the Icelandic volcanic ash.

Many of the English roses proved to be very resilient. The civil servants tended to be smallminded, not least about expenses. The observers' contracts had expired the day they were due to fly out. I had no legal obligation to look after anybody after that date, but I borrowed a large sum of money from a business friend in Khartoum and put up everybody in the former Hilton. Yet some complained about sharing a large (same sex) twin-bed room. I shouldn't give names, but I will say that my journalist colleagues, Irwin Armstrong – who was used to Sudan – and cameraman Marty Stalker were my twin towers of strength. A few military types I can't mention because they weren't supposed to be on loan/leave from the MoD. Professor Stephen Chan was most helpful in writing my final report. David Leach and Judy Larkin led the team who crunched all the numbers from the thousands of check sheets from polling stations. The ten-day enforced stay because of the ash cloud gave me a willing team of helpers who saved me a lot of work when I got home. And the insurance money – not least from an initially reluctant airline – helped to defray my extra expenses. To cap it all, the communications officer, Ben, fell in love with Uthayla, the elegant and energetic Sudanese woman who ran the observer mission office in Khartoum. He converted to Islam and now they live almost next door to me in the Surrey Hills. Ben is a Bray, the family of the traditional lords of the manor in Shere for over 500 years. It was an interesting coincidence that Edwin Lutyens's infatuation with a Bray girl ensured his long stay in the village which did so much to enhance the architectural charm that initially attracted me to the place. Generations later, I was partly instrumental in introducing a Sudanese and Islamic element to the Church of England rituals that had long dominated community life.

I was also reliant on the UN, especially Heidi Modro in Khartoum. The UN did an impressive job – their separate mission in the south (UNMIS – UN Mission in Sudan) had pulled out all the stops, despite their usual lack of resources, especially air transport. The large (and occasionally imperious) EU mission, however, complained of a failure of UN co-operation. As Mission Head, I attended some of the top-level ambassadorial meetings. I was astounded at the vituperation I sometimes witnessed: the most remarkable was the dressing down the deputy head of the EU delegation gave to the UN chief. The EU representative angrily and repeatedly waved and collapsed her fan – she was Spanish – and then used it to metaphorically jab the startled UN man, accompanied by a loud Latin torrent of criticism. The urbane Indian brigadier present had to try to calm the meeting. And they would have to do it all again the following year, for the referendum.

President Bashir felt vindicated – he had held an election under intense international scrutiny and he judged that he had won the approval of the north. Bashir knew that the south would vote the same way again – overwhelmingly for Salva Kiir, who was committed to separation from Sudan. John Garang had been dead for five years. The SPLM would always revere him, but the vast majority of his followers had fought for independence, not federalism. And what had the north fought for? If the south broke away, what had all the lost lives been for? And could the north survive if southern oil was turned off or diverted? Perhaps the majority of northerners had had enough of war and jihad and prayed for that rare thing, an amicable divorce. Some hardliners in the military and intelligence services, however, grumbled that their president had gambled and lost. The potential coup plotters would bide their time and wait for the referendum results and the immediate aftermath of the likely independence.

The southern referendum

South Sudan was set to become the fifty-fourth African state in July 2011 – would premature and triumphalist celebrations prompt the resumption of the long war? This time I was there with a film crew, not as an observer. Irwin, Marty and I were joined by an old American friend, Sam Dealey.

On the flight down to Juba in an ancient plane of questionable airworthiness, Sam said to me, 'I could be sitting next to a nice fire at home in Washington, cuddling a honey, instead of sitting with you in a death trap.'

I mentioned it was my birthday. 'At least we can get a beer in Juba. As long as I have good friends to drink with, I don't mind being in another war-torn dump.'

'So are you going to fly in some friends, then?' Sam asked.

I didn't tell him that, although I valued his friendship and journalist skills, it was also handy to have a prominent American, a former editor of a national newspaper, with us. I didn't expect any hostage situation on this trip, but the Americans tend to kick up a fuss in such circumstances. From long experience I knew the British Foreign Office would do little, except tut-tut and bring a prisoner a bar of soap. The UK embassy in Khartoum had shown little interest in my observer mission the previous year.

We were rarely obstructed in our travels in the south, but media registration was a trial. The UN had repeatedly told GoSS that this was a unique opportunity to attract positive publicity and possibly investment by welcoming the hundreds of hacks who had expended the time, trouble and expense to get to inaccessible Juba. Rip-off prices for accommodation and transport were to be expected, but the expensive obstacle race – $100 per person per stamp, around various government offices to pay cash for a permit to travel, report, write and possibly breathe – angered the most seasoned of old Africa hands. GoSS's corruption and inept bureaucracy were vividly showcased. My team received some of the required

Irwin (obscured by camera) and I filming an interview in South Sudan during the referendum, 2011.

permits and accreditation via urgent UN intercession. It was a bad start for the world's coverage of the referendum, and the new country.

The referendum was held over seven days in January 2011. Previously, 3.9 million of the estimated eight million southerners had registered to vote. And nearly every registered voter turned out, with over 99 per cent opting for an independent south Sudan. Except for isolated incidents, the voting was peaceful. Al Jazeera, which had over forty personnel in the south, played up the possibility of border clashes and northern intervention, but this did not materialize. The referenda were 'delayed' in the three large disputed border areas, however. They remain delayed.

Elsewhere in the ten southern states the voters showed patience and commitment as they queued in the heat after walking miles to isolated polling stations. According to Western international observers, the polling was largely free and fair. Voting by southerners in the north was very low compared with the south, though an estimated 180,000 southerners made their way back, by road or river, to vote in their homeland.

While endorsing the process, international observers did note problems with voter registration, especially eligibility to vote, and a lack of voter education. As in the previous year's election, many enthusiastic would-be voters could not find their names even when they found the correct polling stations. Much assisted voting was witnessed, though this was again usually well-intentioned because of the very high levels of illiteracy. Many examples of security officials, especially police, being present inside the polling centres were also recorded. Nevertheless, it was absolutely clear that southerners voted en masse and freely – often passionately – for independence.

The referendum may have demonstrated a heartfelt desire for independence, but it also showed the shortcomings of the fledgling government of south Sudan. Southerners living in the north – two to three million had fled there during the decades of war – were urged by the southern government to return home. Thousands came by river along the White Nile. Marty, an ex-Royal Marine, displayed a curious obsession with trying to board – from our small speedboat – one of the large Nile barges as they cruised past. To film on board, he said, but it had more to do with his training, I suspected. He and Irwin managed the leap, but Sam and I stayed in our boat, allegedly to look after our kit.

The gruelling river journey usually took two and a half weeks from Khartoum. When the passengers reached Juba port many were exhausted and some, especially children, were ill. In a few cases clergymen brought their whole congregations with them. Stephen Taban, of the Episcopalian church, had lived for twenty-two years in Khartoum. He pointed at the numerous people camped around him at the port: 'Some had relatives here, others don't. Some don't have food to eat. They really need help.' Despite having to squat at the port, most were glad to be home, but complained about the lack of support from GoSS. The government responded by setting up mobile clinics, although the medical reception for the returnees was generally inadequate. Jobs and homes for the many returnees would still have to be found in one of the poorest regions of Africa.

Three men in a boat. On the Nile, with Irwin (centre) and Marty Stalker (left). Marty, the ex-Marine, was obsessed with boarding the large boats passing by at some speed.

Many northerners – often Muslim businessmen – chose to return to the north either temporarily during the referendum, fearing rioting or looting, or in some cases left permanently. Many shops in the Muslim business area of Juba had shut during the referendum. The businessmen said that no local pressure had been put on them, though some had returned to Khartoum because of concerns among their relatives in the north. Yet other northern businessmen – many who had lived in the south for their whole lives – claimed that up to 5,000 merchants – in the countryside *outside* Juba – had not been allowed to get back their farms and shops which had been seized by the SPLA, despite promises from the ruling party.

South Sudan was desperately underdeveloped. Approximately 90 per cent of the inhabitants lived on less than a dollar a day. Half required food aid. Corruption was endemic. The prime issue was still a settled border. Disputes, particularly over oil-rich Abyei, festered. Besides aid, South Sudan was almost totally dependent on oil – 80 per cent of proven reserves were in the south, but the pipelines to the sea from the landlocked south ran through northern Sudan. Peaceful co-operation made sense. Talk of building alternative pipelines, though difficult terrain, to the sea via Kenya did *not* make sense, because of the high costs and the probability that southern oil output would soon peak and then decline rapidly. North and south oil connections were like two lungs in one body.

Even if a resumption of war were avoided, South Sudan had to contend with numerous other difficulties, not least the crisis of expectations of its own people. SPLM leaders insisted that their new country would be like South Africa. They were (understandably) irritated when I suggested it could be another devastated basketcase like Zimbabwe. So would South Sudan be a multi-party democratic state? That was asking a lot of the cocksure dominant party, the SPLM.

I spoke to Joseph Lagu, the veteran military commander, just after the referendum results were announced. He grew rather animated and waved his stick at me, when I asked about the country's poverty. 'I don't know why people call us the poorest people in Africa,' he said, 'when we have oil under the surface of our soil. And we have got other minerals and we have got green agricultural land.' Yes, the country had many prospects but, as the last decades had shown, nothing could happen without peace.

The referendum was peaceful – so would be the reactions of the north, it was hoped. The state would be recognized, not least by their African neighbours. Nevertheless, a successful breakaway worried the African Union, which faced separatist movements throughout Africa. Bashir's visit to Juba and positive comments while in the south helped to soothe tensions. He did not treat the south as an awkward stepchild; rather he would magnanimously be the first to recognize the new republic.

Irwin and Marty had made what we considered a good film on the referendum. Sam had filed stories in the US. We had not been shot at or arrested. Oddly, Marty was avidly reading one of my books about dangerous times in Afghanistan and Iraq (when I was much younger and fitter). The tough ex-marine asked me, 'Is this the safest thing you've done?'

'I am not superstitious, Marty, but I'll tell you when I get home.'

Independence

The independence of the Republic of South Sudan on 9 July 2011 was the culmination of a complicated international peace process that consumed a decade of haggling and intermittent violence. The mood of celebration, especially in Juba, was understandable. The joys of statehood and freedom were tangible. Consignments of the new flag, based on the former emblem of the SPLA, were shipped in from a helpful China. The creation of the new national anthem, the words created by a collective of poets and the music involving a national competition, was on everybody's lips. 'Oh black warriors, let's stand up in silence and respect, saluting our martyrs whose blood cemented our national foundation.' Not a potential Eurovision hit, though it went down well locally. Peace now promised so much; it also created a crisis of expectation – a wish list as long as the Nile.

A new currency was yet to be produced to replace the Sudanese one. And a place had to be found in the UN. The hall of the General Assembly was full. When a place was created, because the listing is in English alphabetical order, the fledgling country would be placed next to South Africa, if it decided on just 'South Sudan'. There was, typically, still much dispute about what the country should be called – 'South Sudan' was seen as a British or northern construct and insufficiently African. Purists preferred 'Nile' somewhere in the title. Juba's UN diplomats had yet to set up an office in New York. When South Sudan became a full member of the UN, it could organize its own postage stamps through the Universal Postal Union. For the time being, the post had to work through the system based in Khartoum.

A new internet domain had to be agreed. One that was possible was 'SS', though that had obviously negative connotations. South Sudan also wanted to develop its own national football team and take part in the 2012 Olympics. So many grand plans and such a pitiful national infrastructure. Freedom was a heady brew, but in the 2011 drought South Sudanese could not eat freedom. Also, the country had one of the worst maternal mortality rates in the world. And over 84 per cent of women were totally illiterate. At least they could aspire to learn to read in English, the official language.

Technically, South Sudan was a rich country, full of very poor people. Around 95 per cent of government revenue came from oil. Agricultural potential was high, yet the farms and estates had been devastated by war. Statistically the country was already a failed state, so how could it rebuild itself? Foreign aid could help to feed the eight million population in the short term, though aid is addictive, undermines local initiative and often fuels corruption and cronyism.

Mass population transfers and religious and ethnic cleansing were then a clear danger, which could have been resolved by a deal on dual citizenship, though even more pressing were tribal conflicts in the south. Border fighting in Abyei and in South Kordofan dragged on throughout 2011. Common sense dictated that the two new countries should settle on an amicable divorce to share the oil wealth. The sharing of the national debt had to be settled too. Many southern leaders tended to blame the Islamist regime in the north for nearly all their woes. This was the central myth. The northern armies had been brutal; they had stirred up ethnic discontent and supported rival southern militias. Most of the southern travails since 2005 were largely self-inflicted due to bad governance, however.

Just as Mugabe's regime blamed all its ills on foreigners instead of rectifying its own domestic follies, so too Juba developed the habit of blaming everything on Khartoum. As one experienced foreign Sudan-watcher observed, 'If someone is run over in Juba, Khartoum will get the blame.' Corruption, tribalism, military overspending, and autocratic one-party rule threatened South Sudan with another Eritrea or, worse, Somalia.

Many of the SPLA leaders were good commanders, though some were feeble politicians. Too much power had been pulled into the centre, with precious little development or authority in the regions. Much of the war was about marginalization, yet this still persisted. The SPLA/M government – only a small opposition had been elected in the national and state parliaments – needed to stop scapegoating Khartoum and start putting its own house in order. Domestic security was much more important than border security. It was very easy to blame all domestic woes on 'tribalism'. The internal fighting was as much intra-tribal as inter-tribal. Security would be difficult while so many citizens were armed. Attempts to disarm local militias often made things worse, however, as everyone complained about their own disarmament, while claiming that rival groups were allowed to keep their guns. It was a case of gun-toting Nimbyism. Many of the domestic fights had nothing to do with tribe, but all to do with politics, local grudges or access to resources in drought areas. Cattle raiding by well-armed gangs of young men, often beholden to no authority, and frustrated, literally, by the surge in bride prices, were often the cause of friction.

The solution to marginalization did suggest more local autonomy, yet this fed ethnic cronyism. On the other hand, over-centralized control in Juba smacked of military authoritarianism. This was the development paradox that Juba and many other African states faced. Professor Tim Allen, of the London School of Economics, headed a large research team during the build-up to independence. His report, *Southern Sudan at Odds with Itself,* indicated that the main peace dividends expected were 'personal security and access to resources'. Certainly, the usual squabbling and disharmony among the numerous layers of international aid from the UN and NGOs caused problems, said Professor Allen. But his main conclusion was that Juba had to put its own affairs in order. Even if northern Sudan did not, *in extremis*, invade to seize the oilfields, South Sudan had to energize every resource to escape being a failed state.

National freedom had come; it was precarious on the border, but even more so *within* the borders. President Kiir had been an able military commander. He had to become a statesman if he were to avoid a warfare state with one-party (or one-tribe) rule. Salva Kiir had won his war, but could he win the peace?

Aftermath

Bashir was still in power in Khartoum, although he had 'lost the south' according to his internal critics, mainly in the military-intelligence nexus. Some securocrats even quietly suggested that their president's International Criminal Court millstone was an impediment to his continuation in office. Most of the senior leaders I spoke to felt that the president had shown courage in risking all for a southern peace deal. One of the most powerful ruling party leaders, Dr Ibrahim Ghandour, told me starkly, 'They [southerners] are not ready for government.' He also said that the president felt 'disheartened' by the breakdown of the CPA. 'But he went to Juba and stated publicly that he would accept the result of the referendum.' The president's take was poignant. He told me in early 2014, 'I saw the suffering of the people in the south and the famine. I decided it was better to have two Sudans with peace.'

Border fighting continued after southern independence. Salva Kiir made his first visit to Khartoum as head of an independent state. Bashir and Kiir had always had a good military man to military man relationship. Bashir confided to me, 'Personally, we're good friends, but sometimes he had some bad guys around him.' So they sat down alone to try to resolve their disputes on the border and oil revenues. Despite their personal rapport, the dynamics of the conflicts, especially in the south, now seemed almost beyond their control. And Khartoum became embroiled in the Arab Spring. Using the oasis town of Kufra, Khartoum sent military support to the rebels in Libya and finally helped topple a bitter enemy, Gaddafi. Ironically, in this war, Bashir was acting as an ally of NATO.

Then the big north-south break erupted. In January 2012 South Sudan turned off the oil because of failure to agree on transit fees. This made little sense for the struggling new state. Nearly all its income came from oil and, although state spending was slashed, the shortfall could not be made up by foreign aid. The influential American *Foreign Policy* magazine graphically summed up the situation: 'World Bank to South Sudan – Are you out of your freaking mind?' The closure was costing at least $20 million a day.

Meanwhile, Juba's new administration was failing. Overstaffing with so much unemployment was understandable, but 90 ambassadors were appointed and, in typically African fashion, the cabinet grew in inverse proportion to the economy.

Corruption had become rampant and blatant in Juba. It was discovered that government payments were being made to individual cows. Although many of the wonderful lyre-horned cows in the country did have their own names, the money was intended for humans. Many SPLM members felt a sense of entitlement: cronyism and graft were dues for fighting in the liberation struggle and for long years in the bush. Even when caught with their hands in the till, the guilty party members would say brazenly to accusers, 'What were you doing when we were fighting?' Salva Kiir had to resort to writing letters to request seventy-five former and serving senior government officials to return an estimated $4 billion in stolen funds. Much of it had ended up in banks in Nairobi and the sums disclosed were just the proverbial tip of the iceberg. The former freedom fighters had become public looters. Graft and the new austerity because of the oil stoppage could not be easy bedfellows. Nor could the oil simply be turned back on – closing and re-opening the pipelines and refineries required months of repair and maintenance to get the black gold flowing gain, even if the politics were sorted. Turning the taps off made no sense.

Despite renewed talks, border fighting continued. At the same time, in the southern Jonglei state, ethnic clashes caused 100,000 people to flee their homes. Things were beginning to fall apart. On 10 April 2012 the SPLA made a surprise push into the north around the Heglig oilfield. Unexpectedly, SPLA armoured units made rapid progress. The SPLA held the area around Heglig for ten days. Although Khartoum had been taken by surprise, the northern army claimed to have killed around 1,000 SPLA-aligned troops. The Sudanese air force retaliated by bombing the Bentiu area in the south. The official Sudanese military explanation was that they initially withdrew to avoid damaging vital oil installations, which may have been partly true, but the revitalized SPLA was now operationally more efficient. Enough American money had been spent on training it, after all.

For once, Khartoum was portrayed in the international media, especially in Africa, as the victim of the south. Many foreign military experts predicted a resumption of fullscale war between the two states. Fortunately, the AU and UN acted quickly to get the SPLA to avoid a counter-attack against the successful northern recovery of Heglig.

A year after independence, the UN claimed that over 650,000 people had been displaced in the border regions, with most of them fleeing south. In the north the termination of oil supplies forced Khartoum to cut subsidies on fuel and other vital goods, generating popular anger. In June 2012 students clashed with police and speculation mounted that the Arab Spring would spread from North Africa and the Middle East. The unrest was soon contained, partly because the unrest in Egypt in particular was caused by factors largely absent in Sudan. For starters, Sudan had undergone its own Islamist revolution as far back as 1989.

Bashir and Salva Kiir met in Ethiopia to try once more to resolve the chronic economic problems facing both countries because of the oil cut-off. As ever, the country was fraying at the edges, but attacks came in the centre too. The capital was on edge in November 2012 when a coup was thwarted at the heart of the security establishment. Saleh Gosh, head of the National Intelligence and Security Service until 2009, was arrested, along with twelve other serving senior military personnel. Nobody was hurt, but the opposition to Bashir from such trusted sources was a

Salva Kiir, the South Sudan leader, was a good military commander but a poor politician.

worrying development for the president. A considerable backlash had built up in the intelligence services because Gosh was seen to represent a consensus view on what was going wrong, especially in the south. Some of the jailed or suspended intelligence and army personnel were quietly rehabilitated for the sake of national unity. When I asked the president about the coup, he was understandably reluctant to discuss it, brushing me off politely with 'It's all sorted now'. But the mini-rebellion in his core constituency probably played a part in his stated desire to retire by 2015 (though he is still in power as I write this in April 2018). Some of his old army comrades had tried to bend his ear about getting out of politics, but Field Marshal Bashir decided to soldier on in the hot seat. Despite strong protests from his own family, he changed his mind and decided to stand again in the next election.

The northern party-political turmoil was nothing compared with what was happening in the south. In July 2013 Salva Kiir fired his *whole* cabinet, including Vice President Riek Machar. I had a soft spot for Riek, despite his shifty politics. I had spent some time with him in the bush in the 1990s. I enjoyed his urbane style – perhaps it was easy to communicate with him because of his doctorate earned in England. He had a lot of charm, not least with women, despite his lazy eye and gap-toothed smile. His involvement with Emma McClune, an English aid worker, was lambasted by southern rivals for her alleged meddling in local politics. It was dubbed 'Emma's War'. The pregnant Emma died tragically and the rifts in the SPLA were eventually healed, after much bloodletting.

By the end of 2013 the contemporary political differences had degenerated into ancient tribal rivalries, especially in elite military units in the capital. It was assumed in Juba that the inveterate troublemaker Riek Machar was trying to stage a coup. According to northern intelligence sources, still very well-informed on the inner workings of the new state, there was no coup. For once, apparently, Machar was innocent of the charges. It didn't matter. Soon, fighting between the two main tribal wings of the SPLA – Nuer, led by Machar, and Dinka, led by Kiir, although the tribal distinction was never that precise – led to all-out civil war. Dissident warlords had already been active in the south before the December crisis. Now the two rival armies, as well as the inevitable militias, tried to occupy their traditional tribal constituencies, especially around the oilfields. Machar's forces initially captured three state capitals, Bor, Bentiu and Malakal. All were devastated in the fighting. Ugandan troops and aircraft came in on the side of President Kiir, who also appealed to Bashir. The northern president shuttled regularly to Juba on peace missions. He was back in the role of regional peacemaker. He knew Machar and Kiir well and tried to bring them together. Towns such as Malakal were captured and recaptured, sometimes two or three times in one week. It was a highly fluid semi-conventional war, with both sides well equipped.

By the summer of 2014 fullscale civil war raged unabated in the new state of South Sudan. Juba had spent some $1 billion on weapons since the start of the civil war in December 2013. In June 2014 China North Industries Group, the country's biggest arms manufacturer, shipped a large consignment of equipment, consisting of missiles, grenade launchers, machine guns and ammunition, to Juba via Mombasa. At exactly the same time humanitarian agencies were appealing for $1.3 billion to feed four million starving people in the country. Even the capital faced acute shortages of basic food. What food there was cost five times more than the same staples in next-door Uganda. So far, independence had been a disaster. The last civil war in the south had lasted for over two decades; millions were killed. If the current war within the SPLA continued for anything like that period, South Sudan would run out of people.

Both parts of the former Sudan faced an uncertain future. South Sudan was already a failed, devastated state at independence; then it became far worse. Visitors to Khartoum would see gleaming office blocks and fancy hotels. Brand new 4x4s jammed the streets. Behind the façade, the inheritor state of the old Sudan faced many of the problems of rapid growth suddenly halted – unemployment, rapid price rises caused by inflation and hidden poverty in the shanty towns on the edge of the capital. Unlike many African cities things by and large worked – even the traffic lights and lifts. And Khartoum was still the safest and friendliest, if also one of the most boring, capitals in Africa. The two parts of Sudan could not survive without peace and each other. They were destined to live or die in each other's economic embrace.

Breakfast with Bashir
From being arrested in my first hour in the country in 1996 I became a house guest of the president and his family in January 2014. Maybe my contacts were

getting better or perhaps I was going a bit native. I don't know. Years before I had originally suggested to one of the president's advisers that I might write the first biography of Bashir. I had not heard anything so I planned later to write the first comprehensive military history of the country. Lots had been written on General Gordon's death in the siege of Khartoum, though not that much military history since independence in 1956, especially in English.

I got a phone call over Christmas 2013. Would I come over straightaway to start interviews for a biography of Bashir? I had missed so many Christmases with friends and my dwindling family over the years, so I said no. It was a religious holiday – the Sudanese would relate to that, and I needed to show respect for the president by taking some time to prepare questions. They got that too. So in early January 2014 I flew out with my photographer friend, Tony Denton, another inmate of Shere. I would try to write both books in one volume – a military history centred on the Field Marshal who had led the 1989 revolution and been in the top job ever since.

For once everything went to schedule – I was given total access to the 'Boss's' family (his mother, second wife and children) as well as his old schoolmates, teachers and, most usefully, fellow generals and intelligence chiefs. I went to his home village and talked to his cousins. For such a secretive family, normally denied all official access to Westerners, it was remarkable. I had interviewed the president before, in formal Arabic using translators. This time he opened up to me in good English, when I spent a day at his small farm outside Khartoum.

I acquired lots of small pieces of gossip – he had been kicked out of the Muslim Brotherhood for smoking when he was 16. His brother admitted that the Arabization and Islamicization of education had done a lot of harm – all the younger members of Bashir's family spoke fluent English with an American accent after their expensive foreign education. More importantly, I learned a great deal about internal politics, especially the fraught struggle with the spiritual leader of the revolution, Hassan al-Turabi.

Despite his reputation as a fiery dictator, and being the first head of state to be indicted at the International Criminal Court, I found 'Omar' to be modest, friendly and rather humble. Unlike most autocrats he seemed a good listener. To use an English cricket term, he played a straight bat. Many of the top politicians he had instructed to talk to me did so with surprising openness.

Bashir's entire family told me that they wanted him to step down. After twenty-five years in the army and twenty-five years as a head of state, he had done enough for the country, they told me repeatedly. Bashir said he would stand down before the next election in 2015 or 2016. He wanted to return to farming, he said; like the proverbial Cincinnatus, I thought. The 70-year-old President was also planning to write his memoirs. I jokingly asked him to wait until my book on Sudan came out.

Breakfast with Bashir (Tony Denton)

I know you are not supposed to like dictators, but I hope my book does justice to a very complex country and its endless conflicts, many inherited from imperial times, as well as to Bashir's genuine, if belated, attempt to end Africa's longest war. Whatever happens, I know I will get flak for trying. When the book was published by Pen and Sword in 2015 I sent some copies for the president and his advisers to read. After a few months I was invited back to Khartoum to discuss the book with the country's boss. This could be tough review time, I thought, as I recalled previous arrests in Sudan.

First I was examined for some hours by three of Sudan's leading academic historians. It was like a doctoral viva on steroids. Then I had a one on one with President Bashir. He was quite friendly, said he hadn't read all the book and hoped it would be translated into Arabic, with my permission. No toe-nail pulling, just traditional Sudanese hospitality.

Conclusion

Writers are supposed to plumb their shallows and distil an elixir of wisdom at the end of these sorts of books. I have no wisdom to share – except perhaps one comment. I must admit to being a recovering interventionist. For years on my desk I had a small sign saying: 'Rome did not create an empire by having meetings – they did it by killing all those who opposed them.' This was more a comment on my dislike of useless meetings in Whitehall. Many civil servants felt they were achieving so much by reaching consensus, but no decisions, after hours of charming, even erudite, chat. I wasn't bloodthirsty in wanting to emulate Rome. I was once quite gung-ho, however, about getting rid of dictators such as Saddam Hussein. The catastrophic occupation of Iraq soon taught me the errors of my ways. I had been wrong about Iraq as equally I had been wrong about thinking Mugabe would not become the traditional African dictator-for-life. So I am less inclined to pontificate about the dangerous state of the world, especially in the Middle East, where I have spent so much time.

I had another Damascene experience regarding Russia. A few years ago, Vladimir Shubin got in touch to arrange to meet me in London. He had once been a major general in Soviet intelligence and had run all Moscow's operations in southern Africa during the time I was covering the wars there. We talked for over three hours. He had read and annotated some of my books on the region and was eager to tell me, in great detail, where I had gone wrong. Mostly it seemed he was correct. Journalists pride themselves on their objectivity, but they are just as prone as anyone else to succumbing to collective wisdom. I always thought I was a competent contrarian, yet Shubin showed me how often I went along – albeit subconsciously – with racist analyses based largely on Rhodesian, South African and British intelligence sources. They, we, I did not really know what the Russians were up to, but we pretended we did. Mostly, we didn't know anything. What surprised me most was Shubin's honest (I believe) assessment of how little Russian agents and military advisers did in southern Africa. Yes, Pretoria and Washington used to point at the tens of thousands of Cubans in Angola, but Shubin told me in detail about how few trained military Russian advisers he had under his command and where. He had retired as a top spook, so I was persuaded to believe him – perhaps. Most intelligence and defence analysts in southern Africa

"I didn't realise that the President could read English and had gone to the trouble of buying a copy of 'What the hell am I doing here?', my first volume of autobiography, on Ebay. I was, of course, quoted out of context, you see..."

Moorcraft's ninth volume of memoirs was always going to be a bit of a touch-and-go affair . . .

Friends comment on my memoir-writing.

for decades totally exaggerated Russian (and Chinese) influence and constantly underplayed the insurgents' ability to make their own (often bad) decisions. Huge errors were made by the Western defence community, as they did again regarding Iraq and Afghanistan. Intelligence is a vital art form and rarely a science. All I am calling for is a little more modesty, and far less politicization of intelligence work as happened over Tony Blair's dodgy dossiers. I am not really nostalgic for the comfortable certainties of the Cold War, especially as Vladimir Putin has revitalized much of that sad old conflict. And I worry about the West sleep-walking into a possible accidental major war over Ukraine or the Baltic states.

Britain has once more voted on war in the Mother of Parliaments (over Syria). Red-tops screamed 'Gulf War 3'. The Middle East is in flames, and I understand why belatedly America and some in the West want to stop the Islamic State. I am pleasantly surprised that some of the Arab states – take Saudi Arabia, which has a much bigger combat air force than Britain – are doing something to protect themselves. Yet the West is sinking into the Sunni-Shia quagmire, the centuries-old core of regional conflict. The Saudis and Qatar had helped the Islamic State, just as Pakistan's two-faced intelligence services have long armed and aided the Taliban against Western interests. I fear that once again Western intervention, no matter how well-intentioned, will make matters worse. I believe that Islamist extremism, and its fifth columnists, are a major threat to Britain (the subject of my recent successful book, *The Jihadist Threat* published first in 2015). More effort should be put into resolving the security issues at home in the UK. I can't help but recall P.J. O'Rourke's comment: 'Wherever there is suffering, injustice and oppression, the Americans will show up, six months late, and bomb the country next to where it is happening.'

If the Islamist extremists did not indulge in beheading, slavery and mass conversions by the sword, there might well be a case for arguing that the revival of an Islamic Caliphate – if that's what many Sunnis really want – should be allowed to emerge, and then deal with it. After all, the West dealt quite successfully with the Caliphate based in Istanbul for many centuries.

I thought that my controversial book on Jihadism might have angered some of my former Islamist friends, whom I dubbed 'moderate beheaders' (though not to their faces). I worried that I might have to don a blond wig and hide in a farm in mid-Wales, as Salman Rushdie apparently did for a while, after the publication of *Satanic Verses.* At least I could then revive my use of the language of heaven, Welsh. And even if I ducked the sword-wielders, then I thought I could take some flak from the British security establishment. As ever, I was a writer who exaggerated his own importance. Instead, the book was shortlisted (six out of 2,000) for the British Army's Military Book of the Year (2016).

I may perhaps sit this Jihad out. I feel no compulsion anymore to prove myself by rushing to cover wars. Not least because I can hardly see them. I had pushed my luck while I had my sight; even more so recently rushing around minefields in Sudan and Sri Lanka, while relying on the vision of whatever cameraman I was with. Philosophically, I am still curious about the nature of courage. Is it a well that can run dry or a muscle that gets stronger with exercise? Personally, in my own case, I think it is the former. I used to think that courage was the ability to do something you think is right even when you are scared. Maybe it is connected with a form of stubbornness. My own experience of military training and war reporting indicates that you can train people to be brave, or at least react automatically under fire. We know that soldiers are prepared to die not for God, Queen and country any more, but to protect their mates. Perhaps it was ever thus, though I suspect that the stoicism displayed in the

Author looking unhappy while on patrol with the British army in southern Iraq, 2003.

two world wars may not be as common now in our more timorous, PC and 'elf and safety' culture. On the other hand, I still believe that the British Army, man for man and woman for woman, still stands in the front rank of military forces. And I spent enough time in the MoD to know that it can be a force for good. Look what the army did to end the war in Sierra Leone, for example. I also saw for myself the good it did in Kosovo, even if perhaps Tony Blair sent it in for some of the wrong motives.

I was still prepared to be an intellectual busybody. I saw Brexit coming and yet I was surprised that Donald Trump won the US presidency in 2016. The Democrats were to blame: *anybody* except Hillary Clinton could have beaten Trump. The Democrats chose precisely the wrong candidate. Nevertheless, even some avowed Republicans voted for her. As P.J. O'Rourke also quipped, better a *bien-pensant* than *pas de pensées*. I threw myself into trying to explain – not least to myself – this new world. Russia, North Korea and China were perhaps greater threats than the ragged, mad survivors of the Islamic State. I scribbled it all down in a new book, *Superpowers, Rogue States and Terrorism* (2017).

I have had enough of other people's wars, however. I grew up in the activism of the 1960s, when Vietnam was the war cry of Western youth. In the 1960s people took acid to make the world weird. In 2018 the world is definitely weird and people now take Prozac to try to make it normal. I haven't given up on talking about wars. I have not yet had a letter from my local undertaker, signed 'Eventually Yours'. I still plan a few more comebacks, just like the guy who grew up in the same Pontypridd street where my mother's family lived: Tom Jones. I have accepted that instead of always wondering why I inevitably sat next to the nutter on the bus, train or plane, I realize that people often thought *I* was the nutter. I spent my working life at places such as Sandhurst or Staff College assuming I was the only sane man in the lunatic asylum. I finally realized that they couldn't all be wrong. So I concede my madness and thank you for reading my stories about my crazy adventures.

Index